Why God Must Do What is Best

Why God Must Do What is Best

A Philosophical Investigation
of Theistic Optimism

Justin J. Daeley

BLOOMSBURY ACADEMIC

LONDON • NEW YORK • OXFORD • NEW DELHI • SYDNEY

BLOOMSBURY ACADEMIC
Bloomsbury Publishing Plc
50 Bedford Square, London, WC1B 3DP, UK
1385 Broadway, New York, NY 10018, USA
29 Earlsfort Terrace, Dublin 2, Ireland

BLOOMSBURY, BLOOMSBURY ACADEMIC and the Diana logo are trademarks
of Bloomsbury Publishing Plc

First published in Great Britain 2022

Series Design by Louise Dugdale
Cover Image © jvphoto / Alamy Stock Photo

A catalogue record for this book is available from the British Library.

A catalog record for this book is available from the Library of Congress.

ISBN: HB: 978-1-3501-0989-6
ePDF: 978-1-3501-0990-2
eBook: 978-1-3501-0991-9

Series: Bloomsbury Studies in Philosophy of Religion

Typeset by Deanta Global Publishing Services, Chennai, India

To find out more about our authors and books visit www.bloomsbury.com and
sign up for our newsletters.

For Melody,
the best

Contents

Acknowledgments

It is frequently stated that no book project comes to completion without any substantial assistance. I could not agree more. I, therefore, express a profound sense of indebtedness and gratitude in completing this project. While all the defects are solely mine, the completion of this book is the result of the investment of many wonderful people into my life and research.

I first wish to thank librarian Becky Schleicher. Becky not only attained for me a number of books and articles related to my work, but did so in an efficient way. I am grateful for her collegiality and friendship. In addition, I thank archivist Greg Rosauer, for his wisdom and counsel regarding material related to biblical studies. I would also like to express my gratitude to my close friends: most notably Anthony Langager, Justin Mihm, and Kevin Wagner. These three men have provided for me a deeper appreciation of the outdoors, especially during my studies. Furthermore, these friends have solidified in my mind the idea that men thrive in life while having close friends and experiencing community.

Much appreciation goes out to a number of people for their insights and conversations regarding the topics of this book: Paul Eddy, Stewart Kelly, Taylor Lindahl, the late Hugh McCann, James McGlothlin, Aaron Regnier, and Edward Wierenga. In addition, I want to express my gratitude to those who provided critical, yet fruitful, assessment on earlier versions of the written material: Jim Beilby, Jesse Couenhoven, Robert Letham, Katherin Rogers, Thomas Senor, and Lloyd Strickland.

Thanks also goes out to the editors of Bloomsbury Academic Press, especially Becky Holland and Colleen Coalter, for their patience and collegial spirit. I am also grateful to the series editor, Stewart Goetz, along with the anonymous reviewers for their invaluable and acute insight on the manuscript.

I also want to express appreciation to the editors and academic journals for granting me permission to reprint some of the previously published material.

While most of the book's content is new, antecedent versions of some of the book's material can be found in the following journals:

- "The Necessity of the Best Possible World, Divine Thankworthiness, and Grace," *Sophia* 58 (2019): 423–35;
- "*Creatio Ex Nihilo*: A Solution to the Problem of the Necessity of Creation and Divine Aseity," *Philosophia Christi* 19 (2017): 291–313;
- "Divine Freedom and Contingency: An Intelligibility Problem for (Some) Theistic Compatibilists," *Religious Studies* 51 (2015): 563–82.

A special thanks goes out to Paul Helm. I am utterly grateful for his friendship, voluminous scholarship, and analytic mind. His character was unmatched as a gracious and patient spirit, along with a modicum of English humor, which always accompanied his critical remarks. I feel greatly privileged for having Paul evaluate and critically assess my work.

I am especially indebted to my family. My parents, John and Jeanette Daeley, have provided unconditional love from the outset of my education, and I will be forever grateful for their example as loving parents. My two sisters, Trichele Smith and Kristy Titus, have produced refreshing comic relief (which I appreciate) during my studies. It is a joy to be in their presence and not only smile but also to be filled with laughter. I also wish to thank my father-in-law, Sydney Stephan, and my mother-in-law, Cinda Stephan, along with Trent and Cathy Nickelson, for releasing me from familial duties, thus providing me with ample time to research and write. I already owe more to my beautiful children, Julius Justin, Felicity Barbara, and Cyrus John, than they will ever know. They have brought an element of joy into my life that I never thought I could experience. In addition, they have taught me in many ways what it means to "fear the Lord" while being a parent.

Finally, and most of all, it is with deep gratitude that I thank my wife, Melody. She has supported me in every way that she could, and I owe more to her than I could possibly say. Nevertheless, her tireless sacrifice, encouragement, and affection for me have undoubtedly made the process of completing this book project possible. It is her sacrificial love that provides me with a daily and tangible reminder of Jesus Christ's love for his people. It is to her that I dedicate this book.

1

Introduction

1.1 Orientation

This book is a study of what I call *Theistic Optimism*. Unsurprisingly, Theistic Optimism is the conjunct of theism and optimism, such that the latter claims there not only is an optimal among a set of alternatives but also that the optimal invariably wins out. According to optimism, then, things exist, and exist as they do, because the best *must* be actual. The theistic element, on the other hand, emphasizes a variation of theism where God, understood as the most perfect being, is a God who does things, that is, a God who acts, wills, and creates. Given this variation of theism, we might say that Theistic Optimism is the outlook that God must do the best (i.e., must do what is optimal). Consequently, if it is better to create rather than not create, then God must create.

With that said, the project primarily sets out to carefully articulate and defend Theistic Optimism against its critics. While such an outlook has an impressive pedigree throughout the Western theistic tradition (as I eventually argue), it is nevertheless not predominant among contemporary theologians and philosophers of religion. Currently, most contemporary theologians and philosophers of religion claim, instead, that either (i) there are a number of good alternatives tied for the best, (ii) the alternatives are incommensurable with one another and so incomparable, or (iii) there are an infinite number of ways in which God could express His goodness via creating, and the created order as it now stands is one such way. According to these three disparate viewpoints, it is not the case that God must do the best simply because there is no best. In addition to these viewpoints, critics of Theistic Optimism argue that there are insurmountable problems that attend this outlook, especially having to do with divine freedom, aseity, praiseworthiness and thankworthiness, along with modality. The common thread that runs through all of these alternative viewpoints along with some of the alleged problems is a commitment to what I will call *divine alternativity*, such that what God does (e.g., create) could have just as easily been done otherwise (e.g., not create).

I argue, however, that the idea that God must do the best is not as problematic as some contemporary theologians and philosophers of religion claim, since the "must" in question finds its origination and ultimate source within God Himself. There is something about God's perfect nature, in other words, that requires Him to do that which is best. Therefore, while there is something about God's perfection (typically though not exclusively His essential moral perfection) that precludes Him from being able to do anything other than the best, He nevertheless exercises His divine excellence without any external coercion. I submit, then, that Theistic Optimism deserves a vigorous and fresh philosophical defense. In this volume I provide one and offer plausible solutions to the contemporary worries it typically encounters.

Before drawing attention to the book's layout and the conclusions of each chapter, three caveats are in order. First, in saying that Theistic Optimism deserves a fresh philosophical *defense*, this implies that the primary aim of this volume considers objections and challenges leveled against Theistic Optimism. To put it differently, while I simply describe some of the possible motivations for Theistic Optimism, I do not offer extended and detailed arguments for it. Accordingly, the overarching thesis of the book is a conditional one, namely, *if* Theistic Optimism holds true, then the charges leveled against it are found wanting. Moreover, I do not offer any critical assessment of the alternative viewpoints to Theistic Optimism that were mentioned earlier. Nevertheless, it goes without saying that the motivations for some particular outlook (in this case, Theistic Optimism) are frequently utilized as objections to some contrary viewpoint. Consequently, it is not surprising that the objections leveled against these alternative viewpoints are also the motivations for Theistic Optimism. I make no claims, however, as to whether or not the motivations for Theistic Optimism are plausible objections to the alternative viewpoints. Second, Theistic Optimism is not to be confused with the psychological sense of optimism. The psychological sense typically emphasizes a cognitive state that reflects a subject's belief, particularly the belief that things will get better. Accordingly, if this psychological sense of optimism is applied to God, then it conjures up the notion that while things are currently quite gloomy for Him, God is nevertheless hopeful that all will get better in the future. However, to be clear, such an outlook of the divine, though coherent, is not the outlook under consideration. Rather, in philosophical circles the term "optimism" has for almost three centuries been applied (often pejoratively) to the idea that ours is the best possible world. Indeed, the word "optimism" was coined for precisely that purpose by Louis Castel. The third and final caveat is that this volume is not an exercise in theodicy. While some of the insights and conclusions which I offer are undoubtedly relevant to the problem of evil, I leave it to the reader to apply those insights and conclusions if he or she feels it necessary to justify God's ways.

1.2 Structure and Layout

With that orientation in mind, Chapter 2, which is primarily descriptive, seeks to accomplish two fundamental goals. The first goal is to articulate the nature of Theistic Optimism. That is, I describe as succinctly as possible what Theistic Optimism is and what it is not. In order to reach this first goal, I locate Theistic Optimism in the thought of Gottfried Wilhelm Leibniz (1646–1716), the paradigmatic philosopher who advances the idea that God does the best. The second goal is to highlight three primary motivations for Leibniz's commitment to Theistic Optimism: (1) that Theistic Optimism best accounts for God's ontological perfection; (2) that Theistic Optimism best accounts for the Principle of Sufficient Reason; and (3) that Theistic Optimism can find support in Sacred Scripture.

In Chapter 3, I examine what might be for some critics the most obvious problem for Theistic Optimism, namely, the charge that it seriously jeopardizes divine freedom. Indeed, a number of philosophers have argued that if God must do the best, then God cannot be free with respect to doing the best. While defending divine freedom given Theistic Optimism, I draw from Leibniz's account of freedom (but do not follow him rigidly) and argue that what Leibniz calls *spontaneity* and *intelligence* provides solid ground for thinking that God is free. In addition, I demonstrate that a number of contemporary philosophers who argue that God can be free even if divine alternativity is denied are basically Leibnizian in their outlook.

Chapter 4 takes a careful look at another stiff challenge for Theistic Optimism, namely, the charge that it cannot account for divine praiseworthiness and thankworthiness. It is typical within the circles of philosophy of religion to claim that if alternativity is denied (as Theistic Optimism does, indeed, deny), then some agent, such as God, cannot be worthy of praise and thanks for performing some token act, such as creating the best possible world. Taking this objection into account, I argue for the conjunction of Theistic Optimism and divine praiseworthiness and thankworthiness. The conclusion of my argument is founded upon the Judeo-Christian doctrine of divine grace, where I first argue for the conditional premise that if God's act to create the best world is/was a gracious act, then God is praiseworthy and thankworthy with respect to that act. I then argue for the conjunctive premise that the idea of Theistic Optimism is consistent with that particular act being a gracious act.

In Chapter 5, I proceed by investigating whether or not Theistic Optimism somehow violates a fundamental attribute theists typically call divine aseity. For, a number of theologians have recently asserted what I will call proposition (A): If God must create (or create this particular world), then God cannot have aseity (i.e., be from Himself). Accordingly, there is an inconsistency between divine aseity and the idea that God must do the best. Here, I develop an argument for the consistency of divine aseity and the idea that God must do the best, thus concluding that proposition (A) is false. An exploration into the Judeo-Christian doctrine of *creatio ex nihilo* will expedite the argument. This doctrine will provide sufficient grounds for thinking that God has aseity. I then argue that the doctrine of *creatio ex nihilo* is consistent with the idea that God must do the best.

Chapter 6 considers the difficult challenge that Theistic Optimism engenders too many problems with respect to our modal intuitions. One might argue, for instance, that if God must do the best (such as create and create the best world), then it is difficult to comprehend in what sense any other worlds are, in fact, possible. Possible worlds, then, are somewhat of a misnomer in the context of Theistic Optimism. In avoiding this challenge I chronicle three possible responses and provide some discussion as to the costs and benefits of each possible solution. Then, I consider the option of conceding the point and how this option would likely result in amending the idea of *possible* worlds in favor of something else.

In Chapter 7, I consider a final problem for Theistic Optimism, namely, the charge that it seriously deviates from the Christian tradition. In fact, some critics go so far as to assert that denying divine alternativity results in a heterodox view of God's freedom. I will argue that Theistic Optimism is, indeed, consistent with the claims of the Christian tradition, and thus show that Leibniz's outlook is a viable option for that particular theistic tradition. If this is so, then one need not be required to accept the proposition that divine alternativity (with respect to God's freedom) is the traditional view. The argument is founded upon establishing a set of conditions for what constitutes a view as "traditional," and demonstrating that Theistic Optimism is consistent with every member of the set of conditions.

Chapter 8 addresses not so much a challenge to Theistic Optimism (like the prior chapters), but, rather, suggests that a certain variation of theism, which I call Theistic Compatibilism, cannot hold to divine alternativity. Consequently, Theistic Optimism ought to be the preferred outlook for the Theistic Compatibilist in the Christian tradition. The primary reason for this conclusion is that the Theistic Compatibilist typically employs the intelligibility problem, thus arguing that alternativity freedom reduces to random, unintelligible events. However, while utilizing the intelligibility problem, what they deny with respect to human choice (i.e., alternativity), they seem to require of God if He is to be free. But can one consistently employ the intelligibility problem with respect to human free choices and at the same time assert and uphold alternativity with respect to *God's* freedom? I argue that one cannot and consequently I suggest that Theistic Optimism is the best option for the Theistic Compatibilist.

Finally, in Chapter 9, I offer some concluding remarks and draw attention to two peripheral issues related to Theistic Optimism. Here, I highlight how one might respond to these peripheral issues by offering some brief comments as to how the discussion might proceed with respect to Theistic Optimism.

Theistic Optimism and the Leibnizian Legacy

2.1 Introduction

The fundamental aim in this second chapter, which will primarily be descriptive, is to understand the nature and rationale of Theistic Optimism. By accomplishing this goal, in Section 2.2 I locate Theistic Optimism in the thought and legacy of Gottfried Wilhelm Leibniz (1646–1716), the paradigmatic philosopher who advances the idea that God does the best. After explicating the nature of Theistic Optimism, I shall then in Section 2.3 draw attention to four auxiliary features of Theistic Optimism. These auxiliary features will provide a more nuanced picture of Theistic Optimism as generally understood and of Leibniz's outlook in particular. Section 2.4 chronicles three primary motivations for Leibniz's commitment to Theistic Optimism. Lastly, in Section 2.5 I close by offering a summary of the chapter.

2.2 The Nature of Theistic Optimism

Theistic Optimism in the most basic sense is the idea that God does the best, that is, God does what is optimal. It can be most famously captured in the thought of German philosopher, Gottfried Leibniz, when he states in the *Theodicy* that

> [I]f we were capable of understanding the universal harmony, we should see that what we are tempted to find fault with is connected with the plan most worthy of being chosen; in a word, we *should see*, and should not *believe* only, that what God has done is the best.[1]

While one can sense in the former quotation that Leibniz is pessimistic about humanity's epistemic ability to understand the universal harmony, he nevertheless clearly affirms that what God has done is the best. Leibniz's God, consequently, is a God who wills, intends, acts, and thus creates the best.

Theistic Optimism, moreover, is expressed by Leibniz in a number of different ways throughout his corpus. He highlights, for instance, the notion of God decreeing the best *universe* when he states, "It is thus one must think creation of the best of all possible universes, all the more since God not only decrees to create a universe, but decrees also to create the best of all."[2] Furthermore, Leibniz draws attention to the concept of the best *series* and how the reality of sin fits within that series. He says, "The true root of the fall . . . lies in the aboriginal imperfection and weakness of the creatures, which is the reason why sin has its place in the best possible series of events."[3] Leibniz goes so far as to argue that "[I]f God had not selected for creation the best series of the universe (in which sin does occur), he would have admitted something worse than all sin committed by creatures."[4]

In addition to the best universe and the best series, Leibniz also expresses Theistic Optimism by focusing on the best *plan* implying that God acts to achieve particular ends:

> Thus love of the best in the whole carries the day over all other individual inclinations or hatreds; it [i.e., love of the best] is the only impulse whose very exercise is absolutely infinite, nothing having power to prevent God from declaring himself for the best; and some vice being combined with the best possible plan, God permits it.[5]

Lastly, and perhaps the most popular expression, Leibniz speaks of God choosing the best *world* when he says, "Since . . . God's decree consists solely in the resolution he forms, after having compared all possible worlds, to choose that one [world] which is best . . . it is plain to see that this decree changes nothing in the constitution of things."[6]

What we can see at this point is that Leibniz expresses his Theistic Optimism in at least four different ways throughout his corpus by focusing on the best universe, the best series, the best plan, and the best world. This is not to say, however, that by drawing attention to these four different ways of expressing Theistic Optimism Leibniz collapses the idea of, say, the best world with the best series.[7] Rather, it is simply to focus on the fact that these four expressions, while perhaps conceptually different, have among them a common denominator that God does the best. So, whether Theistic Optimism is expressed as decreeing the best universe, selecting the best series, actualizing the best plan, or choosing the best world, the core idea remains constant in Leibniz's thought, namely, that God does the best.

In contemporary discussion, Theistic Optimism is frequently rephrased and nuanced in modal terms in which God does the best *necessarily*.[8] According to this modal variant there is something about God's essential perfections, typically divine wisdom and goodness, which preclude Him from being able to do anything other than the best. And, if God's essential perfections preclude Him from doing anything other than the best, then God *must* do the best. It is not uncommon, therefore, for philosophers to speak of "the necessity of creation" or "the necessity of the best possible world," given the idea that God, because of His essential perfections, must do the best. Leibniz appears to embrace something close to this modal variant of Theistic Optimism when he states the following:

> Now this supreme wisdom, united to a goodness that is no less infinite, cannot but have chosen the best. For as a lesser evil is a kind of good, even so a lesser good is a kind of evil if it stands in the way of a greater good; and there would be something to correct in the actions of God if it were possible to do better.[9]

Similarly, he argues:

> One may say that as soon as God has decreed to create something there is a struggle between all the possibles, all of them laying claim to existence, and that those which, being united, produce most reality, most perfection, most significance carry the day. It is true that all this struggle can only be ideal, that is to say, it can only be a conflict of reasons in the most perfect understanding, which cannot fail to act in the most perfect way, and consequently choose the best.[10]

The crucial element here is not only that God does the best, but also that God *cannot fail* to act in the most perfect way, and thus choose the best. For the (essential) divine wisdom and goodness, according to Leibniz, cannot but have chosen that which is best, and to think otherwise would thus find fault in what God has done. Leibniz, in other words, basically thinks that if we have the reasonable supposition that God's actions cannot be corrected given His essential wisdom, this is good reason to think that it is not possible for God to do better. Therefore, given the fact that God's wisdom and goodness are primarily operative within Leibniz's Theistic Optimism, it appears as though he commits himself to this modal variant where God *must* do the best, that is, that God's wisdom and goodness preclude Him from doing anything other than the best.

We can further see that Leibniz is committed to this modal variant of Theistic Optimism when he draws attention to what he calls a "philosophic maxim" which endeavors to ascribe infinity to the divine perfections. Leibniz begins elaborating on the maxim when he states, "The goodness of the infinitely perfect Being is infinite, and would not be infinite if one could conceive of a goodness greater than this."[11] Crucially, he goes on to apply infinity not only to God's goodness, but also to *all* of God's perfections when he says, "This characteristic of infinity is proper also to all his [i.e., God's] other perfections . . . they must be the greatest one can imagine."[12] Now supposing this maxim holds true (i.e., that God's perfections are infinite), Leibniz reaches the following conclusion:

> This maxim [that God's perfections are infinite] is altogether to my liking, and I draw from it this conclusion, that God does the very best possible: otherwise the exercise of his goodness would be restricted, and that would be restricting *goodness* itself, if it did not prompt him to the best, if he were lacking in good will. Or again it would be restricting his *wisdom* and his *power*, if he lacked the knowledge necessary for discerning the best and for finding the means to obtain it, or if he lacked the strength necessary for employing these means.[13]

What Leibniz is basically arguing here is that if it is not the case that God does the very best possible, then God's goodness, wisdom, and power are restricted. However, God's goodness, wisdom, and power cannot be restricted since, as the maxim states, they are infinite, that is, the perfections must be the greatest one can imagine. Therefore, it is the case that God does the very best possible. Leibniz, in short, concludes that God does the very best possible from the maxim that God's perfections must be infinite. Again, it appears as though Leibniz endorses the modal variant of Theistic Optimism where God, given His (infinite) essential perfections, must do the best.

A more explicit commitment to this modal variant of Theistic Optimism is formulated by Leibniz when he applies the notion of *moral necessity* to God's act to create the best. He begins by saying:

> Yet God is bound by a moral necessity, to make things in such a manner that there can be nothing better: otherwise not only would others have cause to criticize what he makes, but, more than that, he would not himself be satisfied with his work, he would blame himself for its imperfection; and that conflicts with the supreme felicity of the divine nature. This perpetual sense of his own fault or imperfection would be to him an inevitable source of grief.[14]

While there has been much discussion on what Leibniz meant by moral necessity, I take him to mean that, given God's wisdom, God cannot but do the best.[15] As he further says, "[F]or it must be admitted that God, that wisdom, is prompted to the best by a *moral* necessity."[16] Similarly, "for it is a moral necessity that the wisest should be bound to choose the best."[17] So, "moral" in "moral necessity" corresponds to God's wisdom, and thus Leibniz frequently couples wisdom and the divine nature with moral necessity.

Nevertheless, to gain further insight into what Leibniz means by moral necessity, he typically distinguishes it from blind necessity and metaphysical necessity. With respect to blind necessity, Leibniz says the following:

> Mr. Hobbes refuses to listen to anything about a moral necessity either, on the ground that everything really happens through physical causes. But one is nevertheless justified in making a great difference between the necessity which constrains the wise to do good, and which is termed moral, existing even in relation to God, and that blind necessity whereby according to Epicurus, Strato, Spinoza, and perhaps Mr. Hobbes, things exist without intelligence and without choice, and consequently without God. Indeed, there would according to them be no need of God, since in consequence of this necessity all would have existence through its own essence, just as necessarily as two and three make five. And this necessity is absolute, because everything it carries with it must happen, whatever one may do; whereas what happens by a hypothetical necessity happens as a result of the supposition that this or that has been foreseen or resolved, or done beforehand; and moral necessity contains an obligation imposed by reason, which is always followed by its effect in the wise. This kind of necessity is happy and desirable, when one is prompted by good reasons to act as one does; but necessity blind and absolute would subvert piety and morality.[18]

Here, moral necessity cannot be blind necessity such that things exist (e.g., our world) without intelligence, reason, and choice (i.e., the act of the will). Instead, moral necessity captures the fact that one is prompted by good reason to act and will as one does, that is, to do what is most fitting. Or, as Robert Adams nicely puts it:

> What is important to Leibniz ... about the types of necessity opposed here is that they are all *blind* necessity, necessity that operates "without intelligence and without choice." Moral necessity is not blind; in its operation "one is carried by good reasons to act as one does."[19]

With respect to metaphysical necessity, Leibniz says the following in his fifth letter to Samuel Clarke:

> We must also distinguish between a necessity that takes place because the opposite implies a contradiction (which necessity is called logical, metaphysical, or mathematical) and a necessity which is moral, by which a wise being chooses the best and every mind follows the strongest inclination.[20]

Notice, again, that Leibniz couples moral necessity with divine wisdom. In addition, this distinction between metaphysical and moral necessity, when applied to God's act to create, captures the idea that the proposition "God does the best" (or chooses the best world) is not logically necessary since its opposite (i.e., it is not the case that God does the best) does not imply a contradiction (e.g., it is not the case that $2 + 2 = 4$). In other words, the proposition that God chose an inferior world in comparison to the best is free from contradiction, and, therefore, an internally coherent idea.

Yet, Leibniz endorses the idea that God does the best necessarily, but only *in relation to* His essential properties, particularly (as we have seen) in relation to His wisdom. These Leibnizian modal distinctions are brought together in *On Freedom and Possibility* when he says:

> [E]ven if God does not will something to exist [e.g., an inferior world], it is possible for it to exist, since, by its nature, it could exist if God were to will it to exist. "But God cannot will it to exist." I concede this, yet, such a thing remains possible in its nature, even if it is not possible with respect to the divine will, since we have defined as in its nature possible anything that, in itself, implies no contradiction, even though its coexistence with God can in some way be said to imply a contradiction.[21]

So, to reiterate, Leibniz is committed to the modal variant of Theistic Optimism which holds that God's infinite wisdom precludes Him from being able to do anything other than the best, and thus God, in a (strong) sense, must do the best. To suppose that God does anything less than the best would be to jeopardize His wisdom and goodness. Importantly, it is this modal variant of Theistic Optimism where God must do the best, unless otherwise noted, that will be under discussion throughout the remainder of this volume.

2.3 Some Auxiliary Features of Theistic Optimism

Nevertheless, despite Leibniz's commitment to the modal variant of Theistic Optimism, there are a number of important auxiliary features that are worth highlighting that closely accompany his idea that God must do the best. Here, we will see that Leibniz's Theistic Optimism is not a stand-alone outlook, but, rather, an outlook that receives and gives life to other components of his thought. Consequently, highlighting these auxiliary features will give us a more well-rounded understanding of Theistic Optimism as generally understood along with Leibniz's outlook in particular.

The *first* feature is that Leibniz's Theistic Optimism implies the idea that there is de facto a best to be done or to be chosen from. If God does the best, in other words, there is, in fact, a best to be done. It would be incoherent to affirm, on the one hand, that God does and thus creates what is best while at the same time denying that there is a best to be done. Unsurprisingly, then, Leibniz goes on to argue "that if there were not the best (*optimum*) among all possible worlds, God would not have produced any [world]."[22] But Leibniz appears to know by empirical observation that it is certain that a world has, indeed, been produced (by God). It follows, therefore, by *modus tollens* that there is a best among all possible worlds. While bolstering the conditional premise that "if there were not the best among possible worlds, then God would not have produced any," Leibniz draws out an analogy between God's perfect wisdom and the orderliness of mathematics:

> As in mathematics, when there is no maximum nor minimum, in short nothing distinguished, everything is done equally, or when that is not possible nothing at all is done: so it may be said likewise in respect of [God's] perfect wisdom, which is no less orderly than mathematics.[23]

What I take Leibniz to be arguing here is that since we have a creation (i.e., something was, in fact, done) as opposed to no creation at all (i.e., nothing at all was done), this is a reasonable indicator, given God's perfect wisdom, that there was a best among worlds for God to choose from and thus to create it. Therefore, Leibniz holds that there was de facto a best world for God to choose from.

A *second* feature (related to the first) that closely accompanies Leibniz's Theistic Optimism is the notion that God examines, compares, and thus deliberates between an infinite number of possibilities. Accordingly, God in His infinite and perfect wisdom knows every possible combination of existents (i.e., possible worlds); compares them exhaustively; and then chooses the one that is the best. Here is what Leibniz says:

> The infinity of possibles, however great it may be, is no greater than that of the wisdom of God, who knows all possibles . . . . The wisdom of God, not content with embracing all the possibles, penetrates them, compares them, weighs them one against the other, to estimate their degrees of perfection or imperfection, the strong and the weak, the good and the evil. It goes even beyond the finite combinations, it makes of them an infinity of infinities, that is to say, an infinity of possible sequences of the universe, each of which contains an infinity of creatures. By this means the divine Wisdom distributes all the possibles it had already contemplated separately, into so many universal systems which it further compares the one with the other. The result of all these comparisons and deliberations is the choice of the best from among all these possible systems, which wisdom makes in order to satisfy goodness completely; and such is precisely the plan of the universe as it is. Moreover, all these operations of the divine understanding, although they have among them an order and a priority of nature, always takes place together, no priority of time existing among them.[24]

While there are a number of sentiments in the former quotation which could be commented on, the point is to draw attention not only to the fact that Leibniz endorses a deliberative outlook with respect to God creating but also to the fact that God's choice of the best is a *result* of comparing possible worlds. God was aware, in other words, of a number of possibilities before He started to create.

The motivation, furthermore, on Leibniz's part to affirm this deliberative outlook in relation to his Theistic Optimism is to sustain the notion that God acts for good and decisive reasons as opposed to, say, acting randomly. In other words, if God does not compare and thus deliberate over which possible world to create, then it follows that God acts randomly. As Leibniz declares, "The careful consideration of these things will, I hope, induce a different idea of the greatness of the divine perfections . . . from any that can exist in the minds of those who make God act at random, without cause or reason."[25] So, according to Leibniz, the only way for God to act in a non-random way is for Him to compare and deliberate over possibilities, and thus to hold that God had something in mind "before" (either temporarily or conceptually) He created the best.

A *third* feature that one finds in close proximity to Leibniz's Theistic Optimism is the notion that the reality of possibilities (which God compares and deliberates over) is dependent on Him. To begin, Leibniz declares in the *Monadology* that "It is also true that God is not only the source of existences, but also that of essences insofar as they are real, that is, or the source of that which is real in possibility."[26] Here, I take Leibniz to hold that since God is the existential source of that which is real in possibility, possibility is therefore dependent on God for its ontological composition. For, as Leibniz goes on to say, "[I]f there is reality in essences or possibles, or indeed, in eternal truths, this reality must be grounded in something existent and actual, and consequently, it must be grounded in the existence of the necessary being."[27] God's existence, in other words, is required for the reality of possibles, which is just to say that if God did not exist, then nothing, such as possibles, could be a part of the fabric of reality. So, in short, Leibniz is motivated to ground the reality of possibles in the necessary existence of God.

Still, Leibniz nuances the dependence relation between God and possibles by drawing attention to the divine ideas that are derived from God's understanding. After declaring that God is, indeed, the existential source of that which is possible, Leibniz gives the rationale for this when he states, "This is because God's understanding is the realm of eternal truths or that of the ideas on which they depend; without him there would be nothing real in possibles, and not only would nothing exist, but also nothing would be possible."[28] Accordingly, Leibniz highlights the notion that it is God's *understanding*, that is, the divine ideas which ontologically ground the reality of possibles. The divine ideas, in other words, are required for the reality of possibles. Leibniz makes this clear also in the *Theodicy* when he says:

In the region of the eternal verities are found all the possibles, and consequently the regular as well as irregular: there must be a reason accounting for the preference for order and regularity, and this reason can only be found in understanding. Moreover these very truths can have no existence without an understanding to take cognizance of them; for they would not exist if there were no divine understanding wherein they are realized, so to speak.[29]

Given Leibniz's commitment to the notion that the reality of possibles is dependent on the divine understanding, he thus nuances but at the same time distances himself from Plato's realism. For, as Leibniz says:

Plato said in the *Timaeus* that the world originated in Understanding united to Necessity. Others have united God and Nature. This can be given a reasonable meaning. God will be the Understanding; and the Necessity, that is, the essential nature of things, will be the object of the understanding, in so far as this objet consists in the eternal verities. But this object is inward and abides in the divine understanding. And therein is found not only the primitive form of good, but also the origin of evil: the Region of the Eternal Verities must be substituted for matter when we are concerned with seeking out the source of things.[30]

Privileging the divine understanding, then, it is not surprising that Leibniz is also exercised against Rene Descartes's voluntarism (or what some call universal possibilism), where the divine will, as opposed to the divine intellect, takes priority. He states that, "[W]e should not imagine, as some do, that since the eternal truths depend on God, they are arbitrary and depend on his will, as Descartes appears to have held."[31] Rather, "This is true only of contingent truths, whose principle is *fitness* [*convenance*] or the choice of the best. But necessary truths depend solely on his understanding, and are its internal object."[32]

Leibniz, therefore, clearly affirms not only that possibles are dependent on God for their ontological composition, but more specifically that it is the divine understanding which is required for their reality. Consequently, Leibniz finds himself in the realist tradition of *divine conceptualism*, which is simply to say that possibles are thoughts in the divine mind.[33] Leibnizian scholar, Roger Woolhouse, nicely summarizes Leibniz's outlook on God's relation to possibles when stating:

Contingent truths too, truths about what is *actually* the case in the created world, depend on God's understanding (as to what world is the best); but they depend on his will too, his decision to create the best. Essential truths however, truths which are true by virtue of essences, truths about what is *necessary* and *possible*, depend only on God's understanding. So Leibniz holds, the divine understanding is the source of "that which is real in such truths." Without God's understanding, Leibniz's view is, there would be no essential truths, such as those of geometry and mathematics. This does not mean that the truths of geometry would be other than what they are; it means, rather, that there would be no truths of geometry at all.[34]

A *fourth* and final auxiliary feature, and one that is often overlooked, is that Leibniz insists that Theistic Optimism provides an underlying basis for one's piety and devotion toward God, particularly one's obligation to glorify God and love Him. With respect to glorifying God Leibniz says, "[T]o believe that God does something without having any reason for his will—overlooking the fact that this seems impossible—is an opinion that conforms little to his glory."[35] With God's glory yet in mind, Leibniz goes so far to say, "I hold that God does nothing for which he does not deserve to be glorified."[36] Whatever God does, in other words, He deserves to be glorified. And, *ex hypothesi*, God does the best. Therefore, according to Leibniz, God deserves to be glorified for doing the best.

Concerning one's love toward God, Leibniz goes on to suggest that Theistic Optimism is foundational to one's obligation to love Him. He claims that "[T]his great truth, that God acts always in the most perfect and desirable way possible, is, in my judgment, the foundation of the love that we owe God in all things."[37] Leibniz provides the support for this proposition when he says, "since he who loves seeks his satisfaction in the happiness or perfection of the object loved *and in his* [i.e., God's] *actions*."[38] In other words, to love God well is to be completely satisfied not only with the perfection of the object loved (i.e., God), but also with the perfection of what He has done. There obtains, accordingly, a close connection between one's appropriate love for God and a complete satisfaction in God *doing* the best. Leibniz elaborates on this connection when he states:

> To will the same and dislike the same is true friendship. And I believe that it is difficult to love God well when we are not disposed to will what God wills, when we might have the power to change it. In fact, those who are not satisfied with what God does [like doing the best] seem to me like dissatisfied subjects whose attitudes are not much different from those of rebels.[39]

He concludes from this:

> Therefore it is sufficient to have the confidence that God does everything
> for the best and that nothing can harm those who love him. But to know
> in detail the reasons that could have moved him to choose this order of
> the universe—to allow sins, to dispense grace in a certain way—surpass the
> power of a finite mind, especially when it has not yet attained the enjoyment
> of the [beatific] vision of God.[40]

So, while Leibniz suggests a healthy dose of agnosticism with respect to God's
reasons for choosing this order of the universe, he nevertheless claims that
God doing the best is utterly important for one's love and commitment to
Him. In short, "in order to act in accordance with the love of God . . . we must
truly be satisfied with everything that has come to us according to his will."[41]
Leibniz is arguing, then, that one's love for God needs to have a complete
satisfaction with respect to what God does, such as doing the best, lest one has
the attitude of a rebel. Who would have thought that a metaphysical outlook
which Voltaire famously chastised as "madness" was so closely connected to a
philosopher's piety and devotion to God?[42]

   Piety aside, we can see at this point that Leibniz's Theistic Optimism is not
a stand-alone outlook, but, rather, an outlook that has other features which
closely accentuate it. In particular, I drew attention to the notion that Theistic
Optimism implies that there is de facto a best world to choose from. I then
highlighted how the deliberative outlook along with divine conceptualism
functions in close proximity to Leibniz's Theistic Optimism. Lastly, we saw
how Theistic Optimism provides grounds for one's piety and devotion toward
God, particularly focusing on one's obligation to glorify and love Him. This is
not to say that all of these features logically entail Theistic Optimism, or even
that Theistic Optimism entails all of these features. For instance, one could
consistently hold to Theistic Optimism while at the same time affirm Platonic
realism (which would be a denial of Leibniz's conceptualism) with respect to
abstract objects. Similarly, one could hold to the deliberative model of God
and creation and yet assert that God chose some inferior world over that of
the best. Again, this goes to show that Theistic Optimism is not entailed by nor
does it entail all the features that were focused on. Rather, it shows that there is
a "connectedness" in Leibniz's thought, dare I say a sort of "systematic" way of
thinking, where particular metaphysical outlooks give life to one another, but
do not logically entail one another.

2.4 The Primary Motivations for Theistic Optimism

Now although it is the modal variant of Theistic Optimism (where God must do the best) that typically gives rise to a number of worries discussed throughout this volume, one might first wonder what Leibniz's motivations are for holding such a position. That is, what is the rationale for thinking that God, because of His essential perfections, must do the best? While formulating a number of "principles" (e.g., the principle of contradiction and the principle of perfection), which are prima facie interconnected throughout his philosophy, Leibniz highlights three fundamental motivations for the idea that God must do the best.

First, there is the intuitive idea that God is most plausibly understood as a perfect being, that is, as the greatest possible being. Leibniz, while amending Descartes's ontological argument, explicitly endorses this notion of the divine at the outset of his 1686 *Discourse on Metaphysics*:

> The most widely accepted and meaningful notion we have of God is expressed well enough in these words, that God is an absolutely perfect being . . . . And, to penetrate more deeply into this matter, it is appropriate to remark that there are several entirely different perfections in nature, that God possess all of them together, and that each of them belongs to him in the highest degree.[43]

Similarly, in the *Monadology* he says:

> God is absolutely perfect—*perfection* being nothing but the magnitude of positive reality considered as such, setting aside the limits or bounds in the things which have it. And here, where there are no limits, that is, in God, perfection is absolutely infinite.[44]

Leibniz here clearly claims that God is best understood as an absolutely perfect *being*, that is, a being that (1) possesses all perfections together and (2) possesses them in the highest degree. The first condition highlights the notion of compossibility, which is just to say that it is possible for a set of properties to be possessed by an entity at the same time or all together. The second condition specifies that a perfection must be of the highest degree. (Or, as we have seen earlier when Leibniz spoke of a philosophic maxim, a perfection must be infinite.) As Leibniz says, "A fairly sure test for being a perfection is that forms or natures that are not capable of a highest degree

are not perfections."[45] He goes on to support the idea that a perfection must
be of the highest degree by stating "the greatest of all numbers . . . as well as
the greatest of all figures, imply a contradiction, but the greatest knowledge
and omnipotence do not involve any impossibility."[46] Leibniz concludes from
this that "power and knowledge are perfections, and, insofar as they belong to
God, they do not have limits."[47] So, if it is not possible for some property to be
of the highest degree (e.g., the greatest of all numbers), then it cannot count as
a perfection. In short, given (1) and (2), Leibniz therefore understands divine
perfection as unlimited compossibility.

Importantly, however, while clearly predicating perfection on God's being,
Leibniz extends the notion of perfection (along with the superlative "best")
to the *acts* or to the *decree* of God as well. So, Leibniz states that, "Whence
it follows that God, possessing supreme and infinite wisdom, *acts* in the
most perfect manner, not only metaphysically, but also, morally speaking."[48]
In addition, Leibniz claims, "It follows from the supreme perfection of God
that he chose the best possible plan in producing the universe."[49] What I take
Leibniz's position to be, given some of what he says here, is that there is a
seamless transition between who God is (i.e., the best) and what God does
(i.e., the best). He commits himself, therefore, to the idea that "to do less good
than one could is to be lacking in wisdom or in goodness."[50] Leibniz's God,
however, cannot be lacking in wisdom and goodness since divine wisdom and
goodness are perfections, and thus belong to Him in the highest degree, that is,
the perfections are infinite. Consequently, God cannot do less good than one
could. God must *do* the best, in other words, simply because He *is* ontologically
perfect. Or, as Lloyd Strickland nicely puts it when commenting on Leibniz:

> [I]t follows that a most perfect being cannot operate in a less than perfect way.
> That is to say, God's nature is such that only the most perfect way of acting
> is consistent with it. This can be summed up in the following proposition:
> (P) The operation of the most perfect being is always most perfect. And it
> follows from (P) that God, if he exists, necessarily creates the best possible
> world.[51]

Accordingly, it is not possible for a perfect being to operate in a less than
perfect way, and, therefore, to do anything less than the best. Perfection,
then, is predicated by Leibniz not only on God's being (what we might call
ontological perfection) but also on the divine operations (what we might call
operational perfection). So, to reiterate, the first motivation for the idea that

God must do the best (i.e., Theistic Optimism) is the fact that God is most plausibly understood as a perfect being, and a perfect being knows nothing other than to do the best. To claim that God does anything less than the best is to call into question God's ontological perfection.

A *second* line of motivation for the idea that God must do the best is Leibniz's unwavering commitment to the Principle of Sufficient Reason (PSR). While it has already been noted that, according to Leibniz, it is incoherent to assert that God can do something without a reason, here we will nevertheless see that the idea that God does the best functions as the sufficient reason for why God chose, say, this world over some other contrary world. In other words, if one were to ask, "What is the sufficient reason for why God chose this world over some contrary world?", Leibniz would likely respond by saying, "The sufficient reason for why God chose this world over some contrary world is simply that this world is the best."

To begin, the PSR, according to Leibniz, starts with the idea that there is no existent (e.g., the actual world) or true proposition (e.g., the world exists) without a sufficient reason or cause. So, he says in *Monadology* that

> Our reasonings are based on *two great principles, that of contradiction* . . . [a]nd *that of sufficient reason,* by virtue of which we consider that we can find no true or existent fact, no true assertion, without there being a sufficient reason why it is thus and not otherwise, although most of the time these reasons cannot be known to us.[52]

Accordingly, while oftentimes ignorant of the exact reason, for any existent it is required to have a sufficient reason to explain why it exists as opposed to not existing. Or, as Leibniz says elsewhere, "nothing takes place without a sufficient reason."[53] In addition, Leibniz highlights the demonstrative power of the PSR in service of metaphysics and theology when he says, "Now, by that single principle, namely, that there ought to be a sufficient reason why things should be so and not otherwise, one may demonstrate the being of God and all other parts of metaphysics or natural theology."[54]

Here we see that Leibniz's understanding of the PSR is wide in scope, and thus covers facts, events, and true propositions. Whether or not Leibniz articulated a careful distinction between facts and events is a debatable topic since his locutions "sufficient reason" and "sufficient cause" appear to be used interchangeably. Nevertheless, for our purposes, it is worth emphasizing that the PSR, according to Leibniz, applies to true propositions and *everything* in the world that corresponds to those propositions.[55] But just what does Leibniz mean by *sufficient* when stating that nothing can exist or take place without a sufficient reason? In his book, *The Principle of Sufficient Reason*, Alexander Pruss offers some commentary as to what Leibniz means by "sufficient" when advocating for the PSR. Pruss's conclusion is that, according to Leibniz, a sufficient reason holds true when an explanans (i.e., that which is doing the explaining) *entails* the explanandum (i.e., that which is explained). Here is what Pruss says in further detail:

> The sort of explanation that the PSR envisions is an explanans that is sufficient for the explanandum. If the explanans [e.g., this world is the best world] fails to entail the explanandum [e.g., that this world exists], then it is not sufficient for it: the explanans could hold even though the explanandum does not . . . . If the reason is to be *logically* sufficient for the explanandum, then one would do better to talk of the Principle of Logically Necessitating Reason (PLNR). Admittedly, when Leibniz and Spinoza used the PSR, they took it to be in some sense equivalent to the PLNR.[56]

Leibniz would likely have problems with Pruss referring to his outlook as the Principle of Logically *Necessitating* Reason (PLNR). However, it is important at this point to note that according to Pruss, when Leibniz speaks of the PSR what he means is that a sufficient reason will *entail* the explanandum.[57]

Franklin Perkins arrives at a similar conclusion to Pruss when commenting on and applying Leibniz's use of the PSR to the experimental method. According to Perkins, if one is to successfully utilize the PSR, then an identical experiment (i.e., the explanans) cannot yield different outcomes (i.e., the explanandum). As he says:

> We see the reliance [on the principle of sufficient reason] most clearly in experimental method. We assume that an experiment can be repeated and that if the same experiment yields different results, there must have been some difference in the experiments. If we did not rely on the principle of sufficient reason, we would have to admit that the identical experiment could yield different results for no reason at all.[58]

Assuming Pruss and Perkins are correct regarding Leibniz's understanding of the PSR, the only way one can employ the PSR is if it is not the case that the identical experiment (i.e., the explanans) could yield different results (i.e., the explanandum). It is incoherent, in other words, to think that an explanans could explain two different and contrary explananda. Perhaps this is what

Leibniz had in mind when he states "that nothing happens without it being possible for someone who knows enough things to give a reason sufficient to *determine* why it is so and not otherwise."[59]

Now in the context of God creating a world, Leibniz demands that there must be a sufficient reason for why God chose this particular world over some contrary world—that is, a reason that cannot explain the existence of two contrary worlds. For, if the same reason could sufficiently explain the existence of two contrary worlds, then one would abandon the PSR. I do not think it would be too far off the mark to hold that the sufficient reason, according to Leibniz, as to why this particular world *W* was chosen over a contrary world *W'* was simply that world *W* is the best world. So, Leibniz says:

> Now, since there is an infinity of possible universes in God's ideas, and since only one of them can exist, there must be a sufficient reason for God's choice, a reason which determines him towards one thing rather than another. And this reason can only be found in fitness, or in the degree of perfection that these worlds contain, each possible world having the right to claim existence in proportion to the perfection it contains. And this is the cause of the existence of the best, which wisdom makes known to God, which his goodness makes him choose, and which his power makes him produce.[60]

So, we can see here how Leibniz brings together the PSR (along with the wisdom and goodness of God) and the idea that God does the best. What makes for the best (world), in other words, functions as the sufficient reason for why it exists as opposed to some other world. To think that God does anything less than the best would not only be a violation of God's ontological perfection (as we saw earlier) but also a violation of the PSR. Consequently, if there is no best world, then God would not have created anything since, according to Leibniz, God must act according to a sufficient reason. Here is how Brandon Look highlights the Leibnizian idea that God doing the best functions as the PSR:

> Leibniz sometimes implicitly, sometimes explicitly, appeals to this principle [i.e., the principle of the best] in his metaphysics, most notably when he is also employing the Principle of Sufficient Reason. Indeed, when it comes to the creation of the world, the "sufficient reason" for God's choice of this world is that this world is the "best" of all possible worlds; in other words, in this case the Principle of Sufficient Reason is essentially the Principle of the Best.[61]

In summary, at this point Leibniz has two primary motivations for the idea that God must do the best, namely, (1) that God is ontologically perfect, and (2) that God must act according to the PSR. He summarizes these two motivations for his Theistic Optimism when he says, "In my opinion, if there were no best possible series, God would have certainly created nothing, since he cannot act without a reason, or prefer the less perfect to the more perfect."[62] So, to assert that God does anything less than the best will doubtless jeopardize God's ontological perfection along with threatening the PSR. But, as we have seen, Leibniz is clearly and fully committed to both God's ontological perfection and the PSR, which thus function as the primary motivation for his Theistic Optimism.

A *final* and less popular motivation that Leibniz offers for the idea that God must do the best is to consult what he calls "Sacred Scripture."[63] While typically considered as a rationalist, where one consults the mind as the sole source for knowing, Leibniz appears to have a strong commitment to Holy Scripture such that the word of God is without falsehoods. So he says:

> It is safer to hold that Holy Scripture contains nothing except the word of God, and that the authors of the books, even with regard to those which do not pertain to salvation, have not asserted a falsehood insofar as they are philosophical, chronological and geographical. If there are errors, however, they have crept in because of the failings of copyists, or have arisen from words that have been poorly understood.[64]

Given his outlook on Holy Scripture, it is clear that Leibniz is operating as a philosopher within the context of Christian theism. He does not, however, refer to any specific biblical text in order to support his Theistic Optimism. Yet, interestingly enough, he does claim "that a great many passages from Sacred Scripture . . . will be found favoring my opinion."[65] Taking into account Leibniz's allusion to Sacred Scripture as favoring his opinion, it is worth pointing out that there are, indeed, a few biblical texts that plausibly underscore his commitment to the notion that the *divine operations* are, in fact, perfect, and by implication underscore his commitment to Theistic Optimism. In Deut. 32:4, for instance, it says, "The Rock!—[i.e., Yahweh God], His deeds are perfect, Yea, all His ways are just; A faithful God, never false, True and upright is He."[66] Similarly, in 2 Sam. 22:31, it reads, "The way of God is perfect, The word of the LORD is pure. He is a shield to all who take refuge in Him."[67] Finally, in the New Testament, Mathew's gospel states that "You therefore must be perfect, as your heavenly Father is perfect."[68]

What are we to make of these texts given our discussion of Theistic Optimism? If we assume that the "deeds" and the "ways" of God refer to what God *does*, then, according to these texts, what God does is, indeed, perfect. These texts, in other words, prima facie highlight the idea of *operational perfection*, where perfection is predicated on what God does, and operational perfection, as we saw, is an essential component of Leibniz's Theistic Optimism. Furthermore, with respect to Matthew's gospel, it appears as though the author has in mind actions and volitions (as opposed to being, that is, ontology) since he or she speaks of *doing* something, that is, loving your enemies. Accordingly, since the author of Matthew's gospel focuses on doing as opposed to being, the exhortation to be perfect as your heavenly Father is perfect fits more plausibly with operational perfection rather than ontological perfection. Perhaps it was these texts that Leibniz had in mind when he declared that Sacred Scripture will be favoring his opinion, or even when he goes on to argue:

> [T]o act with less perfection than one could have is to act imperfectly. To show that an architect could have done better is to find fault with his work. This opinion [that God could have done better] is also contrary to the Sacred Scripture, which assures us of the goodness of God's works. For, if their view were sufficient, then since the series of imperfections descends to infinity, God's works would always have been good in comparison with those less perfect.[69]

So, while Leibniz does not refer to any particular biblical texts in order to support his Theistic Optimism, he nevertheless claims that Sacred Scripture (without falsehoods) supports his outlook. Sacred Scripture, therefore, can plausibly be understood as a source and motivation for Leibniz's Theistic Optimism despite the fact that he is typically deemed your textbook rationalist.[70]

2.5 Conclusion

In this chapter I have offered an overview of Theistic Optimism by locating it in the thoughts of Gottfried Leibniz. By locating Theistic Optimism in the thoughts of Gottfried Leibniz, I offered a summative overview of the modal variant of Theistic Optimism that will be under discussion throughout the remainder of this volume. Following this, I highlighted what I take to be some of the important auxiliary features that accentuate Theistic Optimism. I then focused attention on the major motivating factors and the rationale for them. However, there are a number of contemporary charges typically leveled against Theistic Optimism that cast doubt on its plausibility, especially those having to do with divine aseity, praiseworthiness and thankworthiness, along with the problem of modal collapse. However, one might first object that Leibniz and his commitment to Theistic Optimism cannot account for the fact that God is free, that is, that God was just as equally free to create the best possible world as He was free not to create the best possible world. It is to this charge that I now turn.

Theistic Optimism and Divine Freedom

3.1 Introduction

Chapter 2 was intended to lay the groundwork for understanding the nature and rationale of Theistic Optimism by looking to the thought and legacy of Gottfried Leibniz. Here we found that given the essential properties of divine wisdom and goodness it follows, according to Leibniz, that God *must* do the best. In addition, it was noted that Leibniz's Theistic Optimism was accompanied by a number of other features such as the deliberative outlook with respect to God and possibilities along with divine conceptualism. Lastly, I drew attention to the primary motivations for Leibniz's Theistic Optimism, namely, the argument from (ontological) perfection, the argument from the principle of sufficient reason, and the less popular argument from Holy Scripture.

In this chapter I will begin to take a close look at what might be the most obvious and perhaps the most common problem for Leibniz and his Theistic Optimism, namely, the charge that God cannot be free. Indeed, a substantial number of contemporary thinkers have come to argue that if God must do the best, which is part and parcel of Theistic Optimism, then God cannot be free with respect to doing the best. In this chapter I argue against this objection and then conclude that Leibniz's Theistic Optimism is consistent with divine freedom. While establishing this conclusion, in Sections 3.3 and 3.4 I draw from Leibniz's analysis of freedom (but do not follow him rigidly) and argue that what Leibniz calls *spontaneity* and *intelligence* provides solid ground for thinking that God is free. In Section 3.5 I consider a possible worry for my argument. Before developing my argument, however, in Section 3.2 I first describe why some contemporary philosophers argue that Leibniz cannot save divine freedom, given his Theistic Optimism.

3.2 The Objection from Divine Freedom

In his book, *Leibniz*, Nicholas Jolley offers an argument which he claims
Leibniz to be committed to:

(1) Necessarily, God is good.
(2) Necessarily, if God is good, he creates the best of all possible worlds.
(3) Therefore, necessarily, God creates the best of all possible worlds.[1]

Jolley's argument, consequently, has as its conclusion that it is necessary that
God creates the best of all possible worlds. In other words, "Leibniz is led to
the conclusion which denies the contingency of God's creation."[2]

Similar to Jolley, William Rowe (who has stimulated a wealth of scholarship
on the problem of divine perfection and freedom) constructs an argument
that he also declares that Leibniz cannot escape. Rowe's argument is as follows:

(1) If God exists and is omnipotent, perfectly wise and good, then he
    chooses to create the best of all possible worlds [parallel to Jolley's
    premise 2];
(2) God exists and is omnipotent, perfectly wise, and perfectly good [parallel
    to Jolley's premise 1];
    therefore,
(3) God chooses to create the best of all possible worlds.[3]

While Rowe here, unlike Jolley, does not add the modal qualifiers to each
proposition of his argument, he nevertheless concludes (like Jolley) that
it is necessary that God chooses to create the best of all possible worlds. As
Rowe states:

> Two further points show that he [i.e., Leibniz] cannot escape the conclusion
> that God's choosing to create the best is absolutely necessary. First,
> proposition (2) [God exists and is omnipotent, perfectly wise, and perfectly
> good], the antecedent of (1), is itself absolutely necessary . . . . Second, it is a
> rule of logic that if a hypothetical proposition is itself absolutely necessary,
> and its antecedent is also absolutely necessary, then its consequent must be
> absolutely necessary as well. Thus, if both (1) and (2) are absolutely necessary,
> (3) must be absolutely necessary as well. Since Leibniz is committed to the
> view that both (1) and (2) are absolutely necessary, we are bound to conclude
> that his view commits him to the view that (3) is absolutely necessary.[4]

According to Jolley and Rowe, then, Leibniz is committed to the troubling fact that it is *necessary* that God chooses to create the best of all possible worlds. In fact, Jolley claims that "the conclusion seems tantamount to the Spinozistic thesis that the actual world is the only possible world."[5]

Crucially, it is noteworthy that these formal arguments from Jolley and Rowe as they now stand do not have as their conclusion that "God cannot be free" with respect to doing the best, like choosing to create the best possible world. Rather, the conclusion of their arguments simply captures the notion that it is necessary (i.e., it is not contingent) that God chooses to create the best possible world. Nevertheless, while the "God cannot be free" objection is not explicitly found in their formal arguments, Jolley does comment that

> *[I]f God's choice is not contingent, he is not a free agent.* Ironically . . . the problem which Leibniz faces arises from reflection on God's goodness. The proposition that God is good is clearly a necessary truth: God, by definition, is a being possessing all perfections, and benevolence is one of the perfections. But it would seem that God's very goodness must compel him logically to create the best of all possible worlds; in other words, the conditional proposition: "If God is good, he creates the best of all possible worlds" would seem to be a necessary truth.[6]

In addition, Rowe adds to his argument when he says:

> [I]t is of crucial importance for Leibniz to deny that (3) [i.e., God chooses to create the best of all possible worlds] is absolutely necessary. For whatever is absolutely necessary cannot logically be otherwise. Hence, if (3) is absolutely necessary, it would be logically impossible for God to choose to create any world other than the best. It would not be a contingent matter that God chooses to create the best. *Nor, of course, could God be free in choosing to create the best.*[7]

Here, Jolley and Rowe now make the additional connection between the conclusion of their arguments (i.e., that it is necessary that God chooses to create the best possible world) and the idea that God cannot be free. Importantly, what Jolley and Rowe mean by freedom (in part) is that God is free only if He could have refrained from creating another world or refrained from creating at all. As Jolley states, "This thesis [i.e., that God is essentially good], to which Leibniz is committed, seems to imply that God could not do otherwise than create the best."[8] Furthermore, Rowe adds that "if God could not do otherwise than create the best world, he created the world of necessity, and not freely."⁹ For, "to say that God *freely* created the good world seems to imply that he was free not to do so."¹⁰ Consequently, Jolley and Rowe are committed to what we might call "divine alternativity" where God was just as equally free to create the best possible world as He was free to refrain from creating the best possible world.

Given these additional remarks, it is appropriate and important to add an additional premise to their previous arguments, namely:

(1) Necessarily, if God creates the best of all possible worlds, then God cannot be free (in the sense that that requires alternativity) with respect to creating the best of all possible worlds.¹¹

Because of this additional premise to the argument, we can now offer a clearer and nuanced argument that appears to be problematic for Leibniz and his Theistic Optimism:

(1) Necessarily, if God creates the best of all possible worlds, then God cannot be free with respect to creating the best of all possible worlds. [from the additional remarks made by Jolley and Rowe]

(2) Necessarily, God creates the best of all possible worlds. [from the conclusion of Jolley and Rowe's initial argument]

Therefore,

(3) Necessarily, God cannot be free with respect to creating the best of all possible worlds.

Jolley and Rowe, accordingly, claim that divine alternativity is a necessary condition for God's freedom. Consequently, Theistic Optimism (which denies divine alternativity) is inconsistent with divine freedom.

In the subsequent section, I begin to provide a solution to the problem by denying premise 1, and therefore argue that it is possible that God is free, while at the same time affirming that it is necessary that God does the best, like choosing to create the best possible world. In establishing this conclusion, I glean from Leibniz's understanding of *spontaneity* and *intelligence* that it provides solid ground for thinking that God is free. While Leibniz thought that *contingency* of a peculiar sort is also a necessary condition for freedom, I save the discussion of contingency for Chapter 6, and, therefore, concede the point regarding premise 2. Accordingly, the argument of this chapter is *inspired* by Leibniz (gleaning only from spontaneity and intelligence) but does not follow him rigidly regarding the metaphysics of freedom. The argument, in short, calls into question the idea from Jolley and Rowe that divine alternativity (i.e., that God was just as equally free to refrain from doing the best) is a necessary condition in order for God to be free.

3.3 Leibniz on Spontaneity and Intelligence

Although it is a matter of discussion as to what extent divine freedom resembles human freedom (or vice versa), Leibniz nevertheless thought that human beings, created in God's image, are mirrors of God with respect to the nature of freedom. I follow Jolley, then, when he states that "Leibniz seeks to develop an analysis of freedom which applies to God and to human beings alike."[12] Consequently, what are stated as conditions for human freedom are also to be taken as conditions with respect to divine freedom.

With that caveat in mind, part of Leibniz's analysis of freedom is to hold that the idea of *spontaneity* is a necessary condition for freedom. So, gleaning from Aristotle, Leibniz says:

> Aristotle has defined it [i.e., spontaneity] well. Saying that an action is *spontaneous* when its source is in him who acts. "Spontaneum est, cujus principium est in agente." Thus it is that our actions and our wills depend entirely upon us.[13]

The idea of spontaneity then according to Leibniz, captures the fact that one is free only if the agent is a self-determining agent. That is, the action finds its sole source within the agent. As Roger Woolhouse declares:

> What is required for freedom is that "we determine." Leibniz's criterion of spontaneity, which in fact goes back to Aristotle, spells out that the determination involved in freedom is *self*-determination. In acting freely we are determined, but what determines us, the principle of our action, is internal.[14]

The choice or action, in other words, decisively derives from and finds its origination within the agent itself. So, with respect to human freedom, Leibniz goes on to say, "As for spontaneity, it belongs to us in so far as we have within us the source of our actions."[15] This is not to say that the requirement for freedom is "being spontaneous" as if God (or any acting agent) acts on the spur of the moment or on impulse without planning or forethought. Leibniz would certainly be opposed to such thinking applied to God since, as was indicated earlier, Leibniz holds that God deliberates between possible worlds. The spontaneity condition, rather, simply captures the idea that God Himself causally determines His actions such that there are no causal chains leading up to His actions. So, God's action is not dependent on anything ab extra (i.e., from the outside).

While the spontaneity condition seems straightforwardly satisfied regarding divine freedom, Leibniz nevertheless introduces an intellectual component to freedom which he says is the "soul of freedom."[16] This intellectual component of freedom "consists in intelligence, which involves a clear knowledge of the object of deliberation."[17] A requirement of freedom, in other words, involves Leibniz's idea of deliberation and assessment as to which choice or action is the best. For, according to Leibniz, "when there is no judgment, there is no freedom." It seems to follow, however, given God's omniscience and the idea that He must act for a reason (i.e., the best reason) that God does, indeed, have judgment, and therefore meets the condition for freedom. Leibniz further elaborates on the condition of intelligence when he declares that

> Our knowledge is of two kinds, distinct or confused. Distinct knowledge, or
> *intelligence*, occurs in the actual use of reason; but the senses supply us with
> confused thoughts. And we may say that we are immune from bondage in
> so far as we act with a distinct knowledge, but that we are slaves of passion
> so far as our perceptions are confused . . . . In truth we will only that which
> pleases us: but unhappily what pleases us now is often a real evil, which
> would displease us if we had the eyes of the understanding open.[18]

Intelligence, then, is a (distinct) knowledge and understanding of objects that are deliberated and "God alone has distinct knowledge of the whole, for he is its source."[19]

In addition, Leibniz goes on to say, "Up to this point I have expounded the two conditions of freedom mentioned by Aristotle, that is, *spontaneity* and *intelligence*, which are found united in us in deliberation, whereas beasts lack the second condition."[20] Consequently, the condition of intelligence allows rational agents (e.g., human beings and God) to be set apart from what Leibniz calls "beasts," which apparently lack intelligence, and therefore cannot be free. In other words, while a number of animals can apparently act with spontaneity, they nevertheless lack freedom. Julia Jorati captures well Leibniz's outlook when she states:

> One final capacity that sets human beings apart from non-rational animals is the capacity for acting freely. This is mainly because Leibniz closely connects free agency with rationality: acting freely requires acting in accordance with one's rational assessment of which course of action is best. Hence, acting freely involves rational perfections as well as rational appetitions. It requires both knowledge of, or rational judgments about, the good, as well as the tendency to act in accordance with these judgments. For Leibniz, the capacity for rational judgments is called "intellect," and the tendency to pursue what the intellect judges to be best is called "will." Non-human animals, because they do not possess intellects and wills, or the requisite type of perceptions and appetitions, lack freedom.[21]

So, Leibniz's idea of freedom involves a rationality component or what some (e.g., Aristotle and the Scholastics) call practical reason whereby, in God's case, He always has a reason (i.e., the best reason) for choosing one particular action over a contrary action. Such a condition is, however, completely innocuous (in fact, expected) given Leibniz's notion that God deliberates between possible worlds along with his unwavering commitment to the idea that God must act according to a sufficient reason. In short, while creatures' perceptions are often confused and mixed with tainted emotions, "it is only God's will which always follows the judgments of the understanding."[22]

Now given the idea that God acts with complete spontaneity (e.g., in creating the best possible world) and the notion that God acts with intelligence (i.e., God knows the objects of deliberation), we can now affirm the following two propositions inspired by Leibniz's outlook:

(a) God is the ultimate source of His actions [from the spontaneity condition];

and

(b) God acts in accordance with His assessment of that which is best [from the intelligence condition].

Proposition (a) satisfies the Leibnizian idea of spontaneity, while proposition (b) fulfills the intelligence component. As Leibniz says, "I have shown that freedom, according to the definition required in the schools of theology, consists in intelligence, which involves a clear knowledge of the objects of deliberation, [and] in spontaneity, whereby we determine."[23]

However, one might demand at this point that in addition to (a) and (b) there also needs to be a power element, or what we will call an *efficacious* condition. For, one might concede that God acts with complete spontaneity along with rationally assessing the objects (i.e., possible worlds) He deliberates between while at the same time argue that God is unsuccessful in carrying out what He intends to do. For example, person P might deliberate and rationally assess that jumping across the river is, in fact, the best choice to perform. In addition, person P acts with complete spontaneity when jumping, but, in fact, does not make it across the river, and thus was unsuccessful in fulfilling the act. The act, in other words, was an ineffectual act. Accordingly, one must have the power to fulfill or act in accordance with what is the best, that is, the act must be effectual (or successful) in producing the desired result in order to be free.

While the efficacious condition may be implied by the spontaneity condition, Leibniz nonetheless seems to be sympathetic to something close to the efficacious condition when he states:

> [W]hen one says that *goodness* alone determined God to create this universe, it is well to add that his GOODNESS prompted him *antecedently* to create and to produce all possible good; but that his WISDOM made the choice and caused him to select the best *consequently*; and finally that his POWER gave him the means to carry out actually the great design which he had formed.[24]

So, while Leibniz does not address the efficacious condition in the context of spontaneity and intelligence, it nevertheless seems plausible to think that Leibniz affirms such a condition since God's power is effectual in producing the desired result, namely, creating the best possible world.

Given the addition of the efficacious condition, we now have a Leibnizian outlook that affirms the following three propositions:

(a) God is the ultimate source of His actions [from the spontaneity condition];

(b) God acts in accordance with His rational assessment of that which is best [from the intelligence condition];

and

(c) God's act produces the desired result [from the efficacious condition].

Let us call this the Leibnizian-inspired set of propositions, set (L).

3.4 Divine Freedom Reconsidered

Now if we suppose that set (L) is a coherent set, then we begin to advance a Leibniz-inspired response to premise 1 of Jolley and Rowe's argument that if God creates the best of all possible worlds, then God cannot be free with respect to creating the best of all possible worlds. In short, set (L) seems to capture (or at least comes very close to capturing) the fact that God can be free. Therefore, set (L) calls into question the notion that divine alternativity is a necessary condition in order for God to be free.

To explicate that set (L) plausibly captures divine freedom, consider the approach from three contemporary philosophers, all of whom (though they do not state it as such) resonate with and echo set (L), and therefore with Leibniz's outlook. First, Edward Wierenga begins by highlighting a circumstance for God to be in such that "whenever God is in circumstance *C* in which a certain action *A* is the best action, he would know that *A* is the best action, he would want to do *A*, and he would be able to do *A*."[25] Leibniz would likely have no worries concerning Wierenga's allusion to this circumstance for God to be in. In fact, such a circumstance is prima facie endorsed by Leibniz when he says, "And this [i.e., that there must be a sufficient reason for God's choice], is the cause of the existence of the best, which wisdom makes known to God, which his goodness makes him choose, and which his power makes him produce."[26] These remarks from Leibniz mirror the sentiments from Wierenga that God would know that *A* is the best, would want to do *A*, and would be able to do *A*.

Despite the similarities between Wierenga and Leibniz when considering a circumstance for God to be in, Wierenga argues that

> If God is ever in such circumstances, it would seem that he is unable in those circumstances to refrain from performing the action in question. He could not refrain from performing the action in those circumstances, since it is impossible that he be in those circumstances and not perform it.[27]

Consequently, it is *not the case* for it to be logically and causally compatible for God to either perform or not perform the action in question. In other words, such a circumstance for God to be in provides a logically sufficient condition for why God performs one action as opposed to a contrary action.

Wierenga argues, however, that such a logically sufficient condition does not jeopardize divine freedom. As he declares:

> No doubt . . . an agent is free with respect to performing an action only if there are no antecedent causally sufficient conditions for the agent's performing the action. But why should we . . . extend this to antecedent *logically* sufficient conditions? After all, at least some libertarians are prepared to countenance the *prior truth* that an agent will (freely) perform an action, despite its being a logically sufficient condition of the agent's performing the action.[28]

Thus, he concludes succinctly by saying:

> Even if in some circumstances *C* God's knowing that *A* is the best action, his wanting to do *A*, and his being able to do *A* is a logically sufficient condition of his doing *A* in *C*, it is nevertheless in virtue of *his own nature* that he knows that *A* is the best action, wants to do *A*, and is able to do *A*. There is no long chain stretching back to things separate from him that give him this constellation of knowledge, desire, and ability; it is due to his *own* knowledge and power and goodness. I see no reason not to say, accordingly, that God is free, even when he does what is best.[29]

What I take Wierenga to be concluding, then, is that God can be free in creating the best possible world even though divine alternativity is not a necessary condition of God's freedom since God's knowing, wanting, and being able to create the best possible world ultimately find their source within God Himself. Crucially, such a conclusion seems to resonate quite well with set (L). For, God knowing that *A* is the best action corresponds to the intelligence condition; God being able to do *A* corresponds to the efficacious condition; and the fact that God wants to do *A* is implied by the spontaneity condition.

A similar outlook is advanced by Thomas Senor. Senor begins by highlighting three kinds of cases that strongly motivate alternativity, or what he calls "the 'can refrain' condition."[30] They are as follows:

(a) the problem of past causally sufficient conditions for the action that not only predate the volition to perform the action but also predate the existence of the actor;

(b) concerns about manipulation by other agents;

and (c) worries about internal compulsions (e.g., addiction/psychological disorder cases).[31]

However, with respect to (a) "there are no conditions or events spatially or temporally prior to God which determine God's actions. Yes, God couldn't refrain from X-ing in circumstance C but there is no set of past series of events and causal laws that is responsible for this."[32] Moreover, concerning case (b) "My actions aren't free because another agent is the source of them. Needless to say, this freedom compromising-condition isn't relevant to the volitions and actions of the omnipotent Source of Being."[33] And with respect to (c):

> Since God is perfectly rational and his volitions and actions are produced by his recognition of the best course of action and his desire to do the best, there can be no worry that God's actions are the result of analogues of human cognitive malfunction brought on either by addiction or psychological disorder. Notice too that the claim that God always does the best because it is the best isn't to be understood as God's having some kind of non-rational, knee-jerk response to the goodness of the action in question. Rather, God's reason for having the volition God has, and for performing the action God does, is God's recognition of the reasons for performing the action in question, God's knowing and appreciating all the reasons for refraining from that action, and God seeing that the reasons for performing the action are weightier than the reasons for refraining. It's God's understanding of the reasons that leads God to act as God does.[34]

According to Senor, then, "God's volitions and actions will pass those three tests even though God lacks the ability to refrain from doing what God sees as the best thing to do."[35]

But what then of God's freedom? While Senor argues that God's volitions and actions will pass cases (a), (b), and (c), he nonetheless advances three conditions that God's particular act to create the best possible world will yet satisfy:

(i) God has effective choice over his creative decision [i.e., one has effective choice regarding an action A if and only if one can do A if one so wills and refrain from doing A if one wills];

(ii) Neither the volition to create nor the creative act is strictly the result of an antecedent causal condition that predates God's existence;

(iii) God's creative action is not the result of a nonrational internal force.[36]

Given these three conditions, Senor concludes with a number of rhetorical questions with respect to divine freedom:

> The upshot of all of this is that given that God's creative act satisfies the above three conditions [i.e., (i), (ii), and (iii)], why should God's inability to refrain require us to deny that God's act is free? For what does the "inability to refrain" come to here other than the inability to act against what he has the best reason to do? Can we really say God would only be free in this context if God were to be able to act against what God sees as the clearly best thing to do, the thing that he has every reason to do and no good reason not to do? That is, that divine freedom would entail the possibility of divine irrationality?[37]

Now in the midst of these questions what I take Senor to be arguing here is that if his conditions (i), (ii), and (iii) hold true, then God can be free. While I think Senor is, indeed, correct in his conclusion that God can be free, it is noteworthy to focus on the fact that his conditions are somewhat parallel to what I designated previously as set (L). In other words, Senor's (i) captures the *efficacious* condition within set (L), (ii) highlights the *spontaneity* condition within set (L), and (iii) reflects the *intelligence* condition within set (L). Senor's outlook, in short, is very Leibnizian as it stands. In fact, his "effective choice" condition (i.e., (i)) seems to be propounded by Leibniz when he says, "[E]ven if God does not will something to exist . . . it could exist *if* God were to will it to exist."[38]

The third and final proponent of the idea that God can be free even if divine alternativity is denied comes from the pen of Kevin Timpe. Timpe's overall project is devoted to drawing out connections between an agent's freedom, the reasons for choosing, and the agent's character. Since an agent's reasons for choosing play an important role in his overall outlook on freedom in general it is worth first highlighting the distinctions Timpe makes regarding *reasons* and how these distinctions play a pivotal role in his position on divine freedom.

Timpe begins by making a distinction between *motivational* reasons and *normative* reasons. The former focuses on "reasons that an agent has for doing a particular action and are capable of explaining her choice if she were to perform that action,"[39] while the latter draws attention to "reasons which would morally justify a particular choice by the agent at a particular time, regardless of whether the agent actually considers them or not."[40] He goes on to add that

> Insofar as an action is morally good for the agent in question to do, there is a normative reason for her performing that action. Likewise, insofar as an action would be morally bad for an agent to perform, there is a normative reason for her not performing it. But if the agent is unaware of the moral goodness or badness of an action, or simply does not care about the morality of the action, then her motivational reasons will not track the normative reasons that there are. Which reasons we point to will depend on whether we are merely explaining or morally evaluating the agent's action.[41]

The second distinction he makes is between *intellectual* (motivational) reasons and *affective* (motivational) reasons. On the one hand, "An intellectual motivational reason involves the agent judging that the content of the end is good, and thus desirable."[42] On the other hand, "an affective motivational reason doesn't involve an intellectual judgment by the agent that the content is good, but rather an emotional response toward that content."[43]

Given these distinctions and Timpe's concern that there is a connection between acting for reasons and an agent's freedom, he emphasizes the following conditional proposition, which he calls "reasons-constraint on free choice":

> *Reasons-constraint on free choice*: If, at time *t*, A has neither any motivational intellectual reasons for *X*-ing nor any motivational affective reasons for *X*-ing, then A is incapable, at *t*, of freely choosing *X*.[44]

In other words, according to reasons-constraint on free choice, "necessarily, given her lack of reasons for *X*-ing, A will not freely choose to *X*."[45] Consequently, Timpe argues that some agent A must have reasons for *X*-ing in order to freely choose *X*.

Now applying the above distinctions along with "reasons-constraint on free choice" to God's freedom, Timpe basically argues that if God is perfectly rational (which implies reasons-constraint on free choice), then God cannot but do the best even though He is free in so doing.[46] Accordingly, like Wierenga and Senor hold, divine alternativity is not a necessary condition in order for God to be free. Here is what Timpe says:

> God's choices . . . are done for reasons. That is, there are reasons that motivate why it is that God chooses to do things that He does. Given God's

perfection, God's motivational reasons [i.e., reasons that explain] will always perfectly track the normative reasons [i.e., reasons that justify] that exist . . . . God, being necessarily omniscient, is necessarily aware of all the normative reasons. Necessarily, God will not fail to weigh the normative reasons properly. And necessarily God will not perform an action (or fail to perform an action) that He judges it would be wrong for Him, all things considered, to perform (or not to perform). So in God we see the perfection of rational agency . . . . We need not think that God reasons discursively to think He acts for reasons. Given God's perfection, His motivational reasons and free choice necessarily track the realm of normative reasons. *God always does what is best despite being free.*[47]

An implication (which I assume Leibniz would endorse) of Timpe's claim that God's motivational reasons (i.e., reasons that explain) will always perfectly track the normative reasons (i.e., reasons that justify) is that supposing there is a best possible world it will function and satisfy both types of reasons. In other words, that there is a best possible world is what *motivates* God to choose that world over some contrary world (a Leibnizian idea), and what *justifies* God's choice is that He chose the best. Again, much of these ideas seem very much Leibnizian, especially when Leibniz states that "To show that an architect could have done better is to find fault with his works" since "to act with less perfection than one could have is to act imperfectly."[48] But, as we have seen, Leibniz argues that God acts perfectly when doing the best, and therefore cannot find fault with His work. God's motivational reason for His choice (i.e., to create the best), then, perfectly "tracks" the normative reason (i.e., that God chose to create the best). So, Timpe concludes as follows:

So if there is a single best possible world, then there exist normative reasons for God to create that world rather than any of the less good worlds. Given that God's motivational reasons necessarily track the normative reasons, God would therefore create that world, that is, the best world. Nevertheless, for the reasons given above, since this necessity comes from God's own nature and not from anything outside of Himself, there is no reason to think that God isn't free in performing a morally obligatory action.[49]

In summary, there are a number of relevant points that are worth drawing attention to. First, the most obvious point is that Wierenga, Senor, and Timpe argue that divine alternativity (i.e., that God was just as equally free to create the best possible world as He was free to refrain from creating the best possible world) is not a necessary condition with respect to divine freedom. Second, Wierenga emphasizes the fact that if God knows *A* is the best action, wants to do *A*, and is able to do *A*, then it is because of *His own nature* that He knows that *A* is the best action, wants to do *A*, and is able to do *A*. This conditional proposition appears to be implied by set (L) (especially the spontaneity condition) which is inspired by Leibniz's philosophy. Third, as indicated earlier, Senor's three conditions (i.e., (i), (ii), and (iii)) with respect to God's freedom to create the best possible world are parallel and thus also reflect set (L). Fourth, while Timpe agrees with Wierenga and Senor that God's free choices are ultimately sourced within Himself, he nevertheless focuses on the importance of God's reasons, in particular His motivational reasons for why He chooses what He chooses. Again, I take it that Leibniz would endorse much, if not all, of what Timpe argues for since what he says regarding (motivational) reasons seems to be implied by Leibniz's intelligence condition. Recall that Leibniz said, "when there is no judgment, there is no freedom," which can be expressed as the conditional proposition "if there is no judgment, then there is no freedom." Such a conditional proposition is very similar to Timpe's conditional proposition captured in his "reasons-constraint on free choice."

> *Reasons-constraint on free choice*: If, at time *t*, *A* has neither any motivational intellectual reasons for *X*-ing nor any motivational affective reasons for *X*-ing, then *A* is incapable, at *t*, of freely choosing *X*.

So, while not to take away from the helpful insights provided by Wierenga, Senor, and Timpe, much of what they conclude can be found in the antecedent work of Leibniz. Consequently, set (L) captures the idea that God can be free, and thus calls into question Jolley's and Rowe's premise (1) that if God creates the best of all possible worlds, then God cannot be free with respect to creating the best of all possible worlds.

3.5 A Potential Worry for Set (L)

Now one might be critical at this point and argue that although set (L) sufficiently captures an account of divine freedom, set (L) is nevertheless inconsistent with an act that God *must* do. That is, the fact that it is necessary that God creates the best possible world is inconsistent with set (L). And, if set (L) is inconsistent with the fact that God must create the best possible world, then there remains a problem for the conjunction of divine freedom and Theistic Optimism.

To elucidate, the objection against set (L) at this point can basically be expressed and simplified in proposition (W):

(W) If it is necessary that God creates the best possible world, then set (L) cannot hold true.

Accordingly, there is (alleged) tension between set (L) and the notion that it is necessary that God creates the best possible world. It is difficult, however, to see how one might offer support for proposition (W) without caricaturing set (L) or calling into question something utterly different than set (L). Nonetheless, why might one think that the idea that it is necessary that God creates the best possible world jeopardizes set (L)? Perhaps one states that there is some metaphysical external reality or being that coexists with God which makes it that God necessarily creates the best possible world. While a coherent notion, this metaphysical hypothesis would, in fact caricature set (L) since stipulating that some metaphysical external reality or being that coexists with God would call into question the spontaneity condition within set (L). The necessity in question, in other words, ultimately finds its source in some *external* reality.

Another possible way of lending support to proposition (W) is to claim that God's necessary act is analogous to a drug addict (who cannot but accept or take drugs) or something akin to psychological compulsion. Here, the necessity is internal and therefore satisfies the spontaneity condition within set (L). However, this alleged support for proposition (W) obviously calls into question the intelligence condition since while the necessity is sourced internally, the volition or action is nonetheless irrational or at the very least non-rational. Again, this support for proposition (W) would only be a caricature of set (L).

Given the implausibility of proposition (W), set (L) seems perfectly consistent with the idea that it is necessary that God creates the best possible world. As Senor, then, rightly says, "[E]ven if God's creating the best world is necessary . . . given God's nature, the theist can still claim that God's creative act satisfies the following conditions [i.e., conditions (i), (ii), and (iii)]."[50] That is, set (L) is consistent with the idea that it is necessary that God creates the best possible world. Or, as Thomas Talbott declares:

> God never makes a mistake concerning the best course of action, never acts upon a false belief, and never suffers from any illusion concerning the consequences of his own actions. With respect to the individual who is God . . . it is a necessary truth that *this individual* always knows which course of action is the best, at least when there *is* a best course of action; it is also a necessary truth that he always chooses whichever course of action he knows to be the best. So in that sense, his most important actions flow, as . . . Leibniz also insisted, from the inner necessity of his own being, or more specifically, from the inner necessity of his own rationality.[51]

Consequently, when one argues that God can be free even while affirming that it is necessary that He creates the best possible world, the necessity in question find its origin and ultimate source within God's nature. In short, there is something about God's perfect nature that precludes Him from doing anything other than the best. Such a preclusion, however, does not negate set (L) and therefore does not call into question divine freedom. So, while set (L) is consistent with a necessary act, set (L) also captures (or at least comes very close to capturing) what it could plausibly mean to say that God is free. Consider these final remarks from Talbott, which, again, seem to highlight set (L):

> If you *combine* the absence of external causes [which is captured by (a) of set (L)] with perfect rationality [which is captured by (b) of set (L)] and the power to act in accordance with such rationality [which is captured by (c) of set (L)]—or, in the case of human beings, the power to act in accordance with a reasonable and well informed judgement concerning the best course of action—why do you not then have something close to a sufficient condition of the freedom that pertains to rational agents? What further freedom could a rational agent possibly desire to have?[52]

3.6 Conclusion

In this chapter I began by highlighting a potential problem for Theistic Optimism that purported to show via Jolley and Rowe that if Theistic Optimism holds true, then God cannot be free in creating the best possible world. I argued against this objection by first gleaning from Leibniz's philosophy, which resulted in what I called set (L).

(a) God is the ultimate source of His actions [from the spontaneity condition];

(b) God acts in accordance with His rational assessment of that which is best [from the intelligence condition];

and

(c) God's act produces the desired result [from the efficacious condition].

I then highlighted how three contemporary philosophers (though they do not state it as such) basically argue that set (L) sufficiently captures divine freedom. I then argued that set (L) is consistent with the idea that it is necessary that God creates the best possible world. However, problems still remain. Although God can be free while it is the case that He must create the best possible world, perhaps He cannot be worthy of praise and thanks with respect to creating the best possible world. For, while alternativity is not required for divine freedom, it is, indeed required for God to be praised and thanked. It is this objection from praiseworthiness and thankworthiness that I consider in the following chapter.

Theistic Optimism, Divine Praiseworthiness, and Thankworthiness

4.1 Introduction

In the previous chapter I argued that Theistic Optimism (i.e., the idea that God must do the best) is consistent with divine freedom. To put it differently, I argued that divine alternativity is not required for God to be free with respect to creating the best possible world. My argument was primarily founded upon a Leibnizian set of propositions that I called set (L):

(a) God is the ultimate source of His actions [from the spontaneity condition];
(b) God acts in accordance with His rational assessment of that which is best [from the intelligence condition];

and

(c) God's act produces the desired result [from the efficacious condition].

Consequently, if the spontaneity condition, the intelligence condition, and the efficacious condition together hold true, then God can be free with respect to creating the best possible world. I then argued that set (L) is consistent with the idea that it is necessary that God create the best possible world. Thus, I concluded that divine freedom is consistent with the Leibnizian notion of Theistic Optimism.

Does Theistic Optimism, however, violate some other nonnegotiable proposition within Leibniz's philosophical theology, namely, the idea that God is worthy of praise and thanks? In this chapter, contrary to what a number of contemporary analytic philosophers of religion propound, I argue that God can, indeed, be worthy of praise and thanks with respect to creating the best possible world. In short, I argue that Theistic Optimism is consistent with the idea that God is worthy of praise and thanks. To begin, Section 4.2 offers some preliminary remarks concerning praiseworthiness and thankworthiness. Section 4.3 draws attention to the primary problem for Theistic Optimism expressed in what I call proposition (T):

> (T) If God must create the best possible world (i.e., if Theistic Optimism holds true), then God cannot be worthy of praise and thanks with respect to creating the best possible world.

Section 4.4 advances a solution to proposition (T). Finally, Section 4.5 points to the summary and conclusions of the chapter.

4.2 Some Preliminary Remarks on Praiseworthiness and Thankworthiness

While Leibniz does not say much concerning thankworthiness, it is evident in the following argument that he is committed to predicating *praise*worthiness on God. Here is what he says:

> Let us assume . . . that God chooses between A and B and that he takes A without having any reason to prefer it to B. I say that this action of God is at the very least not praiseworthy; for all praise must be based on some reason, and by hypothesis there is none.[1]

Leibniz here holds as a premise in the former argument that acting for a reason is a requirement for being praiseworthy concerning the act in question. While this premise is unsurprising given his unwavering commitment to the principle of sufficient reason, it nonetheless highlights the fact that Leibniz is, indeed, committed to the notion that God can be worthy of praise.

In addition, what is notable about Leibniz's argument is that divine praiseworthiness is correlated with *what God has done*, that is, whether or not God is worthy of praise for His action(s). Philosophers of religion frequently differentiate God being worthy of worship concerning *what He has done* from the idea of God being worthy of worship regarding *who He is*, where the former concentrates on God's actions, while the latter draws attention to God's being or character. For example, Richard Swinburne states:

Theism . . . does make this further claim—that God is worthy of worship by men. The theist normally claims that God is worthy of worship both in virtue of his having such essential properties as I have discussed and also in virtue of his having done of his own free will various actions (e.g. rescued the Jews from Egypt and brought them to the Promise Land).[2]

Similarly, while also focusing on Christian theism, W. Paul Franks puts it this way:

Central to any conception of Christian theism is the idea that God is worthy of worship. This worthiness can be spelled out in various ways, but two themes are likely to emerge. One is that God is worthy of worship simply for being who he is. God, as a perfect being, commands the respect and admiration of any other being. The second theme, that follows from the first, is the idea that God is worthy of worship because of what he does. On traditional Christian theism it is taken to be true that God not only created, and sustains, the universe, but also interacts with it, and this interaction produces great goods.[3]

In the view of some, then, there is a substantive difference between God being worthy of worship for what He does and God being worthy of worship for who He is. Applying this difference to our study of Theistic Optimism, then, divine praiseworthiness will be discussed in relation to God creating the best possible world since creating the best possible world is an instance of something that God has done. Moreover, given the fact that Leibniz discusses divine praiseworthiness in the context of what God has done, it seems reasonable to conclude that Leibniz would have no problems with this distinction between God being worthy of worship concerning what He has done and the idea of God being worthy of worship regarding who He is.

Thomas Senor, however, (in common with Swinburne and Franks) draws attention to this plausible distinction, but at the unfortunate expense of claiming that divine praiseworthiness corresponds *only* to who God is, while thankworthiness corresponds *only* to what God has done. Here is what Senor says:

When theists claim that God is to be praised, they often distinguish this from saying that God is to be thanked. Why? Because God is to be praised for *who God is*; God is to be thanked for what *God has done*. Now God's praiseworthiness is surely not just a function of our helplessness before God,

of God's ability to do with us as God will . . . . What makes God praiseworthy
is God's power together with God's nature as fair, merciful, and loving—
God's embodying all that is valuable.[4]

What are we to make of these sentiments from Senor? Is Leibniz mistaken
when he speaks of praiseworthiness correlated with and in the context of
what God has done? While it is commendable that Senor draws attention to
the plausible distinction between who God is and what God has done, it is
nevertheless misleading to claim that praiseworthiness is confined to who God
is. Praiseworthiness, on the one hand, captures only admiration and veneration,
while thankworthiness, on the other hand, highlights only gratitude and
appreciation. The theist's motivation, therefore, for distinguishing "God is to
be praised" from "God is to be thanked" is not to be found in correspondence
with the distinction between who God is and what God has done. The theist's
motivation, rather, is to be found in the fact that when praise is offered to
some object (e.g., God) it captures something entirely different from that of
thankworthiness, namely, admiration and veneration as opposed to gratitude
and appreciation.

Now if the theist's motivation for distinguishing praiseworthiness from
thankworthiness has nothing to do with the distinction between who God is
and what God has done, then it seems coherent (contrary to Senor's position)
that praiseworthiness can also be correlated with what God has done. In short,
does it not seem appropriate for Leibniz to express admiration and veneration
for what God has done? Expressing admiration and veneration (i.e., praise), in
other words, is not limited only for the subject to focus on the ontology of the
object. To offer an analogy, often in the context of watching athletes perform
we say things like: "Wow! Did you see that fade-away jump shot at the end of
the game by Lebron James? That was awesome!" Or, "What an unbelievable
pass that was by Tom Brady! He put the ball only where the receiver could
catch it!" Typical expressions like these seem to suggest that it makes sense
for praise to be correlated with something that an agent does, say, shooting a
basketball or passing a football.

Nevertheless, creaturely analogies aside, Ps. 105:1-2 reads "Praise the LORD;
call on His name; *proclaim His deeds* among the peoples. Sing praises to Him;
speak of all His *wondrous acts*."[5] Here, the exhortation found in the Psalm to
praise God is closely linked to what God has done, and thus substantiates the
idea that God can be praised for His (wondrous) acts. Similarly, the Catechism

of the Catholic Church states that "Praise is the form of prayer which recognizes most immediately that God is God. It lauds God for his own sake and gives him glory, quite beyond what he does, but simply because HE IS."[6] While this statement from the Catechism explicitly supports the idea that God is to praised for who He is (which I take as uncontroversial), the phrase "quite beyond what he does" seems not to rule out the idea that God can be praised for what He does, but, rather, presupposes it. I take the Catechism to be teaching, in other words, that when praise is "quite beyond what he does" it *includes* rather than precludes what God does. In short, because it is natural to look at creation and praise God for what He has done, the Catechism is exhorting its readers to go beyond that and praise God also for who He is. Consequently, if we take seriously what the Psalm and the Catechism teach, then we have good reason to conclude (with Leibniz) that divine praiseworthiness is not limited to praising God for who He is, but, rather, that it is also rightly linked to what God has done.

4.3 Proposition (T)

Despite the coherence of Leibniz's position that divine praiseworthiness can correlate to what God does, we now come to the heart of the issue in this chapter for Theistic Optimism, namely, that a number of analytic philosophers of religion have asserted what we will call proposition (T):

> (T) If God must create the best possible world (i.e., if Theistic Optimism holds true), then God cannot be worthy of praise and thanks with respect to creating the best possible world.

According to (T), there is inconsistency between God being worthy of praise and thanks with respect to creating the best possible world and the idea that God must create the best possible world. Robert Adams, for instance, asserts that the praise and thanks to God found within the Judeo-Christian Psalms "seem quite incongruous with the idea that God created us because if He had not He would have failed to bring about the best possible states of affairs."[7] Similarly, Laura Garcia claims that "On this scenario, gratitude towards God as creator seems inappropriate."[8] In addition, more recent and polished expressions of proposition (T) have been advanced by William Rowe and Daniel Howard-Snyder. Rowe has forcefully argued that "if God's being essentially perfectly good makes it *necessary* for him to do what he sees as the best thing to be done, then it is difficult to make any sense of thanking him and praising him for doing what is best for him to do."[9] He retains this focus with respect to thankworthiness when he states that

> [A]lthough believers should be thankful for the fact that there necessarily exists an omnipotent, omniscient, perfectly good being who is incapable of refraining from doing what he knows to be the best act that can be done in the circumstances, all things considered; it makes no sense to thank that being for doing an act that, given his necessary properties, he is incapable of refraining from doing.[10]

Howard-Snyder, on the other hand, expresses proposition (T) this way:

C. If God is worthy of thanks and praise for what he does [e.g., creating the best possible world], then it redounds to his credit that he does it.

D. If it redounds to his credit that he does it [i.e., creates the best possible world], then he is able to do something worse in place of it.[11]

However, according to Howard-Snyder, if D is false, then it is possible that

> (II) An act of God's [e.g., creating the best possible world] redounds to his credit . . . and he was *unable* to do something better instead.[12]

But Howard-Snyder in support of D claims (II) is impossible, and thus concludes that "If his [i.e., God's] act was the best, then it does not redound to his credit since he was never able to do anything about any of the factors that entailed his performing that act."[13] Consequently, an act that God *must* perform (even if God is the sole agent-cause of the act) cannot be an act worthy of praise and thanks, which is just another way of saying that Theistic Optimism is inconsistent with divine thankworthiness and praiseworthiness. Similar to God's freedom, then, divine alternativity is required in order for God to be worthy of thanks and praise when doing the best, that is, worthy of thanks and praise when creating the best possible world.

One might initially respond to proposition (T) by insisting that it is a mistake to assume the same criterion (i.e., alternativity in this case) by which we judge our fellow human beings can apply to God. Katherin Rogers has recently advanced this type of response and draws attention to the mistaken assumption by first stating:

[E]ven those who subscribe to the view that God is necessarily good, almost always assume that if human beings are not to be praised and blamed unless they choose between open options, then the same must be true for God. And often they argue that, while God cannot do something wrong, His significant options must include a better and worse.[14]

But this assumption, according to Rogers, that God must have alternativity in order to be worthy of praise (and thanks) is simply wrongheaded since "created agents only *have* a reflected justice, while God *is* the independent Justice which the creature can only mirror."[15] Consequently, "our reason for praising the created agent is different from, though related to, the reason for praising God."[16] Here is the focal point of her argument:

Suppose you are a huge Elvis Presley fan. You attend a contest for Elvis impersonators and you judge some to be good and some to be bad based on how well they imitate Elvis. But suppose, now, that The King himself appears. He cannot be judged to be a good or a bad Elvis impersonator, because he is not, and cannot be, an Elvis impersonator at all. The same criteria by which we judge the Elvis impersonators good or bad cannot be applied to him, since he cannot *imitate* Elvis. None the less these criteria are clearly related to the actual Elvis. He is the standard against which the impersonator is measured. We praise the impersonator for accurately imitating Elvis, but The King himself we praise simply for doing what he does so well. And so with God and man. The imitation of God requires that we hold fast to the good on our own, and hence requires open options. We are praiseworthy when we choose to cling to the good God has given. God Himself *is* the good, and is praiseworthy, or better "*worship*worthy," simply for being what He is.[17]

Accordingly, open options (i.e., alternativity) cannot apply to God, and, therefore, it makes sense for God to be worthy of praise simply for doing what He does so well. Rogers concludes that "It is just a mistake to insist upon the same criteria for praise and the same mechanics of free will with respect to God, the standard, and man, the imitator."[18]

While this response from Rogers is a reasonable response given certain theological commitments (e.g., divine simplicity), I nonetheless develop below my own response to proposition (T) by consulting the Judeo-Christian doctrine of divine grace. This doctrine applied to God's act of creating the best possible world provides sufficient grounds for concluding that God is worthy of praise and thanks for creating the best possible world. Along the way, I will consider possible objections to my argument.

4.4 Divine Grace as a Response to Proposition (T)

While there is frequent contention over the nature and attributes of God within philosophical theology, there is nevertheless widespread agreement that the Judeo-Christian God (at least) is a God of grace, that is, a gracious God. In Exod. 34:6, for example, we read of God revealing Himself to Moses: "The LORD passed before him and proclaimed: 'The LORD! The LORD! A God compassionate and gracious, slow to anger, abounding in kindness and faithfulness.'"[19] Similarly, Ps. 145:8 states that "The LORD is gracious and compassionate, slow to anger and abounding in kindness."[20] In addition, in the New Testament we read in 1 Pet. 5:10 that "[A]fter you have suffered a little while, the God of all grace, who has called you to his eternal glory in Christ, will himself restore, confirm, strengthen, and establish you."[21] Finally, Leibniz, not to be forgotten, speaks of what might have moved God "to dispense his saving grace in a certain way."[22]

Given the fact that grace is predicated on the Judeo-Christian God, God typically has a disposition to love and express goodness, thus exerting favor over some subject or recipient. As Gen. 6:8 reads: "But Noah found favor with the LORD."[23] These characteristics highlight what we might call the "favor condition" in order for God to be gracious. Given this condition, God is gracious only if there is a divine disposition to love and express goodness toward some subject or recipient. The twentieth-century Catholic theologian, Ludwig Ott, puts it this way:

> In the terminology of Holy Writ, grace (χαρις= gratia) in its subjective sense, signifies a disposition of condescension or benevolence shown by a highly-placed person to one in a lower place, and especially of God towards mankind (gratia = benevolence).[24]

Although it may seem obvious that the favor condition is a required component of divine grace, such a condition is not sufficient. God's disposition to love and express goodness, it is also said, must be independent of the merit of the recipient being loved. For, it seems plausible to think that God may have a disposition to love some subject, but such a disposition to love could be *dependent* on the merit of the subject being loved. Such a scenario, however, cannot be an instance of divine grace. These characteristics underscore what we might call the "unmerited condition" in order for God to be gracious. Consider how the contemporary theologian John Feinberg highlights the unmerited condition:

> As for the concept of grace, it is best understood as unmerited favor. That means that something good happens to you even though you have done nothing to merit or earn it. Scripture portrays God as a God of abounding grace. It is important to understand that God owes no one any grace. This is so not just because God is not *prima facie* obligated to any of us, and not just because none of us have done anything that merits such favor. It is so as well by the very nature of grace as *unmerited* favor. If God or anyone else were obligated to give grace, it would no longer be grace—blessing would simply be a matter of justice.[25]

Consequently, according to Feinberg, the unmerited condition is part and parcel of what it means to say that God is gracious. As Feinberg further states, "The very nature of grace . . . is that it is never owed or earned."[26] Generally, then, what distinguishes the love of God from the grace of God is that the latter is always unmerited.

Now if we bear in mind both the favor condition and the unmerited condition that I have earlier drawn attention to, then the crucial understanding of the concept of divine grace (DG) begins to emerge:

> (DG) For any property of divine grace, God is gracious if and only if (i) God has a disposition to love and (ii) the divine disposition to love is independent of the merit of the subject or recipient being loved.

On the face of it, DG has some intuitive plausibility and appears to be the historical understanding of divine grace with respect to the Judeo-Christian religion. In fact, Herman Bavinck, a nineteenth-century advocate of DG, captures it quite nicely when he says:

> Objectively, χαρις means beauty, charm, favor (Luke 4:22; Col. 4:6; Eph. 4:29); and, subjectively, it means favor, a positive disposition on the part of the giver, and gratitude and devotion on the part of the recipient. Ascribed to God, grace is the voluntary, unrestrained, and unmerited favor that he shows to sinners and that, instead of the verdict of death, brings them righteousness and life. As such it is a virtue and attribute of God (Rom.

5:15; 1 Pet. 5:10), demonstrated in the sending of his Son, who is full of grace (John 1:14ff.; 1 Pet. 1:13), and additionally in the bestowal of all sorts of spiritual and material benefits, all of which are the gifts of grace and are themselves called "grace" (Rom. 5:20; 6:1; Eph. 1:7; 2:5, 8; Phil 1:2; Col. 1:2; Titus 3:7, etc.), thus radically excluding all merit on the part of humans (John 1:17; Rom. 4:4, 16; 6:14, 23; 11:5ff.; Eph. 2:8; Gal. 5:3-4).[27]

What I take Bavinck to be highlighting here is that in order for God to be gracious, He must not only have a disposition to love, but also that the disposition to love thus expressed must be unmerited. Of course, God may, indeed, have a disposition to love, but such a disposition to love could be dependent on the merit of the subject being loved. Such a scenario, however, would not be an instance of grace since condition (ii) of DG is not met. In a different scenario, the disposition to love may surely be independent of the merit of the subject being loved, but it may be the case that God did not, in fact, have the disposition to love. Here condition (i) of DG is not met, and so this also is not an instance of divine grace. Therefore, according to Bavinck (and others such as Feinberg), (i) and (ii) are necessary (and perhaps jointly sufficient) in order for God to be gracious.

Yet, it is important at this point to highlight the fact that we are focusing on God's *act* of creating the best possible world. One might be tempted, furthermore, to think that while (i) and (ii) of DG are necessary conditions for a divine gracious *act*, they nevertheless are also jointly sufficient. For, as we have seen, the *concept* of grace is typically defined as "unmerited favor." However, it seems plausible when speaking of a token gracious act that the act in question would need also to be *motivated* by that loving disposition toward the subject or recipient of the act. For instance, a rich man may have a disposition to give to everyone $100 (while at the same time that disposition to give everyone $100 is independent of any merit), but, in fact, not have the motivation to do so. That is, God could have a disposition to love some subject or recipient, indeed act toward the subject or recipient, but if that token act is not motivated by unmerited love, then the act is still not a divine gracious act. Accordingly, there is a substantive distinction between having a disposition (to love) and having a motive (to love), and thus when speaking of a token *act* DG must be amplified by the idea of motivation. We might call this the "motivation condition" in order for God to *act* graciously.[28]

Since, then, there is prima facie good reason to think that conditions (i) and (ii) are not constitutive of the Judeo-Christian doctrine of God *acting* graciously, we will understand a divine gracious act (DGA) as now stated:

(DGA) For any divine gracious act, God acts graciously if and only if (i) God's act expresses a disposition to love, (ii) the divine disposition to love is independent of the merit of the subject or recipient being loved, and (iii) God's act is motivated by unmerited love.

4.5 The Necessity of the Best Possible World and Divine Grace

Robert Adams, a contemporary advocate of the idea that God is gracious, claims, however, that God's gracious love for the best possible world is inconsistent with His having a (necessary) preference for creating the best possible world. In addition, if Adams (and others) are correct, then this raises a problem for the fundamental argument of this chapter, namely, that DG provides a solution to the problem that God cannot be worthy of praise and thanks with respect to creating the best possible world necessarily. Adams begins by defining DG "as a disposition to love which is not dependent on the merit of the person being loved."[29] Given this definition of DG, he then concludes that while God would, indeed, be equally free to create the best possible world as opposed to some other world, God nevertheless cannot have as the *grounds* for choosing to create a world the fact that the world is the best possible world. To think otherwise would jeopardize not only God's freedom but also the notion that God is gracious toward the world He creates. Here is what Adams says:

A God who is gracious with respect to creating might well choose to create and love less excellent creatures than He could have chosen. This is not to suggest that grace in creation consists in a preference for imperfection as such. God could have chosen to create the best of all possible creatures, and still have been gracious in choosing them. God's graciousness in creation does not imply that the creatures He has chosen to create must be less excellent than the best possible. It implies, rather, that even if they are the best possible creatures, that is not the ground for His choosing them. And it [i.e., divine grace] implies that there is nothing in God's nature or character which would require Him to act on the principle of choosing the best possible creatures to be the object of His creative powers.[30]

Similarly, theologian David H. Kelsey adds:

> [N]othing about the stories of God's creating entails that God must necessarily also draw what is created to eschatological consummation or that God must reconcile them if they were alienated from God. Were it otherwise, neither God's relating to draw creatures to eschatological consummation nor God's relating to reconcile estranged creatures would be grace or gracelike. For grace is, by definition, not necessitated.[31]

Accordingly, the appeal to DG is motivated on the part of Adams and Kelsey in order to preserve the alternative possibilities account of God's freedom in creating some particular world (e.g., the best possible world). Laura Garcia (a proponent of proposition [T]) also highlights a similar outlook where she states that

> God is traditionally viewed as creating out of gracious love and kindness toward his creatures *rather than out of necessity*, whether of an internal or external kind. To deny divine freedom is to see the universe in all its aspects as a necessary emanation from God's nature, so that God had no choice but to create us and our fellow creatures.[32]

What we see here from Adams, Kelsey, and now Garcia, is that an act, such as creating the best possible world, cannot both be an instance of DG and one performed necessarily. Therefore, according to these philosophers and theologians, the idea of DG implies an alternativity with respect to creating a particular world, where God was just as equally free to create the best possible world as He was free not to create the best possible world.

Now if Adams, Kelsey, and Garcia are correct, then the notion of DG has the consequence that in order for God to be gracious with respect to, say, creating the best possible world, God must have been just as equally free to create the best possible world as He was free not to create the best possible world. However, have Adams, Kelsey, and Garcia given us another required component to add to our understanding of a DGA act (i.e., DGA)? I do not think so, for the idea of DG has no implication concerning what the grounds are for God creating a particular world over, say, some other world. And, if DG carries no such implication, then God can, indeed, act graciously with respect to creating the best possible world while the act to create the best possible world was performed necessarily. Perhaps these remarks from Rowe can shed light on the shortcomings of Adams, Kelsey, and Garcia. He begins by asking:

In what, then, given that God has a reason for creating one world over another, would that reason reside? It would reside, I suggest, in his desire to create the very best state of affairs that he can. Having such a desire does not preclude gracious love. It does not imply that God cannot or does not equally love the worst creatures along with best creatures. Loving parents, for example, may be disposed to love fully any child that is born to them, regardless of whatever talents that child is capable of developing. But such love is consistent with a preference for a child who will be born without mental or physical impairment, a child who will develop his or her capacities for kindness toward others, who will develop his or her tastes for music, good literature, and so on. And in the like manner, God will graciously love any creature he might choose to create, not just the best possible creatures.[33]

Rowe continues by saying:

[I]f God is not reduced to playing dice with respect to selecting a world to create, there must be some basis for his selection over and beyond his gracious love for all creatures regardless of merit. And that basis, given God's nature, as an absolutely perfect being, would seem to be to do always what is best and wisest to be done. And surely the best and wisest for God to do is to create the best world he can. Doing so seems to be entirely consistent with God's gracious love of all creatures regardless of their merit.[34]

How is this argument to be understood? According to Rowe, God, as a perfect being, must have the desire to create the best states of affairs that He can. Such a desire, however, does not preclude gracious love. Further, God must have some basis for creating one world over another world other than gracious love. That basis, according to Rowe, is that God always does what is wisest and best; and what is wisest and best can include expressing gracious love.

Therefore, Rowe's argument (which is quite Leibnizian), if more plausible than its negation, would provide further reason to uphold the proposition that God must create the best possible world is consistent with that particular act being done graciously. We might conclude with Rowe at this point (*contra* Adams, Kelsey, and Garcia) that "It is doubtful, therefore, that the Judeo-Christian concept of grace rules out the view . . . that God must create the best world if there is a best world to create."[35]

One might object at this point and state that while divine grace is consistent with God creating the best possible world out of *metaphysical* necessity, divine grace is nevertheless inconsistent with God creating the best possible world out of *moral* necessity. In addition, one might, indeed, think that when Adams, Kelsey, and Garcia use such locutions as "necessity," "must," and "required" applied to God's act to create the best possible world, they have a *moral* (as opposed to a metaphysical) notion in mind. Accordingly, if the distinction between acts that are morally required and acts that are supererogatory apply to God, one might think that God's nature necessitates His doing what duty requires, but, of course, not necessitating those acts of supererogation (such as creating the best possible world). So, while it may be granted according to this objection that divine grace is consistent with God creating the best possible world out of metaphysical necessity, divine grace nevertheless is inconsistent with God creating the best possible world out of moral necessity.

How might we respond to this objection? First, while I do not develop an argument here, perhaps an act of supererogation is not required for a gracious act. One might see that while God's nature necessitates His doing what duty requires of Him, He nevertheless acts graciously with respect to these duties. Consequently, going beyond the call of duty is not a necessary condition for a gracious act, and thus God could act graciously without performing a supererogatory act. A second and perhaps more promising response would be to argue that the distinction between dutiful acts and supererogatory acts cannot apply to God. For, supposing a particular metaphysics of divine freedom, God out of metaphysical necessity does what is best. Freely doing an act of supererogation is an option only for beings who are free to fail to do what is best. But, it is not the case, given our supposition, that God is free to fail to do what is best. Thus, it is not the case that freely doing an act of supererogation is an option for God. Moreover, supererogation depends on the notion of duty, and one might plausibly argue that God (at least as traditionally understood) does not have duties. Rather, while the Euthyphro dilemma cannot be addressed here, God (or, more specifically, God's nature) is typically seen as the standard or source of moral duties, and I take it that Leibniz would be sympathetic to the outlook that there does not exist a set of (Platonic) moral standards for God to abide by, especially given his commitment to divine conceptualism. In other words, given Leibniz's commitment to divine conceptualism (covered in Chapter 2), necessary truths concerning morality can plausibly be ontologically grounded in God's understanding. So, Leibniz would likely deny the idea that God has duties.

To further support the consistency of God acting graciously while performing some token act necessarily, it seems implausible to think that before he existed the subject or recipient would have any sort of claim on the divine token act. Creating the best possible world, say, is a gracious gift not because it could have been otherwise in an alternativity sense but, rather, because for any creature it is undeserved, and thus it is a fitting expression of God's goodness for that creature. As Jesse Couenhoven nicely puts it:

> A necessary creation remains gratuitous in that we have no claim on it: it is an undeserved and bounteous gift to those who are created. Even if the Father, Son and Holy Spirit necessarily create, this does not mean that they owe creation to us . . . or that we should be anything other than thankful for it! Creation is a gracious gift not because it is unnecessary, and thus free in a libertarian sense, but because it is an undeserved yet fitting expression of God's loving kindness, and thus free in the normative sense.[36]

To reiterate, then, simply because God performs the act of creating the best possible world necessarily, it does not follow that what is created *deserved* or *merited* being created. Moreover, given the fact that God exists prior (whether temporally or nontemporally) to that which He creates, it follows that what is created cannot deserve or merit being created. Therefore, being gracious while performing some token act (such as creating the best possible world) is consistent with that act being performed necessarily.

4.6 Back to Praiseworthiness and Thankworthiness

Now with license to employ DGA, one begins to have a powerful argument against the notion that divine praiseworthiness and thankworthiness with respect to creating the best possible world is inconsistent with the idea that God must create the best possible world, and thus proposition (T) (i.e., if God must create the best possible world, then God cannot be worthy of praise and thanks with respect to creating the best possible world) is called into question. In order to see this, consider an earthbound illustration where we suppose that God, because of His perfect nature, healed a child from cancer necessarily. Suppose further that this act of healing expressed a disposition to love the child, the disposition to love could not be dependent on the merit of the child being loved but, rather, on its need, and that God's act of healing was motivated by unmerited love for the child. That is, God was *gracious* in performing this act of healing. In addition, if the parents of the beloved child realize that these things are so, does it not seem reasonable that the parents would assert the following?

(1) We recognize this is, indeed, a token act necessarily performed;

(2) We affirm that God was the sole source for performing it;

(3) We are full of joy that God expressed a disposition to love our child and that God was motivated to act according to this disposition;

and,

(4) We consider ourselves to be in debt to God since nothing in ourselves or our child merited this act.

It seems the parents could, indeed, assert all of (1)–(4) even though they realize that, because of God's perfect nature, God healed this child from cancer necessarily. However, if the parents can assert these things, then they can reasonably praise and thank God for healing their child of cancer. What this illustration highlights is the fact that if God is gracious while performing some token act, then God is, indeed, praiseworthy and thankworthy for that particular act.

In addition, one might think that the parents are obligated to praise and thank God from the sheer fact that the parents (and the child!) *benefitted* from God's gracious act. Thomas Senor has recently advanced this line of thought where he gives the illustration of a benevolent aunt bestowing gifts upon her niece or nephew. Here, while the niece or nephew benefitted from the aunt's kindness, the aunt nevertheless was unable to refrain from giving. The aunt, in other words, gives necessarily. Such a necessity, Senor argues, does not result in the fact that the aunt ought not to be (at least) thanked. Here is what he says:

> Suppose that you have a benevolent aunt who frequently sends you gifts. Suppose you knew that this woman did what she did was because of her upbringing and very strong religious convictions. Indeed, suppose you knew that given your relative need and her relative plenty, her relationship to you, and her belief in the importance of giving (particularly to the family) she was not really able to resist giving you generous gifts. Would your understanding

of her situation release you of a duty to thank her for her kindness toward you? Of course not. We owe our [benefactors] a debt of thanks when, motivated by a concern for our well being, they bestow benefits upon us. In fact, it might be that the condition that the gift is given out of a "concern for our well being" is overly restrictive. If I have a self-serving uncle who gives me a gift primarily because it will provide him with a significant tax write-off, I still have a duty to thank him provided that he was able to see that the gift would benefit me.[37]

Two things are noteworthy here with respect to Senor's remarks. First, although he does not explicitly refer to the idea of grace with respect to this illustration, it nevertheless seems plausible to think that what he has in mind is something akin to the notion of grace since the aunt gives generously to someone who does not deserve it. Second, according to Senor, one is obligated to thank the aunt simply because of benefitting from the aunt's kindness, even on the supposition that the condition to give out of concern for one's well-being is, indeed, overly restrictive. The beneficiaries (i.e., the niece or nephew), in other words, owe the benefactor (i.e., the aunt) thanks for the benefit they received. Therefore, even though Senor does not refer to the idea of a gracious act, it is plausible to think that one benefits from a gracious act, and is thus thankworthy for that act.

Richard Swinburne advances a similar outlook where he seeks to defend the position that "there is clearly an even stronger case for a duty to pay explicit respect to benefactors."[38] Although Swinburne emphasizes the notion of respect, his argument is nevertheless in the context of God being worthy of worship, where God is the benefactor. The following is the essence of his hypothesis:

If a man has done much for us, he is entitled to our explicit respect. By virtue of their status benefactors are entitled to a special degree of respect. We show this by our mode of address, by giving them places of honour, perhaps by the occasional present. Sometimes to show him respect is the only return one can make to a benefactor for what he has done. Now of course some men may think that there is no obligation on the recipient of the benefit to show respect to the benefactor. They should, however, reflect on that fact that all societies from Tsarist Russia to Communist China, from primitive tribes to capitalist U.S.A., have shown such respect and thought it right to do so. They have shown such respect often when the benefactors were in no position to confer further benefit.[39]

Accordingly, what Senor's and Swinburne's earthbound illustrations highlight is that an action is worthy of praise and thanks (and respect a la Swinburne) so long as the benefitting action is undeserved. Applying their outlook to our current discussion, then, it is plausible to affirm that God is, indeed, praiseworthy and thankworthy in light of being gracious while performing some token act, even if the token act was done necessarily.

Finally, in the spirit of the Judeo-Christian religion, a sidelong glance at the Judeo-Christian Scriptures seems to support the idea that God acting graciously is sufficient for His being worthy of praise and thanks. For example, in Eph. 1:5-6 , the Apostle Paul's letter reads, "In love he predestined us for adoption as sons through Jesus Christ, according to the purpose of his will, *to the praise of his glorious grace*, with which he has blessed us in the Beloved."[40] Similarly, in 1 Cor. 1:4, Paul writes, "I give *thanks* to my God always for you *because of the grace of God* that was given you in Christ Jesus."[41] What we see from these texts is that praise and thanks are closely correlated with God's grace. So, while of course these texts are silent on the question of whether or not God could have acted otherwise in an alternativity sense (especially with respect to creating the best possible world or refraining from creating the best possible world), they nevertheless highlight the fact that being gracious provides the basis for admiration and gratitude expressed toward God when He performs some token act.

4.7 Conclusion

We have seen that a number of analytic philosophers of religion endorse what we have called proposition (T): If God must create the best possible world (i.e., if Theistic Optimism holds true), then God cannot be worthy of praise and thanks with respect to creating the best possible world. In this chapter, however, I have argued against proposition (T), thus concluding that divine praiseworthiness and thankworthiness are consistent with the idea that God must create the best possible world. In order to reach this conclusion, I first argued that the idea that God must create the best possible world is consistent with the fact that God's act of creating the best possible world was a gracious act. I then argued that if God's act of creating the best possible world was a gracious act, then God can be worthy of praise and thanks with respect to that act.

Theistic Optimism and Divine Aseity

5.1 Introduction

We have seen in Chapter 4 that Theistic Optimism does not call into question the fact that God is worthy of praise and thanks. In other words, God can be praiseworthy and thankworthy with respect to creating the best possible world even if He must create the best possible world. Consequently, divine alternativity is not a required condition in order for God to be worthy of praise and thanks. At this point, however, another important question arises and needs to be dealt with, namely, does Theistic Optimism somehow call into question a fundamental divine attribute theists typically call *divine aseity*?

In this chapter, I explore this question and conclude that it is not the case that Theistic Optimism threatens divine aseity. The conclusion of my argument is primarily founded upon the doctrine of *creatio ex nihilo* (CEN), where I argue in Sections 5.3 and 5.4 that it provides plausible grounds for thinking that God possesses aseity. Then in Section 5.5 I argue that the doctrine of CEN is consistent with the idea that God must create the best possible world (i.e., consistent with Theistic Optimism). Before developing my argument, however, Section 5.2 describes the tension between Theistic Optimism and divine aseity.

5.2 The Tension Between Theistic Optimism and Divine Aseity

The term aseity, by itself, is derived from the Latin phrase *a se*, meaning "from or by itself."[1] Aseity thus applied to God captures the absolute independence, self-sufficiency, and self-existence of God, such that He is *from Himself* in all respects. In addition, divine aseity does not entail the view that God creates

Himself. The phrase *a se* is typically taken in a negative way, which is just to say that God does not have some lack or need that must be satisfied by the existence of some external person or principle, nor is He a product of factors or agencies working independently of Him. William Lane Craig, while contrasting aseity with God's necessary existence, understands the doctrine this way:

> Minimally speaking, God exists a se if and only if He exists independently of everything else. Were everything other than God to disappear, God would still exist. Such a minimalist or "thin" conception of divine aseity entails that God exists independently of anything else in every possible world in which He exists but does not entail that God exists in every possible world. God's existing in every possible world is a function of His attribute of metaphysically necessary existence. But conjoin divine aseity with divine necessity, and we lay the foundations for a truly great concept of God, a being which eternally exists in every possible world independently of anything else.[2]

According to Craig, then, that God exists independently of everything else is necessary and sufficient for God to have aseity. Leibniz would likely agree with Craig that God exists independently of everything else, but routinely calls God *ens a se* (i.e., being from itself). As he says, "God's *independence* means that he is necessary and eternal in existing, which is called *ens a se*."[3] In addition to predicating *ens a se* on God, Leibniz expresses God's self-existence and ontological independence when committed to his cosmological argument for the existence of God. Here is what Leibniz says:

> God is the first reason of things: for such things are bounded, as all that which we see and experience, are contingent and have nothing in them to render their existence necessary, it being plain that time, space, and matter, united and uniform in themselves and indifferent to everything, might have received entirely other motions and shapes, and in another order.[4]

He concludes the argument by saying:

> Therefore one must seek the reason for the existence of the world, which is the whole assemblage of *contingent* things, and seek it in the substance which carries with it the reason for its existence, and which in consequence is *necessary* and eternal.[5]

Here, Leibniz is basically arguing that in order to account for the whole assemblage of the contingent order, the explanation needs to be found in a substance which has within itself the sufficient reason for its own existence.

In other words, God (i.e., the explanation of the contingent order) must exist by necessity of His own nature. To assert otherwise is to beg the question as to what sufficiently explains the existence of God, if He exists. Hugh McCann highlights Leibniz's point about divine aseity correlating with the cosmological argument when he says:

> Without this feature of *aseitas* or aseity, the God hypothesized in the cosmological argument would not be qualified for the role he is to fulfill: that of explaining the existence of entities such as we find in the world— entities that lack aseity, whose existence can only be explained, if at all, as derived elsewhere. It would do no good to argue that a creator is needed to account for the existence of the world, only to face the objection that some further agency is required to account for the creator's existence. Postulating aseity in God renders that objection futile. If such a being exists, then to ask what causes him to exist is like asking what makes water H_2O. Nothing makes water H_2O; it simply *is* H_2O by nature. And in the same way, a being possessing aseity exists by its own nature.[6]

So, there is for Leibniz (and for McCann) an interconnectedness between his cosmological argument for God's existence and his affirmation that God does, indeed, have aseity. It is a hopeless endeavor, in other words, to claim that the cosmological argument can have plausibility without a God having aseity.

Nevertheless, despite Leibniz's commitment to the self-existence and ontological independence of God, a number of theologians have asserted what we will call proposition (A):

> (A) If God must create (as opposed to not creating), then God cannot have aseity (i.e., be from Himself).

According to (A), then, there is an inconsistency between divine aseity and the idea that God must create. Consider, for example, the way in which John Frame highlights proposition (A):

> We are inclined to say that God would still be God, even if he had chosen not to create Steve Hays. So we say that God's creation of Hays is a free act, not a necessary one. The same consideration applies equally to all of God's creative acts. Not only Hays, but the whole world is, we say, a free creation of God, not one in which he was constrained, even by his own nature. The same may be said of providence and especially redemption, for the very idea of grace seems to imply that God might have chosen otherwise. God's nature, it seems, does not force him to create or redeem. For if he must

create or redeem, even if the necessity comes from his own nature, it would seem that he owes something to the creation, that the creation has a claim on him (contrary to his aseity; see chapter 26).[7]

Similarly, James Beilby claims that

> [W]hile God's choice was free in that it was self-determined—it was neither indeterminate nor externally determined—for divine aseity to be maintained, self-determination is necessary, but not sufficient. Divine aseity requires that God's decision to create the world be free in a libertarian sense of the word—God possessed *power to the contrary* of his choice. While he was not and could never be "disinterested" in his decision, there was nothing—either external to him or *part of his internal nature*—that necessitated one choice or made another impossible. Divine aseity, therefore, requires not only that God's choice be free—that is, self-determined—but that it not be internally necessitated.[8]

As a last proponent of proposition (A), K. Scott Oliphant argues:

> (2) God's will is free, in that he is able to and *does* make choices and commits himself to actions that were in no way necessary . . . . If we give up 2, then creation becomes necessary, and, again, his essential aseity is compromised.[9]

There are two items here that are important to highlight given these remarks from advocates of proposition (A). First, these critics argue that divine alternativity with respect to creating is *required* for divine aseity, and thus the idea that God "must" create (even if the must is sourced in God's nature) renders it impossible for God to be an independent, self-sufficient, and self-existent being.[10] Second, these critics are focused primarily on God *creating in general* as opposed to God creating a particular world, such as the best possible world.[11] That is, these critics do not explicitly claim that Theistic Optimism is a problem for divine aseity since Theistic Optimism focuses on God creating a particular world, namely, the best possible world. So, it does not appear on the face of it that these advocates of proposition (A) also hold to the notion that Theistic Optimism jeopardizes divine aseity.

Keep in mind, however, that it is part and parcel of Theistic Optimism that God must do the best. In addition, the fact that there exists a created order as opposed to no created order (sometimes referred to as the "null world") is a reasonable indicator that creating something *is/was better* than not creating at all. Given, then, that God must do the best along with the idea that creating something is better than not creating at all, creating in general (as opposed to not creating at all) is just as inevitable as creating a particular world, namely, the best possible world. Consequently, Theistic Optimism is not only applied to God creating a particular world (i.e., the best possible world) but also applied to God creating in general since creating is better than not creating at all. So, it is not a stretch at this point to conclude that proponents of proposition (A) would claim that Leibniz's Theistic Optimism is in tension with divine aseity.[12]

With that caveat in mind, I now develop an argument for the consistency of divine aseity and the idea that God must do the best, thus claiming that proposition (A) is false. An exploration into the doctrine of CEN will expedite the argument. This doctrine, along with some of its implications, will provide sufficient grounds for thinking that God has aseity. I then argue that the doctrine of CEN is consistent with the idea that God must create. The following is a summary of my argument where M = God must create; A = God has aseity; and C = God creates ex nihilo:

(P1) $(C \rightarrow A)$
(P2) $(M \wedge C)$

Therefore,

(C1) $(M \wedge A)$

Along the way, I will consider possible objections to my argument.[13]

5.3 Creatio Ex Nihilo and Existential Priority

While it is a matter of dispute whether or not the idea of CEN is explicitly found in the Judeo-Christian Scriptures, it is nevertheless affirmed throughout the history of the Judeo-Christian tradition.[14] In *Theophilus to Autolycus*, for example, written in the late second century, Theophilus (120–190) held that:

> [I]f God is uncreated and matter [is] uncreated, God is no longer, according to the Platonists, the Creator of all things, nor, so far as their opinions hold, is the monarchy [i.e., the existence of God as the sole first principle] of God established. And further, as God, because He is uncreated, is also unalterable; so if matter, too, were uncreated, it also would be unalterable, and equal to God; for that which is created is mutable and alterable, but that

which is uncreated is immutable and unalterable. And what great thing is it if God made the world out of existent materials? For even a human artist, when he gets material from some one, makes of it what he pleases. But the power of God is manifested in this, that out of things that are not He makes whatever He pleases.[15]

In this passage, while clearly arguing against the Platonic idea of the eternal existence of matter, Theophilus, by implication, endorses what we might call the doctrine of CEN, where the central idea is that God willed into existence from nothing what formerly did not have existence. A later advocate of the doctrine of CEN was Saint Augustine. Augustine characterizes the doctrine this way:

In the beginning, that is from yourself, in your wisdom which is begotten of your substance, you made something and made it out of nothing. For you made heaven and earth not out of your own self, or it would be equal to your only-begotten Son and therefore to yourself. It cannot possibly be right for anything which is not of you to be equal to you. Moreover, there was nothing apart from you out of which you could make them, God one in three and three in one. That is why you made heaven and earth out of nothing, a great thing and a little thing, since you, both omnipotent and good, make all things good, a great heaven and a little earth. You were, the rest was nothing.[16]

In addition, in his *Monologion*, Saint Anselm held that

[S]ince all existing things exist through the supreme essence, and nothing can exist through him unless he either makes it or is the matter for it, it follows necessarily that nothing but him exists unless he makes it. And since nothing exists or has existed except him and the things made by him, he could not make anything at all through any instrument or assistance other than himself. Now whatever he made, he certainly made it either from something as its matter or from nothing. Therefore, since it is perfectly obvious that the essence of all things that exist, other than the supreme essence, was made by that same supreme essence, and that it does not exist from any matter, there is undoubtedly nothing more evident than this: the supreme essence alone, through himself, produced so great a mass of things ... from nothing.[17]

An important element of the doctrine of CEN is what we might call the "ontological difference" component. As Augustine states, "For you made heaven and earth *not out of your own self*, or it would be equal to your only-begotten

Son and therefore to yourself."[18] What the ontological difference component asserts is the fact that there is a difference between the being of God and the being of any creation. To put it negatively, according to CEN, creation cannot be an extension of God's own being. Consequently, the ontological difference component highlights what is typically called the "Creator-creature" distinction.

In addition to the ontological difference component, there is also what we might call the "preexisting matter denial" component. The preexisting matter denial component claims that God created the world without consulting or using any preexisting matter, typically referring to Plato's eternal matter, as we saw from the remarks of Theophilus. God, rather, simply brings the created order into a state of existence from a state of nonexistence by his will or decree. Therefore, in light of the preexisting matter denial component, when one speaks of CEN, he ought not to think of "nothing" as a kind of eternal matter, or as an ethereal "something" from which God created the world, or even a physical vacuum which God filled.

Given both the ontological difference component and the preexisting matter denial component (collected from Theophilus, Augustine, and Anselm), the key idea of CEN begins to emerge:

> (CEN) For any doctrine of *creatio ex nihilo*, God creates out of nothing only if (i) that which is created is ontologically distinct from God's own being and (ii) God does not create from any preexisting, eternal matter (not even a physical vacuum).

On the face of it (CEN) has some intuitive plausibility. In fact, Leibniz appears to endorse (CEN); that is, it seems as though he affirms both conditions (i) and (ii). With respect to the ontological difference component (i.e., (i)), we can infer that Leibniz holds to this given that a substantial portion of his philosophy is explicitly devoted against Spinoza's metaphysical monism. It would be odd, in other words, for Leibniz to be so zealous against Spinoza's metaphysical monism while at the same time thinking that creation is simply an extension of God's own being, which is a denial of the ontological difference component of (CEN). Here is a sampling of Leibniz being exercised against Spinoza regarding this point:

> I have many other arguments to present and several of them serve to show that according to the view which completely robs created things of all power and action, God would be the only substance, and created things would only

be accidents or modifications of God. So those who are of this opinion will, in spite of themselves, fall into that of Spinoza, who seems to me to have taken furthest the consequences of the Cartesian doctrine of occasional causes.[19]

Whether or not Leibniz is correct in arguing that occasionalism implies the idea that there is only one substance (i.e., God), here he is clearly exercised against Spinoza's doctrine of metaphysical monism. Because of this we have good reason to think that Leibniz does, indeed, affirm the ontological difference component, and therefore holds to (i) of CEN.[20]

In addition to Leibniz affirming (i) of CEN, we have good reason to also conclude that Leibniz affirmed the preexisting matter denial component. If Leibniz was not committed to (ii) of CEN, then he would find himself resonating with Plato's idea that there exists eternal matter coexisting with God. However, Leibniz does, in fact, distance himself from Plato's notion of the existence of eternal matter. In the *Confessio philosophi* he says, "I reply *first* that all things are created ex nihilo, not from preexisting matter at any moment whatever, for even matter itself is created."[21] Leibniz here, while conversing with Nicolas Steno, affirms the preexisting matter denial component, that is, (ii) of CEN, since he clearly distances himself from Plato's notion of eternal matter. Or, as Daniel Cook says:

> Leibniz does believe that the "eternal truths" or Platonic forms exist, but only in God's mind [as we saw from Leibniz's divine conceptualism]; they have no independent reality. Leibniz's theory of Creation does substantially differ from Plato's, whose Creation story in the *Timaeus* has the Demiurge creating the world out of pre-existing matter, in that Leibniz does rule out the possibility of eternal matter.[22]

So, on the face of it, it does appear as though Leibniz is committed to (i) and (ii) of CEN, and therefore finds himself resonating with the collected thoughts of Theophilus, Augustine, and Anselm concerning CEN. To think that Leibniz denied (i) or (ii) of CEN would collapse his outlook into either Spinoza's metaphysical monism or Plato's doctrine of eternal matter. Leibniz, however, is clearly exercised against both of these metaphysical outlooks and thereby committed to (i) and (ii) of CEN.

However, Paul Copan and William Lane Craig, contemporary advocates of CEN, have recently argued that in order to sustain CEN God must also have created, *if they exist at all*, abstract objects (e.g., numbers, sets, properties, relations, propositions, and possible worlds).[23] Here is what they say:

> The chief theological failing of Platonism, and therefore the reason it is unacceptable to orthodox theists, is that Platonism is incompatible with the doctrine of *creatio ex nihilo* and so fundamentally compromises divine aseity. For Platonism posits infinite realms of being [i.e., abstract objects] that are metaphysically necessary and uncreated by God.[24]

Here, one might think that Copan and Craig are advising that one denies the existence of abstract objects by the following argument: if CEN holds true, then abstract objects (assuming they exist) cannot exist. But Craig (at least) is not submitting that proposal. Rather, he states, "But it is no part of my [anti-platonism] project to deny that abstract objects exist; I maintain only that *uncreated* abstract objects do not exist."[25] With this caveat in mind, Craig further argues:

> If confronted by a modern-day platonist defending an ontology which included causally effete objects which were *ageneta* and so co-eternal with God, they [i.e., the ante-Nicene Church Fathers] would have rejected such an account as blasphemous, since such an account would impugn God's aseity by denying its uniqueness and undermine *creatio ex nihilo* by denying that God is the universal ground of being. The Fathers could not therefore exempt such objects from God's creative power, since He is the sole and all-originating *agenetos*.[26]

Now if Craig is correct, then CEN has the consequence that abstract objects, *if they exist at all*, must be *created* by God. Has Craig hereby given us another required component (i.e., that abstracts objects must be created by God) to add to CEN on the assumption that abstract objects exist? Much, of course, will depend on one's outlook with respect to the problem of God and abstract objects, that is, whether or not one thinks traditional theism is compatible with Platonism.

While the literature on this issue is vast and quickly growing, I simply cannot go too far afield with respect to the problem of God and abstract objects. Suffice it to say, however, that the theistic activist (who is motivated to harmonize Platonism with traditional theism) could *accept* Craig's (and Copan's) point that abstract objects, if they exist at all, must be created by God since the theistic activist does, indeed, hold that abstract objects are created by God, though eternally and perhaps necessarily.[27] However, since Craig is exercised against *any* variant of Platonism he argues that theistic activism suffers from two principal difficulties:

> *First,* modified Platonism [i.e., theistic activism] misconstrues either the scope or nature of creation. If we think of abstract objects as part of the order of dependent beings existing external to God, then the scope of *creatio ex nihilo* becomes miniscule. For as we have argued, a biblically robust doctrine of creation involves God's bringing into being the objects of his creative activity and thereby implies a temporal beginning of existence of created things. But on the proposed view (i.e., theistic activism) the realm of dependent beings, with the exception of concrete objects, exists coeternally with God. Hence, scarcely anything, relatively speaking, is created *ex nihilo* by God . . . . *Second,* the more serious problem with absolute creationism [i.e., theistic activism] is that it appears to be logically incoherent. On this view all abstract objects, including properties, are created by God. But then what about God's own properties? Does God create his own properties? . . . . But to maintain that God does create his own properties pulls us into a vicious circle: in order to create various properties, God must already possess those properties.[28]

Accordingly, if Craig is correct at this point, then theistic activism is necessarily false.[29] If, however, one wants to *deny* Craig's requirement that abstract objects, if they exist at all, must be created by God but still maintain that abstract objects are *dependent* on God for their necessary existence, then it seems one might defer to Leibniz's divine conceptualism or at least some contemporary variety of it. Perhaps one could endorse the recent work by Greg Welty. According to Welty, "AOs [i.e., abstract objects] are necessarily existing, uncreated divine ideas that are distinct from God and dependent on God."[30] Welty further states:

> As a "theistic conceptual realist" I reject (3) [i.e., If abstract objects exist, then they are independent of God], though for a different reason than theistic activists. I argue that the platonistic tradition can accommodate AOs being *necessarily dependent* on God, in virtue of their being uncreated divine ideas that "play the role" of AOs with respect to all created reality. I think there are good reasons for thinking that AOs cannot *causally* depend on God, and so I part ways with theistic activists in this respect. Still, I maintain that AOs are *constitutively* dependent on God, for they are constituted by the divine ideas, which inhere in the divine mind and have no existence outside of it.[31]

Similarly to Leibniz and Welty, Walter Schultz denies the proposition that abstract objects must be created by God while focusing on the idea of "omnicompetence," that is, "that God is aware of his ability *ad extra*."[32] The idea of divine omnicompetence, according to Schultz, accounts for "real possibilities," and thus "*God's eternal awareness of his omni-competence* is the [ontological] ground of all existence *ad extra*."[33] He highlights "five things" concerning real possibilities that capture the essence of his outlook:

> The first is that these possibilities—these "thoughts"—are eternal. They are constant features of God's being . . . . Second, these representations are necessary . . . . [A] third feature, that whatever is possible, is *necessarily* possible. Fourth, the eternal *actuality* of these representations lies in God's omni-competence and in their being aspects of God's eternal awareness of such . . . . Finally, it follows from these that God does *not* "create" these eternal and necessarily existent abstract objects *by* thinking them as though thinking were an instrumental cause of their existence . . . . Here we have a general answer to the *Abstract Objects Problem* which shows how they can be eternally and necessarily existent while being ontologically dependent on God.[34]

While resonating with Leibniz's idea that *abstracta* are ontologically grounded in God's understanding, what we see here, according to both Welty and Schultz, are two plausible ways in which one might deny the proposition that God must create abstract objects, yet at the same time affirm that abstract objects are dependent on Him.[35] Of course, one might think that these two variations of divine conceptualism have serious costs and thus need to be abandoned. Craig, for instance, argues that the divine conceptualist (such as Welty) is confused in stating that *abstract* objects exist as divine ideas. As Craig states,

> He [i.e., Welty] therefore risks misleading his readers in affirming that *abstract objects* exist as ideas in the mind of God. For as a form of concrete realism . . . divine conceptualism denies that abstract objects exist. Welty should say, rather, that mathematical objects, for example, are ideas in the mind of God. Only in a note do we learn that Welty is speaking merely "functionally" when he affirms that abstract objects are divine ideas. Properly speaking, there are, according to his view, only concrete objects, some of which are mental, rather than physical, in nature.[36]

The point in drawing attention to both Welty and Schultz is not to adjudicate their position over a contrary position, say, Craig's. I am simply showing how one might plausibly deny that abstract objects (if they exist at all) must be created by God, yet at the same time affirming that they are dependent on Him. The motivation here, on my part, is to stipulate a more "minimalistic" approach to CEN while not compromising divine aseity. Therefore, if this minimalistic approach to CEN can plausibly account for divine aseity, then *quanto magis* will the added requirement from Copan and Craig (i.e., that abstract objects, if they exist at all, must be created by God) similarly account for divine aseity.

Since, then, there is prima facie good reason to be skeptical of the idea that abstract objects, if they exist at all, must be created by God, we will hereafter understand CEN as previously stated:

> (CEN) For any doctrine of *creatio ex nihilo*, God creates out of nothing only if (i) that which is created is ontologically distinct from God's own being and (ii) God does not create anything from any preexisting, eternal matter (not even a physical vacuum).

Although CEN is arguably the fundamental principle of the doctrine of CEN, it nevertheless is not the only principle. Another principle operative within CEN that will be of major concern is what we will call the "Principle of Existential Priority I" (PEP I):

> (PEP I) For any x and y, if x's existence is prior (whether temporally or non-temporally) to y's existence, then x cannot existentially depend on y's existence.

According to PEP I, if x's existence is prior to y, then x's existence cannot depend on y's existence. This may be because the dependence relation (i.e., existential dependence) is asymmetrical. As Aristotle in the *Metaphysics* puts it, "Some things then are called prior and posterior . . . in respect of nature and substance, i.e. those which can be without other things, while the others cannot be without them."[37] Therefore, while y may (or may not) depend on x for its existence, x cannot depend on y for its existence if x's existence is prior to y's existence.

One might initially wonder if there are counterexamples to PEP I. It is difficult, however, to see what such a possible counterexample might look like. How could x's existence depend on y's existence provided x's existence is *prior to* y's existence? To expose the difficulty of a possible counterexample to PEP I, consider first a nontemporal notion of priority where we make the claim that "sets existentially depend on their members." It is plausible, here, that {Plato} depends in some way on Plato for its existence but that Plato does not depend in the same way on {Plato}. The dependence relation, in other words, is asymmetrical. Moreover, the type of dependence at hand here is not causal dependence since it could be plausibly argued that Plato does not cause {Plato}. Rather, it is an existential dependence, that is, a dependence that highlights the notion of existence. Therefore, the fact that {Plato} depends on Plato for its existence can be seen in the proposition "Plato is *prior* to the existence of {Plato}."

In addition to the nontemporal notion sketched previously, temporal examples can also highlight the difficulty of a possible counterexample to PEP I. Consider secondly the fact that children existentially depend on their parents. However, given that children existentially depend on their parents, parents cannot existentially depend on their children—the dependence relation is, again, asymmetrical. Of course, this not to say that some child *C* existentially depends on his or her parents *P* and *Q* for *sustaining* his or her existence moment by moment since it is obvious that child *C*'s parents could go out of existence and child *C* still exists. The point, rather, is that if parents *P* and *Q* did not exist, then some child *C* could not have come into existence. What this temporal example highlights is that child *C*'s initial existence depends on parents *P* and *Q*. So again, like Plato and his singleton, {Plato}, that child *C* existentially depends on parents *P* and *Q* can be captured in the proposition "Parents *P* and *Q* are *prior* to the existence of child *C*."

Now in drawing attention to both a nontemporal and temporal scenario, which are motivated to cast doubt on a possible counterexample to PEP I, I have not given an account, analysis, or even a definition of existential dependence.[38] Instead, I have appealed to two different examples by highlighting that the notion of existential dependence is an asymmetrical relation. Therefore, while PEP I is certainly not proven at this point, we nevertheless have good reason to think that PEP I is more plausible than its negation.[39]

5.4 Divine Aseity Again

If one employs PEP I at this point, then one begins to have a strong argument against the idea that divine alternativity with respect to creating is required for divine aseity, and thus proposition (A) (i.e., If God must create, then God cannot have aseity) is called into question. In other words, PEP I seems to accentuate the idea of divine aseity. To see this, consider the notion that God is existentially prior to creation captured by the early ecclesiastical theologian, Tertullian (155–240):

> The fact of God being the One and only God asserts this rule, for He is the One-only God for the only reason that He is the sole God, and the sole God for the only reason that nothing existed with Him. Thus He must also be the First, since all things are posterior to Him; all things are posterior to Him for the reason that all things are by Him; all things are by Him for the reason that they are from nothing . . . for there is no power, no material, no nature of another substance which assisted Him.[40]

According to Tertullian, if CEN holds true, then "all things are by God." Further, if all things are by God, then "all thing are posterior to God." It follows, therefore, that if CEN holds true, then all things are posterior to the creator.

Now what I take Tertullian to be emphasizing when concluding that all things are posterior to the creator is—what I have designated as—that the created order is *existentially* posterior to God. That is, the created order's existence is posterior to God's existence. For Tertullian, this is simply another way of asserting that God is existentially prior to creation: God's existence is prior to the existence of the creation. But what is perhaps most important at this point is that if the antecedent of PEP I holds true when applied to God and creation (i.e., that God is existentially prior to creation), then God cannot existentially depend on creation, and is thus *a se* in respect of the creation. God's existence, in other words, cannot depend on the existence of the created order provided He is existentially prior to creation. To think otherwise would be to put the cart before the horse. Consequently, God's existence is from Himself. A more succinct way of putting this portion of my argument is as follows:

(1) If CEN holds true, then God's existence is prior to the created order's existence [from Tertullian];

(2) If God's existence is prior to the created order's existence, then God's existence is independent of the created order's existence [from PEP I];

(3) Therefore, if CEN holds true, then God's existence is independent of the created order's existence.

However, one might object at this point and state that while God's *existence* is, indeed, prior to creation and thus from Himself, He nevertheless is dependent on creation in some other way, a way that has nothing to do with His existence. Perhaps, instead God is dependent on creation for His *essence* (or similarly, for His identity) if He must create.[41] For as critics such as Frame and Beilby claim, "if his very deity requires him to create and redeem, then it would seem that his *deity* depends . . . on the world";[42] and "if it [i.e., God's choice to create] was internally necessitated, then God's nature would be such that he needed to create the world *to be who he was*."[43] Beilby, at least, further amplifies divine neediness provided God creates from an internal necessity when he says:

> Granted. God is not lacking . . . . But even if it is granted that there is no deficiency or lack in God . . . it does *not* follow that God has no unfulfilled needs. It is possible to be needy either because of a deficiency—a lack that needs to be filled—or an abundance—a surplus that must be distributed. Either way, there is an unfulfilled need, a need that is met in the creative act.[44]

So, while it may be granted according to this objection from Frame and Beilby that God has *existential aseity* (i.e., His existence is from Himself), He nevertheless cannot have what we might call *essence aseity* (i.e., His essence is from Himself) if He must create.[45]

How might we respond to this type of objection? Does God's essence (e.g., His essential happiness a la Beilby) depend on creation provided He creates while His existence survives unscathed? First, one might respond to this objection by arguing that the distinction between existential aseity and essence aseity cannot have application in God's case given *classical* theism. For, according to classical theism, as an aspect of His aseity God cannot be composed of parts, and thus it denies that He is a metaphysical composite. Rather, God is simple in that He is identical to His essence and His essence is identical to His existence. According to divine simplicity, then, God's existential aseity would be identical to His essence aseity, and thus the distinction cannot be applied to God as critics would have it.

To better understand this response from divine simplicity here is an analogy inspired by William Mann:

> When Jones says that the highest mountain in the world is Everest while Smith counters that the highest mountain in the world is Chomolungma,

we can say that the dispute between them is merely verbal, or merely epistemological: Jones and Smith are necessarily reporting the same fact (if they report a fact at all.) The dispute evaporates once one realizes that Everest = Chomolungma.[46]

Similarly, then, a proponent of divine simplicity can regard existential aseity as referring to the same reality as His essence aseity.[47]

But even if the demands of classical theism are laid aside, a second response would be to argue more generally that existential aseity implies essence aseity. Let us assume with the essentialist that x's essence is constitutive of a set of essential properties, and an essential property is a property which x possesses at all times and which x cannot cease to possess until ceasing to exist.[48] Consider, then, another important principle of CEN that we will call the "Principle of Existential Priority II" (PEP II):

(PEP II) For any x and y, if x's existence is prior (whether temporally or non-temporally) to y's existence, then x cannot depend for its essence on y's existence.

To see the plausibility in PEP II as it applies to God, we might ask the following types of questions: *Who* is this God that has existential aseity? Does He not also have an essence, that is, a set of essential properties prior to creation? If critics such as Frame and Beilby reply, "this God who has existential aseity also has essence aseity prior to creation," then aseity undoubtedly is upheld and there does not seem to be a problem. If, however, they say, "this God who has existential aseity does not have essence aseity prior to creation," then they seem to commit themselves to a God who has deficiencies ab initio, and thus much of their effort and commitment to proposition (A) (i.e., if God must create, then God cannot have aseity) is simply question-begging from the outset. Consequently, if God's existence is prior to the created order's existence (which Frame and Beilby seem to grant via the distinction between existential aseity and essence aseity), then God's essence cannot depend on the created order's existence.

In addition, while the plausibility of PEP II is not dependent on such support, one might nevertheless consult Brian Leftow's critique of what he calls "deity theories" in order to bolster PEP II. Deity theories, according to Leftow, stipulate "that God's nature makes necessary truths true or gives rise to their truthmakers—that the content of God's nature, deity, is the ultimate reason that 2 + 2 = 4 or that hydrogen atoms have one proton."[49] He offers two critical "strikes" against deity theories. The following is the first:

> It seems . . . that deity has just one ontological job. Just as having redness makes one red and having doghood makes one a dog, having deity makes one divine. Just as redness's *only* job is making red, deity's only job is making divine. So . . . if one has deity, that makes true of one just things that help make one divine. Now on a deity theory, deity provides a truthmaker for every necessary truth, and so for 'water = H_2O'. So on a deity theory, water's being H_2O is part of deity's content. But in fact . . . it is not. Water's being H_2O doesn't help make one divine. It doesn't help make God what or who He is. So . . . 'water = H_2O' is not something having deity makes true: strike one against deity theories.[50]

What I take Leftow to be arguing here is that if water's being H_2O is part of deity's content, then water's being H_2O contributes to making one divine. Much of this worry is nuanced further in his second strike against deity theories. Here is what Leftow says:

> Consider the claim that

> 1. if (it is untrue that water = H_2O) → then God does not exist.

> (1) is true simply because it has an impossible antecedent. We are sure of this because the antecedent's impossibility suffices to explain (1)'s truth and (1)'s antecedent appears irrelevant to its consequent. (If water goes down the drain, why should it take God with it?) Thus (1) is true trivially, as are all impossible-antecedent strict conditionals, but only trivially. But suppose that a deity theory is true. Then if God exists, deity provides a truthmaker for 'water = H_2O'. If 'water = H_2O' has a truthmaker, it is true. So on a deity theory, if it is untrue that water = H_2O, God does not exist. Thus on a deity theory, (1) reflects a fact about the divine nature (that deity provides a truthmaker for 'water = H_2O'). So (1)'s truth is overdetermined. Unintuitively, it is true for substantive as well as trivial reasons. Further, a truth-to-truthmaker connection provides a hidden link between (1)'s antecedent and consequent. Unintuitively, (1)'s antecedent is relevant to its consequent. Strike two against deity theories.[51]

Accordingly, the fact that water's being H_2O contributes to making one divine results in God's nature being *dependent* on created natures, and thus God's existence and essence depend ontologically on creatures. As Leftow concludes, "deity theories commit us to the claim that God's existence depends on there being truthmakers for particular necessary truths about creatures."[52] Therefore, while these two strikes advanced by Leftow are not only strikes against deity theories, they can nevertheless also be consulted in support of God's independent existence and essence, that is, consulted in support of PEP II.[53]

5.5 Creatio Ex Nihilo and the Idea that God Must Create

At this point, while a critic may concede the argument of the preceding subsection (i.e., if CEN holds true, then God has aseity with respect to both his existence and his essence), he or she may nonetheless object in claiming that CEN is *inconsistent* with the fact that God must create. In addition, if this objection is sound, then divine aseity is, indeed, inconsistent with the idea that God must create. So, in this section I will defend the consistency of CEN and the idea that God must create, that is, I will defend (P2) of my basic argument.

To begin, one might wonder what sort of support an objector would offer for the proposition that CEN is inconsistent with the idea that God must create. Consider the remarks by Thomas McCall, where he first summarizes two options with respect to divine action:

(A) Divine action with respect to creation is necessary (though still free in the compatibilist sense of freedom);

or

(B) Divine action with respect to creation is contingent.[54]

Taking into consideration these two options concerning divine action, McCall argues as follows:

> If (A) [i.e., divine action with respect to creation is necessary though free in the compatibilist sense], *then we are right back to panentheism*. The assessment of [Jonathan] Edwards made by the Reformed theologian John W. Cooper would be appropriate here as well: This view [i.e., (A)] is "best construed philosophically as a panentheism that borders on Spinozan pantheism." Historical considerations aside, we can see that with (A) comes the necessity of creation—thus God could not exist without creation . . . . What is this once again but the denial of divine aseity?[55]

Similarly, Frame makes a distinction between God's "necessary" actions (i.e., the Father generating the Son) and God's (libertarianly) "free" actions (i.e., creating).[56] But, like McCall, in light of the idea that God must create, Frame claims there to be a problem:

> Now . . . no such distinction [between God's necessary actions and God's free actions], apparently, is possible. If . . . God's only freedom is freedom from external constraint, then God's redeeming us is just as necessary to his nature as the eternal generation of the Son from the Father. *But anyone trained in theology should be able to see the pantheizing tendency here.*[57]

According to both McCall and Frame, the dreadful consequence of the idea that God must create is that panentheism (a la McCall) or pantheism (a la Frame) seems to follow. Panentheism, speaking in general, is the view that states that all reality is in God ("all-in-God-ism"), that is, an ontological emanation from Him.[58] Pantheism, on the other hand, makes the stronger identity claim asserting that all reality *is* God. Therefore, McCall and Frame allegedly argue that if God must create, then either all of reality is a component of the divine nature or all of reality is identical to God's own being.

Now, before responding to McCall's and Frame's argument (i.e., if God must create, then some form of metaphysical monism follows), I want to express a minor quibble regarding McCall's usage of John Cooper's work, *Panentheism, The Other God of the Philosophers*. McCall, like Beilby, is also exercised against Jonathan Edwards and those who follow him (i.e., Edwardsian-Calvinism). McCall, accordingly, claims that if *Edwards* asserts that God must create, then Edwards is committed to panentheism. In support of this claim, as we can see from the previous quotation, McCall draws from the sentiments of Cooper. However, upon a closer look at Cooper's claims I fail to see that Cooper is arguing (apparently as an ally with McCall) that if Edwards (or anybody for that matter, say, Leibniz) holds to McCall's (A) (i.e., divine action with respect to creation is necessary though still free in a compatibilist sense), then he is committed to panentheism. To see this, here is a lengthier quotation from Cooper that McCall refers to:

> It is clear why scholars debate whether Edwards is a panentheist or pantheist. Like Spinoza, he regards God as the only substance and embraces a

deterministic view of God's relation to the world. Creatures are simply direct projections of God's mind and power, individual divine thoughts and acts. This sounds like pantheism. Yet Edwards affirms God's transcendence of creation in ways impossible for Spinoza. He cannot say that *God* and *Nature* are two terms for the same substance. He does not regard the productivity of nature (*Natura naturans*) as divine. Moreover, although he agrees with Spinoza that humans are not substances, Edwards affirms that humans retain their individual existence everlastingly, a doctrine that Spinoza denies. These factors point away from pantheistic monism. But Edwards lacks the robust ontological Creator-creature distinction of classical theism. For him, creatures are divine thoughts. All things considered, his affirmation that "the whole is *of* God, and *in* God, and *to* God" is best construed philosophically as panentheism that borders on Spinozan pantheism.[59]

Nowhere here does Cooper state that panentheism *follows* from the idea that God must create, much less from what McCall calls a compatibilist outlook of divine freedom. Rather, what I take Cooper to be claiming is that panentheism perhaps follows for Edwards simply because "For him [i.e., Edwards], creatures are divine thoughts."[60] The issue, then, (if there is one) appears to be that there is a logical relation between panentheism and some variation of idealism, or even divine conceptualism. So, I fail to see that these sentiments from Cooper could function as support for McCall's argument that panentheism follows from the idea that God must create.

Yet, despite this minor quibble, although McCall and Frame do not explicitly state that CEN is inconsistent with the idea that God must create, there is nevertheless good reason to think that this is an implication of what they are arguing. Recall that one of the required conditions for CEN is (i): *what is created by God is ontologically distinct from God's own being.* However, if McCall and Frame are correct that either panentheism or pantheism follows from the fact that God must create, then it is not the case that what is created by God is ontologically distinct from God, and is thus a denial of CEN. McCall and Frame, in other words, argue that (i) of CEN is called into question given the fact that God must create. Here is an augmented version of McCall and Frame's argument, as I understand it:

(1) If God must create, then either panentheism or pantheism follows.
(2) If either panentheism or pantheism is true, then it is not the case that the created order is ontologically distinct from God.

(3) If it is not the case that the created order is ontologically distinct from God, then CEN does not hold true.

(4) Therefore, if God must create, then CEN does not hold true.

While this is, indeed, a valid argument, I fail to see the plausibility in premise (1) which is where McCall's and Frame's main contention lies. For traditional theism stipulates that there is a conceptual distinction, as we have seen, between what God is and what God does *ad extra* such that what He is, is prior (temporally or nontemporally) to what He does. To think otherwise would be to blur the distinction between God's being and the being of creation. It is simply incoherent to assert the character of what God does *ad extra* without conceptually presupposing the existence and being of God as distinct from the creation. But the stipulation of traditional theism that there is a conceptual distinction between the being of God and the actions of God *ad extra* seems to be consistent with the idea that God must create. And if so, then premise (1) of Frame's and McCall's argument is false.

An earthbound illustration should further help drive home the point that premise (1) is false, and thus highlight the fact that the proposition God must create is consistent with CEN. Suppose you find yourself along a beach and observe "Johnny" playing in the sand. Suppose further that Johnny is so full of joy that he cannot help but build a sandcastle. That is, Johnny *must* build the sandcastle, namely, from his own joy. However, taking into account this illustration, it seems rather obvious that Johnny is not ontologically identical with the sandcastle nor is it the case that the sandcastle is a participant in the very being of Johnny. In other words, just because Johnny must create the sandcastle, it does not necessarily follow that Johnny is ontologically one with the sandcastle or that the sandcastle is part of Johnny's being.[61]

Of course, it may be objected that this analogy breaks down since Johnny's building of the sandcastle is not an instance of CEN. Fair enough. However, highlighting this fact would in effect bolster my argument instead of detracting from it. For, it seems reasonable to think that if Johnny (who does not create ex nihilo) is not ontologically one with the sandcastle, then *quanto magis* it is not the case that God (who does create ex nihilo) is ontologically one with creation. Therefore, even if it holds true that God must create, the relationship between God and world in all other regards could affirm the absolute Creator-creature distinction of traditional theism, which denies that the created order is ontologically identical to God or ontologically a participant in the divine nature. It is simply a mistake on the part of McCall and Frame to think that panentheism or pantheism follows given the fact that God must create. The idea that God must create is, therefore, consistent with the doctrine of CEN.

5.6 Conclusion

We have seen that a number of theologians propound what we have called proposition (A): If God must create, then God cannot have aseity (i.e., be from himself). However, I have argued that the idea that God must create is consistent with divine aseity, and thus that proposition (A) is false. The conclusion of my argument was founded upon the doctrine of CEN along with two operative principles implied by this doctrine, namely, PEP I and PEP II. I then argued that the doctrine of CEN is consistent with the idea that God must create.

Theistic Optimism and Modal Collapse

6.1 Introduction

In the previous chapters I have argued that Theistic Optimism (i.e., the idea that God must do the best) can plausibly account for divine freedom, divine praiseworthiness and thankworthiness, along with divine aseity. Theistic Optimism, however, might well be criticized and perhaps even rejected on other grounds. Perhaps it engenders too many problems with respect to our *modal intuitions*. Some might worry, for instance, that if God must do the best (such as create and create the best world), then it is difficult to comprehend in what sense any other worlds are, in fact, possible. Laura Garcia puts the problem this way:

> [W]e should note one unfortunate consequence of accepting (1) [i.e., If God's willing a certain universe is rational, then that universe must be the optimific alternative] and (2) [i.e., There is an optimific universe, a best of all possible worlds]. If these were correct, it would follow that the actual world . . . is the only possible world, since it is necessarily the only world which could have been created by the necessarily existing creator. If God's existence is necessary and his eternal act of will is also necessary, then . . . there is only one possible world . . . . In the end, [one] must simply accept the counter-intuitive result that many things which appear to us to be eminently contingent . . . are in fact metaphysically necessary.[1]

Similarly, Edward Wierenga adds:

> The assumption that there is a best possible world thus has an extraordinary consequence, namely, that it is necessary that God creates it. If "the best possible world" is a rigid designator, as it would seem to be if it designates at all, then it is hard to see in what sense any other worlds are so much as

possible. No other world could possibly be actual, so no other world would be possible. And every true proposition would turn out to be necessarily true. Nothing could be different from the way it is.[2]

Accordingly, if Theistic Optimism holds true, then it seems that no world other than the best possible world could be actual. What this suggests is that the idea of *modal collapse* emerges: no other world is possible, in which case every fundamental constituent (whether that be propositions and/or state of affairs) in the actual world is necessary and not contingent. Or, as Mark Heller says, "God, being necessarily all good, cannot do less than the best. Any description of a world that includes God doing something less than the best does not describe a possible world at all, no matter how much it seems to."[3] So, given the idea that God must do the best, it seems that nothing could be different from the way it is since truth (i.e., contingency) collapses into necessity, and this, apparently, unduly violates our modal intuitions and judgments. The problem can be captured more precisely in the following conditional proposition (CP):

(CP) If God must do the best (i.e., if Theistic Optimism holds true), then the best possible world (i.e., the actual world) is the only possible world.

How to avoid this challenge and thus argue for the conjunction of Theistic Optimism and the idea that other worlds are possible will be the focus of the chapter. What counts for a contingent possible world will be front and center since contingency, broadly speaking, is typically taken as a variation of possibility that yet excludes necessity.

6.2 Possible by Its Own Nature Solution

The first way of undermining (CP) is to appeal to some of what Leibniz says concerning modality. He primarily accounts for possibility (and thus *possible* worlds) by holding that a world is "*possible by its own nature*," or by claiming that a world is "*possible in itself*." While "possible by its own nature" and "possible in itself" are quite ambiguous phrases for those unfamiliar with Leibniz's philosophy, those phrases nevertheless amount to saying that what is necessary and sufficient for a world to be possible is that a world *does not imply a contradiction*. Accordingly, some world *w* is possible in its nature if and only if world *w* does not imply a contradiction. We can see this

Leibnizian solution unfold in the following passage in "On Freedom and Possibility":

[W]e must say that God wills the best through his nature. "Therefore," you will say, "he wills by necessity." I will say, with St. Augustine, that such necessity is blessed. "But surely [you will also say] it follows from this that things exist by necessity." How so? Since the nonexistence of what God wills to exist implies a contradiction? I deny that this proposition is absolutely true, for otherwise that which God does not will would not be possible. For things remain possible, even if God does not choose them. Indeed, even if God does not will something to exist, it is possible for it to exist, since, by its nature, it could exist if God were to will it to exist. "But [you say] God cannot will it to exist." I concede this, yet, such a thing remains possible in its nature, even if it is not possible with respect to the divine will, since we have defined as in its nature possible anything that, in itself, implies no contradiction, even though its coexistence with God can in some way be said to imply a contradiction.[4]

What Leibniz is basically arguing here is that the created or actual world (which is the best possible world) along with its fundamental constituents is contingent since all other worlds are possible, if they are properly understood as worlds that do not imply a contradiction. These possible worlds, in other words, are an internally coherent set of states of affairs and/or propositions. He continues this theme in the later published *Theodicy* when he says the following:

[F]or since there are many things which have never happened and never will happen, and which nevertheless are clearly conceivable, and imply no contradiction, how can one say they are altogether impossible? M. Bayle has refuted that himself in a passage opposing the Spinozists, which I have already quoted here, and he has frequently acknowledged that there is nothing impossible except that which implies contradiction . . . . In a word, when one speaks of the possibility of a thing it is not a question of the causes that can bring about or prevent its actual existence: otherwise one would change the nature of the terms, and render useless the distinction between the possible and the actual . . . . That is why, when one asks if a thing is possible or necessary, and brings in the consideration of what God wills or chooses, one alters the issue.[5]

Crucially, given what Leibniz says in the previous passages, it is not required for God to be able to create or actualize worlds other than the best in order for those worlds to be possible. For, according to Leibniz, to bring God's existence and will into the discussion would inevitably muddy the waters, that is, one "alters the issue" as to what is possible. Again, it is necessary and sufficient for some world *w* to be possible provided it does not imply a contradiction. Here is how Roger Woolhouse nicely summarizes Leibniz's view:

> Leibniz faces the objection that this actual world, which is the best possible, is really the *only* possible world . . . . His response is that it does not follow, for other possible, but less good worlds, "remain possible, even if God did not choose them." Certainly such a less good world is "not possible with respect to the divine will"; but it "remains possible in its nature." It "implies no contradiction, even though its coexistence with God can in some way be said to imply a contradiction." For this world to be contingent it is sufficient that, even if it were not possible for God to choose them, there are other worlds possible in themselves, worlds which involve no contradiction.[6]

So, in short, Leibniz proposes that other worlds are possible *in themselves* (i.e., they do not imply a contradiction) apart from the divine will. And, if other worlds are possible in themselves and do not imply a contradiction, then the actual world (i.e., the best possible world) is contingent.

Whatever this outlook amounts to, divine alternativity is not a necessary condition for worlds to count as possible, and therefore divine alternativity is not required for the contingency of the actual world, that is, the best possible world. Rather, contingency (of a world), according to Leibniz, is "*that whatever is more perfect or has more reason is true.*"[7] That is, "all truths concerning contingent things or the existence of things, rest on the principle of perfection."[8] Leibniz more explicitly notes the connection between contingency and perfection when he says:

> [T]he reason [*causa*] why some particular contingent thing exists [e.g., the best possible world] rather than others, should not be sought in its definition alone, but in comparison with other things. For, since there are an infinity of possible things which, nevertheless, do not exist, the reason [*ratio*] why these exist rather than those should not be sought in their definition . . . but from an extrinsic source, namely, from the fact that the ones that do exist are more perfect than others.[9]

Given this understanding of possibility and contingency, Leibniz thinks it is therefore coherent to hold that God must do the best while at the same time deny that all other worlds are impossible. In addition, if Leibniz is successful in regarding possibility as simply that which does not imply a contradiction and contingency as that which is more perfect, then the actual world (i.e., the best possible world) is contingent, and thereby eschews the objection from modal collapse.[10]

Is Leibniz's proposal, however, a successful solution to the problem of modal collapse? While I have thus been sympathetic in this volume to some of what Leibniz says, I do not think his proposal here is the best solution to the problem of modal collapse. The main reason for this is that it is odd that Leibniz would account for modality, in particular possibility, while excluding God's existence and perfect nature from his account. It is worth noting, however, that when Leibniz and others speak of possible worlds (and thus possibility in general), there seem to be two levels or different senses of reality operating. On the one hand, possible worlds are ontologically grounded in God's *understanding*, given Leibniz's commitment to divine conceptualism. Possible worlds, then, are a part of the fabric of reality but only at that particular level, that is, at the level of the divine understanding. On the other hand, however, worlds possibly existing or not existing specifies only that which can be *actualized by God* apart from His mind. Given these two ontological notions, perhaps it is beneficial to refer to possible worlds within the divine mind as subsisting (but not existing) and the actual world as existing.

Yet, while Leibniz proposes that a "thing" or state of affairs is possible if and only if it does not imply a contradiction, this is not to say that he advances the idea that the state of affairs could de facto exist, that is, be actualized by God. For, recall that he is willing to concede the point that anything less than the best "is not possible *with respect to the divine will*." Moreover, Leibniz goes so far as to say that despite a thing or a state of affairs being possible *in itself*, "its coexistence with God can in some way be said to imply a contradiction." Existence, here, (or rather coexistence) obviously does not refer to reality at the level of the divine understanding. For, if existence does refer to reality at the level of divine understanding, then that would collapse existence into subsistence. Rather, possibly existing is captured by what can or cannot be actualized by God. So, when Leibniz excludes God's existence and perfect nature from his account of possibility, he commits himself to the proposition that a world which could not possibly exist (i.e., be actualized by God) is, indeed, a possible world. In other words, Leibniz holds that if there is subsisting an internally coherent set of thoughts in the divine mind, then that set is a possible world. Is it plausible, then, to hold that something could never exist apart from God's mind but is nonetheless possible? While Leibniz would wholeheartedly answer "yes" to the question, this solution is on the face of it contrived. Therefore, I submit that while a world that does not imply a contradiction is necessary for being deemed possible, it is not sufficient. In order for some world to be possible, it must also be able to be created or actualized by God. In opposition to Leibniz, then, we thus have two necessary conditions with respect to our understanding of a *possible* world:

> For any possible world *w*, *w* is possible only if (1) *w* does not imply a contradiction, and (2) *w* is actualizable by God.

6.3 The Contingency of the Criterion of Perfection Solution

The second possible response to the problem of modal collapse is to argue that contingency is to be found in the criterion of perfection, that is, in what makes a possible world count as perfect or the best. Leibniz writes in the *Discourse on Metaphysics* that God chooses the world that most effectively combines (1) the simplest in hypotheses/laws with (2) the richness in phenomena. Here is what he says:

> Thus, one can say, in whatever manner God might have created the world, it would always have been regular and in accordance with a certain general order. But God has chosen the most perfect world, that is, the one which is at the same time the simplest in hypotheses and the richest in phenomena, as might be a line in geometry whose construction is easy [i.e., simplest in hypotheses] and whose properties and effects are extremely remarkable and widespread [i.e., richest in phenomena].[11]

Similarly, in *Principles of Nature and Grace*, he states:

> It follows from the supreme perfection of God that he chose the best possible plan in producing the universe, a plan in which there is the greatest variety together with the greatest order. The most carefully used plot of ground, place, and time; the greatest effect produced by the simplest means; the most power, knowledge, happiness, and goodness in created things that the universe could allow.[12]

What I take Leibniz to mean by simplest in hypotheses/laws and richness in phenomena is that God creates the greatest variety of things (perhaps substances) by the simplest/easiest way possible. He likens this outlook not only to a geometer, but also to a good architect, a good householder, a skilled machinist, and a learned author.[13] The architect, for instance, designs a building with a great variety of different rooms, shapes, and accents. Variety, in other words, adds to the goodness of the blueprint.

Yet, it would be unthinkable, according to Leibniz, for a skilled architect to use complex and inefficient means when designing the blueprints for an edifice when something simpler was readily at hand. In other words, while designing the blueprints for such a building, the architect does not consult a complex and inefficient way to fulfill his purposes. Rather, the ideal architect designs the building with all its great variety using the simplest and most efficient way possible, which thereby results in a perfect balance and harmony between the simplicity of his ways and the richness of his effects. As Leibniz says:

> As for the simplicity of the ways of God, this holds properly with respect to his means, as opposed to the variety, richness, and abundance, which holds with respect to his ends or effects. And the one must be in balance with the other, as are the costs of a building and the size and beauty one demands of it.[14]

So, God uses the simplest means when creating a great variety of things in His world. To think otherwise would jeopardize God's perfect wisdom and the intelligibility of His creation. We might say, in scholastic terms, that Leibniz holds that creating is an exercise of the practical (not theoretical) reason. In short, the combination of simplest in hypotheses/laws and richness in phenomena is what characterizes a possible world as best.

However, given Leibniz's criterion for what characterizes a possible world as best, one might propose that such a criterion of perfection (or any such criterion of perfection), though in fact true, is contingently true, and thus the best possible world is not necessary. Furthermore, if Leibniz's criterion for what makes a world perfect were to be contingently true, then what is in fact the best possible world is contingently the best. Consequently, while God must do the best, what is in fact the best is a contingent matter. This type of solution has recently been advanced and nuanced by Martin Pickup where he proposes that contingency ought to be located in Leibniz's criteria for perfection, that is, in the criteria of simplicity in laws and richness in phenomena.[15] As Pickup says:

> Simplicity in laws and richness in phenomena . . . are not necessarily the properties that make a world good. A proposition is necessary if its negation entails a contradiction. But there is no obvious contradiction is supposing that, for example, sheer volume of existence is what ranks the quality of worlds . . . . Worlds certainly can be ranked according to such criteria, and there is nothing that appears to prevent these being rankings of perfection. In other words, it's hard to see why the properties these criteria track could not be the properties upon which perfection supervenes. The alternatives seem perfectly internally consistent, and they do not conflict with any mathematical or metaphysical truths. Thus the negation of the proposition that perfection is ordered by the criterion it is in fact ordered by doesn't lead to contradiction and is not necessary. It is thereby really contingent.[16]

Pickup's suggestion, then, that Leibniz's criteria of perfection (i.e., simplicity in laws and richness in phenomena) are thereby really contingent allows for the conclusion that

> [W]hile it is necessary for God to choose to create the best possible world, it is not necessary for any world to be the best possible. This is because the criterion for judging perfection can itself be contingent. Different criteria will judge different worlds as the best. Thus it is necessary for God to create the best, but not necessary which is the best.[17]

Pickup basically takes up Nicholas Jolley's suggestion that one can argue for the contingency of the best possible world by employing the distinction between referential and attributive uses of the phrase "the best possible world." According to Jolley, while the referential use of a phrase captures a particular subject or object that is under discussion (in this a case a possible world), the attributive use of a phrase, on the other hand, focuses on whoever or whatever might fit the description. Here is what Jolley says:

> A more subtle approach to the problem [of modal collapse] would accept that there is a sense in which it is necessarily true that God chooses the best of all possible worlds. But it would add that there is also a sense in which it is only contingently true. In other words, this approach seems to exploit ambiguity in the phrase "the best of all possible worlds." In technical terms, the ambiguity in question is between referential and attributive uses of the phrase. The phrase is understood in the referential sense when it is used

simply to pick out a particular possible world; by contrast, it is used in the attributive sense when it means "the best possible world, which ever it may be."[18]

Accordingly, if one employs the distinction between referential and attributive uses of the phrase "the best possible world," then one (e.g., the Theistic Optimist) can argue that it is a necessary truth that "God chooses the best possible world" when understood in the attributive sense, but is contingently true when understood in the referential sense. Or, as Jolley further puts it, "[I]t is not logically necessary that God chooses this particular world which is, as a matter of fact, the best of all possible worlds."[19] So, while God must choose to create the best possible world (understood in the attributive sense), the best possible world is nonetheless contingent (understood in the referential sense) since, according to Pickup, the criterion for perfection is contingent.[20]

What are we to make of this solution to the problem of modal collapse? While such a solution is a coherent emendation of Leibniz's outlook, I imagine that Leibniz and those who are sympathetic to his Theistic Optimism would not endorse this solution. The primary reason for this rejection is that the solution is in direct opposition to the primary motivations for Theistic Optimism in the first place. In other words, if one were to accept this solution to the problem of modal collapse and thus save Theistic Optimism from this charge, then the motivations for Theistic Optimism would need to be abandoned. Or, to put it another way, if one sustains one's commitment to the ontological perfection of God along with the PSR, then these motivations can be used as objections against the contingency of the criterion of perfection solution.

To see this, recall that the two primary motivations for Theistic Optimism (which were highlighted in Chapter 2) are (1) that Theistic Optimism best accounts for God's ontological perfection, and (2) that Theistic Optimism best accounts for the Principle of Sufficient Reason with respect to why God chooses one world over a contrary world. Now given (1), one might argue that if the contingency of the criterion of perfection holds true, then God cannot be ontologically perfect. For, according to this solution (following Pickup), it appears that God not only uses a criterion of perfection to choose between possibilities, *but He also initially chooses between the different sets of criterion of perfection which govern His choice of possibilities.* What this results in is that while divine alternativity is not required to choose between possibilities, divine alternativity is nevertheless assumed (perhaps required) when God chooses between the different sets of criterion of perfection. This assumption, however, seems correct in order for Pickup's solution to have any traction. For, it is senseless to claim that God uses a criterion of perfection when choosing between possibilities yet at the same time denying that God prefers or chooses a particular criterion of perfection. But, as we have seen in Leibniz's philosophy, for God to do anything less than the best is to call into question His perfection. And, given the supposition that God initially chooses between the different sets of criterion of perfection which govern His choice of possibilities, the fact that one set of criterion of perfection was actualized and all others were not is a good indicator that the actual set was the best set. That is, according to Leibniz, if there is (in God's understanding) no best set of criterion of perfection, then God would simply not choose a criterion of perfection. But, on our supposition, God has, indeed, chosen a criterion of perfection, and this functions as a plausible indicator that the actual set of criterion of perfection is the best set. In summary, Leibniz would likely argue that if there were no best criterion of perfection, then God would not have actualized any set of criterion of perfection, since He cannot prefer the less perfect to the more perfect.

Given (2), one might similarly argue that if the contingency of the criterion of perfection solution holds true, then the Principle of Sufficient Reason with respect to why God chooses (or, as Pickup says "used") one set of criterion of perfection over a contrary set of criterion of perfection cannot be sustained.[21] In other words, if one were to ask, "What is the sufficient reason for why God chose (i.e., used) this set of criterion of perfection over some contrary set of criterion of perfection?", Leibniz would likely respond by saying, "The sufficient reason for why God chose this set of criterion of perfection over some contrary set of criterion of perfection is simply that this criterion is the best." Accordingly, if there were not a best set of criterion of perfection, then God would not have used any set of criterion since God cannot act without a sufficient reason, that is, a reason that cannot explain the existence of two contrary sets of criterion of perfection. If the same reason could explain why God actualized or used one set of criterion over a contrary set of criterion, then the criterion of perfection is glaringly arbitrary, and thus one would abandon the PSR. Supposing, then, that God chose between different sets of criterion, Leibniz would likely hold that the sufficient reason as to why this particular set of criterion was chosen and used over a contrary set of criterion was simply that the actual criterion was the best criterion.

In short, it appears that the contingency of the criterion of perfection solution assumes divine alternativity at the level of choosing the criterion of perfection which thereby governs the necessity of God's choice as to which possibility to actualize. But, in assuming divine alternativity at the level of choosing the criterion of perfection, this solution ultimately results in abandoning Theistic Optimism and the primary motivations for it.

6.4 The Contingency of Human Alternativity Free Choices Solution

The third and final possible response to the problem of modal collapse is to argue that contingency is not so much to be found in the criterion of perfection as in the fact that alternativity is a requirement for *human* free will (supposing that humans are, indeed, free). Moreover, if humans have free will and alternativity is a requirement for that freedom, then what constitutes the best possible world can differ from one possible world to another possible world. In short, what may or may not count as the best possible world is *dependent on* humans exercising alternativity freedom. Consequently, like Jolley's suggestion, while God must do the best, what is, in fact, the best is a contingent matter since human alternativity free choices are taken as contingent. Wierenga suggests (in a footnote) this outlook when he says:

> We will later distinguish possible worlds generally from feasible possible worlds, where the latter are ones that God is able to actualize. Whether there is a best possible feasible world and, if so, which world it is, is something that could vary from world to world. Thus, if it should turn out that, necessarily, God actualizes the best feasible world, *it would not follow that only one world is possible*. So even if the assumption that there is a best possible world is implausibly strong, the issue taken up in the text is worth pursuing, because it would arise if God's goodness and power constrains him to actualize the best feasible world.[22]

Here, Wierenga employs the typical Molinist distinction between "possible worlds" and "feasible worlds," where the latter are worlds that God is able to actualize. Accordingly, while every feasible world is a possible world, not every possible world is a feasible world, which is just to say that not every possible world is actualizable by God. Consequently, the proposition "actualizable by God" is not a necessary condition for what counts as a possible world.

Wierenga develops this proposal (i.e., the proposal that human alternativity freedom saves contingency) further when he draws attention to how God might make a world. In doing so, Wierenga takes up the distinction between God "strongly actualizing" versus "weakly actualizing," where the former focuses on God causing or directly making to be the case a *part* of, say, world *W* while the latter aims at God bringing about the rest of world *W* (indirectly) via human alternativity freedom. To put it in the negative, God does not cause it to be the case nor does He directly bring something about when weakly actualizing. As he declares:

> [W]e can say that God weakly actualizes a possible world by directly or strongly actualizing a part of that world. God does his part [by, say, creating necessarily], and then any [alternativity] free agents he creates add their share. More precisely . . . we can say that for any given possible world, *W*, there is the largest state of affairs included in *W* that God strongly actualizes, *T(W)*. But since *T(W)* does not determine all of *W*, there is some other possible world, *W'*, such that *T(W)'* = *T(W)*. Whether God can actualize a world *W* then depends on which of the following is true:

(i) If God were to strongly actualize *T(W)* then *W* would be actual, or

(ii) If God were to strongly actualize *T(W)* then *W'* would be actual.[23]

Given the truth-value of these two CPs, Wierenga concludes as follows:

> Just as God's ability to actualize a world depends on one these "counterfactuals of world-actualization" being true, for whichever one is false, there is a world that God is unable to actualize even though it's possible that he do so. For example, if (ii) is false, then God cannot actualize *W'*. To do so, he'd have to strongly actualize *T(W)*, but if he were to do that, he'd get *W* instead of *W'*.[24]

Accordingly, if (i) is true and (ii) is false, then world *W'* is a possible world without it being a feasible world, which is just to say that *W'* is possible without God being able to actualize it. Yet, what is important for our purposes is to highlight the fact that human alternativity freedom (in particular, counterfactuals of human freedom per Molinism) is part and parcel of feasible worlds. The best feasible world, say, is contingent simply because, as Wierenga says, "counterfactual circumstances ("counterfactuals of freedom") are taken, by Molinists, to be both contingent and independent of God's will."[25] In short, the best feasible world derives its contingency from the contingency of creaturely counterfactuals of alternativity freedom.[26]

Still, while Wierenga focuses on the best feasible world, the idea that human alternativity freedom saves contingency might not be limited to a Molinist outlook. Katherin Rogers, for instance, though not appealing to the Molinist notion of feasible worlds, nevertheless states that components of a possible world are partially up to human alternativity free choices, and thus she (like the Molinist) relies on the distinction between what is actualizable by God and what is not actualizable by God. So Rogers says:

> Is ours, then, "the best of all possible worlds?". . . . If created agents have libertarian freedom [i.e., alternativity freedom], then the state of the world is partially up to us. Clearly we do not always do what is best. We sin . . . . God can bring about the best results consistent with our choices, but it is not clear that . . . this entails the best possible world *simpliciter.* Thus it is probably better to say that God brings about the best "actualizable" world, that is, the best world He can, taking into account created choices. Given God's omniscience and omnipotence, God's plans cannot really be thwarted, but given creatures with libertarian freedom, the free choices of created agents must immutably and eternally play a role in those plans.[27]

So, while Rogers does not employ the typical Molinist notion of *feasible* worlds, she nonetheless relies on a similar distinction between "the best possible world simpliciter" and "the best actualizable world," where the former is apparently not actualizable by God. Again, given Rogers' distinction between what is actualizable by God and what is not, the best actualizable world derives its contingency from the contingency of creaturely alternativity freedom.[28] The fundamental idea, then, that Wierenga and Rogers are proposing is that while God *must* do the best, what is, in fact, the best is a contingent matter since human alternativity free choices are taken as contingent.

The contingency of human alternativity free choice solution is promising, but there are two important points that need to be highlighted. The first and most obvious point is that this outlook commits itself to a metaphysics of human freedom which stipulates that alternativity is a required condition for human freedom. This type of freedom is no doubt a variation of incompatibilism (where freedom is incompatible with determinism) which typically goes under the name of libertarian freedom. While this is not the place to offer a full critique and complete assessment of this type of freedom, it goes without saying that those committed to some variation of determinism (whether theological or not) would likely have problems with alternativity as a required condition of human freedom, and by extension have problems with this particular solution to modal collapse. So, if one is committed to determinism, as most scholars take Leibniz to be, then this solution does not look like a viable option for that variant of theism and the Leibnizian.[29]

Determinism aside, the second and perhaps more important point with respect to this outlook is that it seems to commit itself to a notion of possibility very much similar to that of Leibniz. To see this, the contingency of human alternativity free choice solution is dependent upon the distinction between actualizable possible worlds and nonactualizable possible worlds, or for the Molinist, between feasible possible worlds and possible worlds generally. This outlook, in the wake of the problem of evil, is influenced by Alvin Plantinga where he proposes that there may be a possible world which contains moral good but no moral evil. Yet, while such a world is a possible world, it is nevertheless, according to Plantinga, a world that is nonactualizable.[30] Accordingly, like Leibniz, "actualizable by God" is not a necessary condition for a world to count as a possible world. What this distinction allows for is that while there may be for all we know a best possible world (e.g., a world which contains moral good but no moral evil), such a world is nonactualizable by God. Instead, God creates the best actualizable world, that is, in Wierenga's words, the best feasible world. But, notice that those who are committed to making this distinction between actualizable possible worlds and nonactualizable possible worlds (or between feasible possible worlds and possible worlds generally) are also committed to the (Leibnizian) idea of worlds counting as possible despite the fact that they are not actualizable by God. Again, this is very much like Leibniz's notion that worlds are possible (understood as not implying a contradiction) yet not able to be actualized by God. So, it is worth focusing on the fact that if one has a problem with Leibniz's "possible by its own nature" solution, then one would similarly have a problem with Wierenga and Rogers' outlook (and by extension Plantinga's) since both outlooks are committed to the idea that nonactualizable worlds are *possible* worlds even though it is *impossible* for them to exist apart from the mind of God.

6.5 Conceding the Point?

Given some of the concerns and the previous discussion with respect to each solution regarding the problem of modal collapse, would it be such an outrage for one to basically concede the point? That is, would it be philosophically respectable to conclude that the best possible world is the only possible world, given Theistic Optimism along with the theistic idea that for a world to be possible it must be actualizable by God? Perhaps so, but it would come with an obvious cost for the Theistic Optimist, namely, amending the idea of *possible* worlds in favor of something else. One might plausibly jettison the concept of "possible worlds" and substitute it for a simpler notion of, say, "worlds." God, then, does not compare and deliberate within His mind among possible worlds but, rather, among *worlds*. This viewpoint has been suggested by Lloyd Strickland when he declares the following:

> God will of necessity create the only possible world . . . . [F]irstly, because God is perfectly good, and secondly, because the world he favours is unsurpassed by any other. "Unsurpassed by any other what?" we may ask, for we know that there are no other possible worlds. The response is disarmingly simple: unsurpassed by other *worlds*. Not possible worlds. Worlds. While the only possible world cannot be the best of all possible worlds, it is still the best world, or best of worlds, and we thus have our answer: the world God necessarily creates will not be the best *of all possible worlds*, but it will be the best *world*.[31]

Strickland goes on to state that a world "is a completely determinate and contingent set of things that is free from internal contradiction."[32] For him, then, God must create the best set of things that is free from internal contradiction and it is only that set of things that meets the necessary conditions for a world to count as a possible world. Consequently, "[a]ll the worlds inferior to the best are impossible by the same criteria, for while they are internally consistent, they have no chance of ever being granted existence."[33]

Yet, in favoring *worlds* as opposed to *possible* worlds, Strickland notes that one might object and ask, "[H]ow can it be meaningful to compare a possible thing [e.g., the best possible world] with other things that aren't possible at all [e.g., other inferior worlds]? Is it not just as absurd as saying that a square can be compared in size with a square triangle?"[34] He thinks not since it confuses two distinct types of impossibility. So, Strickland declares:

> In the case of worlds, there are two ways in which they could be impossible. The first way is when a world is like the square triangle in nature, that is, it involves contradiction. Such worlds may include and exclude the same thing, or involve some other breach of the laws of logic. . . . But there is of course another way in which a world can be impossible: not because of some violation of a logical rule within the concept of the world itself, but rather because these worlds are inferior to the best, and thus not attractive enough to a perfect being to make him want to create them. Thus it is the very fact that these impossible worlds *can* be compared to the only possible world that makes them impossible in the first place![35]

Now while Strickland at this point might offer us some headway, one may nevertheless demand that the talk of mere "worlds" needs some adjectival substantiating, that is, modifying the quality of what a world amounts to. Since "possible" is ruled out as a modifier, perhaps it is coherent to refer to these worlds as *conceivable*. Moreover, given Leibniz's commitment to divine conceptualism (where worlds are thoughts in the divine mind) and his deliberative outlook on God and creation, appealing to conceivable worlds seems quite plausible. To see this, conceivability is typically taken as an epistemic notion, and if worlds in Leibniz's philosophy are ultimately grounded in God's *understanding* (another epistemic notion), then it makes sense to call these worlds conceivable worlds. In fact, Leibniz seems to equate possibility with conceivability when he says "since there are many things which have never happened and never will happen, and which nevertheless are clearly conceivable . . . how can one say they are altogether impossible?"[36] Here is how Roger Woolhouse puts it:

> Leibniz's account of God's understanding plays a central role in his philosophy, not only because it explains the creation of this particular world, but also because it is the foundation for the status of necessary truths and is the model for human understanding, which he says mirrors or expresses that of God. What is this understanding that God has? What does it contain? All possibilities in all combinations, that is, everything which can be conceived.[37]

In short, these worlds are worlds that God conceives or has in His understanding. But building on from Strickland, keep in mind that calling these worlds conceivable worlds is not to say that these worlds are possible, thus distancing from Leibniz. Consequently, one will quickly notice that if one holds that these worlds are properly understood as conceivable worlds, then the Theistic Optimist will now be committed to a controversial claim, namely, while possibility entails conceivability, conceivability does *not* entail possibility, at least at the divine level. For recall that, although there are a number of conceivable worlds (i.e., worlds in God's understanding), only one of those worlds is, in fact, a possible world (i.e., the best world). But, as David Chalmers reminds us, "conceivability . . . is relative to a speaker or thinker."[38] So, if Chalmers is correct, then perhaps it is plausible to conclude that conceivability does not entail possibility at the divine level.

6.6 Conclusion

In this chapter I considered the difficult problem of modal collapse: if God must do the best, then the best possible world is the only possible world. I highlighted three possible solutions to this problem, namely, (1) the possible by its own nature solution a la Leibniz, (2) the contingency of the criterion of perfection solution a la Pickup, and (3) the contingency of human alternativity freedom solution a la Wierenga and Rogers. While drawing attention to these three solutions, I also noted some of the possible costs and benefits of each viewpoint hoping to advance the discussion regarding the plausibility of each solution. Finally, I considered the option of conceding the point that the best possible world is, indeed, the only possible world. However, such a concession results in jettisoning the notion of *possible* worlds in favor of *worlds*, or more specifically in favor of conceivable worlds.

Theistic Optimism and the Christian Tradition

7.1 Introduction

We saw in Chapter 2 that there are three primary motivations for Leibniz's Theistic Optimism, namely, God's ontological perfection, the Principle of Sufficient Reason, and Sacred Scripture. What of the Christian tradition? While Leibniz does not explicitly consult particular historical figures as support for his outlook, he nonetheless states the following:

> I also believe that . . . the holy fathers will be found favoring my opinion [that to act with less perfection than one could have is to act imperfectly], but scarcely any will be found favoring the opinion of these moderns, an opinion which is, in my judgment, unknown to all antiquity and which is based only on the inadequate knowledge we have of the general harmony of the universe and of the hidden reasons for God's conduct. . . . Besides, these moderns insist on certain subtleties, for they imagine that nothing is so perfect that there is not something more perfect—this is an error.[1]

Here, Leibniz has a straightforward appeal to the "holy fathers" favoring his outlook. Despite lack of a referent, however, in this chapter I will take a close look at a final problem for Theistic Optimism, namely, the charge that it seriously deviates from the Christian tradition. In fact, a number of philosophers claim that divine alternativity is the traditional view, particularly the traditional view of God's freedom. I will argue that Theistic Optimism is, indeed, consistent with the claims of the Christian tradition, and thus show that Leibniz's outlook is a viable option for that particular theistic tradition. If this is so, then one need not be required to accept the proposition that divine alternativity is the traditional view. The argument for this is founded upon establishing a set of conditions for what constitutes a view as "traditional," and demonstrating that Theistic Optimism is consistent with every member of the set of conditions. I close the chapter by considering a possible objection to my argument.

7.2 The Objection from the Christian Tradition

A substantial number of thinkers have claimed that, contra Theistic Optimism, the *traditional view* is anything but the idea that God must do the best, and therefore by implication Leibniz and his commitment to Theistic Optimism grievously depart from the established Christian tradition that he is indebted to. For instance, in his book, *Anselmian Explorations*, Thomas V. Morris asserts the following:

> The traditional view is that God is a free creator of our physical universe: He was free to create it or to refrain from creating it; he was free to create this universe, a different universe, or no such universe at all. Of course, the range of God's creative freedom must be consonant with his nature as a maximally perfect being. That renders divine freedom interestingly different from human freedom. He could not have done morally otherwise than as he did. He could not have produced a physical universe which was ultimately, on balance, evil. But there are innumerably many ways in which he could have done otherwise than as he did, sufficient for his creation of our worlds being free.[2]

While the objection from divine freedom was discussed in Chapter 3, it is clear that what Morris posits as the traditional view is of an entirely different outlook than that of Theistic Optimism. For the traditional view, according to Morris, basically states that it is not the case that God must do the best, and therefore concluding that Theistic Optimism abandons the Christian tradition. Morris, then, would have serious reservations about the idea that God *must* do the best fitting within the realm of what he calls "the traditional view."

In addition, William Hasker argues that "if God is not free in this sense [i.e., in the alternativity sense which Theistic Optimism denies], then the divine act of creation must be somehow necessitated by the nature of God; the creation will then be *necessary for God*, and not a free and gracious act as the Christian tradition has affirmed it to be."[3] Hasker, then, concludes that one must attribute to God a similar outlook as that posited by Morris. In fact, "they must do so if they wish to be orthodox Christians."[4] Similarly, Paul Copan and William Lane Craig state that "In orthodox Christian thought creation is seen as the freely willed act of God. He does not create by a necessity of nature, and there are possible worlds in which God refrains from creation and so exists alone."[5] Consequently, Hasker, along with Copan and Craig, seems to claim by implication that the idea that God must do the best is part and parcel of *un*orthodox thought. Lastly, Sandra Menssen and Thomas Sullivan argue that Leibniz's Theistic Optimism is an outlook "against the traditional position," where the traditional position denies the Leibnizian idea that God must do the best.[6] Accordingly, we have an argument against Theistic Optimism from the Christian tradition. That is, if one affirms Theistic Optimism, then one deviates from the traditional view within (orthodox) Christian thought.[7]

Before engaging this problem, it is noteworthy that this objection basically states that if one *believes* or *affirms* Theistic Optimism, then one is outside the bounds of the Christian tradition. Consequently, this argument from the Christian tradition against Theistic Optimism is doxastic in nature (i.e., having to do with belief) rather than conceptual. For the argument focuses on one *believing* or *affirming* Theistic Optimism rather than supposing that Theistic Optimism holds true. The charge, in other words, is not that if Theistic Optimism holds true, then one deviates from the Christian tradition. The charge, rather, is that if one *believes* in Theistic Optimism, then one deviates from the Christian tradition. So, again, that the objection has a doxastic feature to it rather than a conceptual one makes the problem slightly different from those considered in previous chapters.

With this caveat in mind, how might one respond to statements like those of Morris, Hasker, Copan and Craig, along with Menssen and Sullivan? Is divine alternativity the traditional view? While the aforementioned philosophers do not give (or even hint at) a possible desideratum for what counts as a traditional view, it will nevertheless be important that we first consider what might make for a traditional view. In other words, whether we accept the criticism that Theistic Optimism deviates from the Christian tradition will undoubtedly depend on what the requirements are for a traditional view. I see only two possible conditions, each sufficient, which may support a particular view as *the traditional view*. First, it could be argued that a certain outlook (let us call it *O*) is what we find in either the testimony of Scripture or in Ecumenical Creeds. It is these *authoritative writings* that represent the Christian tradition regarding outlook *O*. Or second, perhaps a particular outlook is to be found in the affirmations of *significant theological figures* in the history of the Christian tradition—that is, that the post-canonical religious authorities, when explicating outlook *O*, clearly propound and are in harmony with one another regarding outlook *O*. I will argue that in each case these arguments do not yield the conclusion that Theistic Optimism grievously deviates from the Christian tradition. In fact, given certain theological representatives of the Christian tradition, there is a case that Leibniz and his Theistic Optimism ought to be the preferred outlook. Let us now consider each of these requirements.

7.3 Authoritative Writings

Authoritative writings have typically played an important role in the development of what can or cannot be deemed as a traditional theological position. Most notably these include the witness from Scripture and the declarations of Ecumenical Creeds: the Nicene Creed (325), the Apostles' Creed (390), the Chalcedonian Creed (451), and the Athanasian Creed (fifth century). Accordingly, one might initially apply a Holy Scripture condition since there is good reason to think that the Bible is the foundation and wellspring of what the Christian tradition has always professed. In fact, this is exactly what at least Menssen and Sullivan hold to while exercised against Theistic Optimism, and conclude that their outlook is the "Scriptural teaching."[8] The texts to which they refer are the following:

> Our God is in the heavens; he does all that he pleases (Ps. 115:3);

and

> In him we have obtained an inheritance, having been predestined according to the purpose of him who works all things according to the counsel of his will. (Eph. 1:11)

Similar texts which could be highlighted are

> I will be gracious to whom I will be gracious, and will show mercy on whom I will show mercy (Ex. 33:19);

and

Worthy are you, our Lord and God, to receive glory and honor and power, for you created all things, and by your will they existed and were created. (Rev. 4:11)

Are these texts representative statements which cast doubt on the idea that God must do the best? I conclude "No" since the denial of the idea that God must do the best is neither explicitly nor implicitly found in these texts. Moreover, there is simply no mention in these texts of divine alternativity, which would rule out Theistic Optimism. Rather, what these texts highlight is the simple fact that nothing metaphysically external to God could function as the ultimate explanation for why God does one thing rather than another. In other words, according to these texts, God is not constrained, coerced, determined, or even influenced by anything *outside of himself*.

It needs to be noted, however, that these statements found in the Holy Scriptures do not demand Theistic Optimism either—there is simply nothing in the texts which speaks of the notion that God must do the best. Therefore, in general, a philosophical conception of divine alternativity or Theistic Optimism is not entailed by the biblical statements. To think otherwise would simply read too much into the text. Here is a case where the language of Scripture with respect to the metaphysics of God's act of creating a particular world is not sufficiently precise as to provide a definitive resolution of the issue one way or another. Because of this insufficient precision, it would be unwise for anyone to claim that divine alternativity or Theistic Optimism is entailed by the language of Scripture. To put it simply, there is underdetermination regarding the specifics of God creating a particular world with respect to the biblical evidence. But, given this underdetermination, these texts are consistent with Leibniz's Theistic Optimism and the overall framework of having a high view of Scripture (as we saw in Chapter 2).[9]

Supposing, then, that the precise metaphysics of God's act of creating a particular world is underdetermined with respect to the Scriptural data, what sort of account can be gleaned from the Ecumenical Creeds? Here the data is even more scarce, but in this case the two most relevant statements come from the Apostles' Creed and the Nicene Creed. The Apostles' Creed reads:

I believe in God the Father, almighty, Maker of Heaven and Earth.[10]

And the significant part of the Nicene Creed states:

We believe in one God the Father all powerful, maker of all things both seen and unseen . . . through whom all things came to be, both those in heaven and those in earth.[11]

What we see from both these creedal statements is that they similarly affirm God as "almighty" (or "sovereign") and "maker" of heaven and earth. The core ideas seem to be that (1) God is powerful enough to create, (2) God created all that exists, and (3) nothing external to God influenced or determined Him to act as He did. Further, I do not think it would be too far off the mark to also state that the doctrine of *creatio ex nihilo* is in the background here. Nevertheless, what the church fathers produced in these creeds is not a metaphysical explanation of divine freedom but, rather, a set of parameters, or a sort of guideline, through which specific theological views are filtered. In other words, the creeds function as a way of letting the church know what is and what is not acceptable concerning the doctrine of God and creation.

To further illustrate this point, a parallel example can be seen from what Sarah Coakley has recently pointed out regarding what Chalcedon can (or cannot) solve regarding a plausible model of the Incarnation of Christ.[12] She argues that some of the essential terms in the Chalcedonian definition (e.g., *physis* [i.e., nature] and *hypostasis* [i.e., person]) are simply left undefined, and therefore leave the definition somewhat flexible. She argues nevertheless that Chalcedon should be approached as a theologically regulatory and binding text—as a grid through which our metaphysical reflections on the Incarnation must pass. So, Chalcedon does not, she says, "intend to provide a full systematic account of Christology, and even less a complete and precise metaphysics of Christ's makeup. Rather, it sets a 'boundary' on what can, and cannot be said"[13]—hence the use of negative expressions in the Chalcedon formula.

Similarly, then, just as there are many important Christological issues that Chalcedon cannot solve, so too there are many important metaphysical issues about the specifics of God creating that the Apostles' Creed and the Nicene Creed cannot solve either, or even hint at. These two latter creeds, for instance, do not tell us whether or not God could have acted otherwise in an alternativity sense, or whether freedom is or is not consistent with necessity, or even whether God is free! This is not to say, however, that Theistic Optimism is *inconsistent* with the creeds. On the contrary, the creedal statements are consistent with Theistic Optimism such that they can be interpreted in that way. Whether the church fathers intended by their statements to teach Theistic

Optimism is certainly a more complex question since these texts, admittedly, can equally well be interpreted in a non-Theistic Optimism way, that is, in a divine alternativity way. Similarly regarding Holy Scripture, then, I conclude that these two Ecumenical Creeds are underdetermined with respect to the precise metaphysics of God and creation.

7.4 Significant Theological Figures

But what about significant theological figures? Can post-canonical religious thinkers help us further on the question whether or not divine alternativity is the traditional view? In what follows, I will consider three influential figures upon the Christian tradition, namely, Saint Augustine of Hippo (354–430), Saint Anselm of Canterbury (1033–1109), and Jonathan Edwards (1703–1758). Undoubtedly, there are other prominent thinkers that could be consulted, such as John Duns Scotus, William of Ockham, Thomas Aquinas, and John Calvin. However, in selecting Augustine, Anselm, and Edwards, I hope to demonstrate that Leibniz's Theistic Optimism has not been summarily rejected by these influential thinkers, but, rather, to some extent supported by them. So, our current question is now as follows: What can be gleaned from Augustine, Anselm, and Edwards regarding the notion that divine alternativity is the traditional view within the Christian tradition?

Although Augustine does not give a systematic treatment of God and creation (which is rather unfortunate), he nevertheless seems to posit that there is an internal necessity of the divine will such that for God to create *anything* less than the best is a failure of perfect goodness. To begin, Augustine claims (in the context of why God made souls he knew would sin) that it would be foolish to think that souls should not have been made, while also thinking it foolish that souls should have been made otherwise. Here is what he says in *On Free Choice of the Will*:

> Whatever right reason suggests to you as more perfect, you may be sure that God has already made it, for He is the Creator of all things good. Whenever you suppose that something better should have been made, because you are unwilling to have anything less perfect exist, this is not right reason but a want of understanding stemming from envy.[14]

And,

> There may be something in nature which you do not conceive of in your
> mind, but it is impossible that something not exist which you truly conceive
> of in your mind. You cannot conceive of anything better in the creation
> which has escaped the knowledge of the Creator.[15]

Although created souls are in context (as mentioned), Augustine goes on to
highlight two further examples, namely, angels and the souls of the damned.
He goes so far as to say that the souls of the damned must exist since their
misery "contributes to the perfection of the whole by ensuring that it includes
even those souls who deserved to be made unhappy because they willed to be
sinners."[16]

Further, when one rightly reasons that something is better than another,
even though one does not see it, that particular thing *ought* to have been
created. In other words, the *a priori* reflection of that which is best is capable
of deducing what God has, indeed, created. As Augustine further declares:

> So the soul must believe that God has made what his right reason tells him
> should have been made, even though he fails to see it among the things
> created. Even though a man were unable to see the heavens with his eyes
> and yet could rightly conclude by his reason that such a thing should be
> made, he would have to believe it was made, though he could not see it
> with his eyes. Only in the light of those [Divine] Ideas, after which all
> things have been made, could he see in his mind why something had to
> be made. One cannot form a true conception of anything not present in
> these [Divine] Ideas any more than he can find something there which is
> not true.[17]

What we see here from Augustine is a connection between what God knows
and what God creates. Augustinian scholar, Roland Teske, offers the following
reconstruction of Augustine's argument:

> If ones sees correctly, that is, with true reason, that X should have been
> made, then he can be sure that X already has been made, even if he cannot
> by observation check that it has been made. One sees what he sees correctly
> in the divine ideas, and the divine ideas are the patterns in God's mind in
> accord with which God produces whatever he produces. The text does not
> imply that something apart from God, for example, the goodness of X,
> causes God to create it. But what we know in the divine ideas, God obviously
> knows as well. If we can be certain that he has created X because we see X in

his ideas, it would seem that, given this knowledge of his, he could not but create X.[18]

Teske argues from this reconstruction that, "If the Augustinian God knows only what he creates, then he could not create anything other than what he does create. And thus he would not be free in the sense that he could have created other things than he did create."[19] Teske thus concludes by rhetorically asking: "Given such texts, does it not seem that God could not but create the world and could not but create the best possible?"[20] It goes without saying that an affirmative answer to Teske's questions resonates quite well with Theistic Optimism. Indeed, with respect to Augustine's outlook on God's will, Teske goes so far as to find himself "admitting an optimistic determinism of the divine will."[21]

Katherin Rogers arrives at a similar conclusion as Teske but for different reasons. While Teske found support in *On Free Choice of the Will*, Rogers finds her main support in *The Literal Meaning of Genesis*, where "Augustine presents an argument which shows that a perfectly good God could not fail to create."[22] Here is what Augustine says:

> Of what good things could he laudably feel no need if He had not made anything? For He also could be said to need no good things, not by resting in Himself from the things He has made, but just by not making anything. But if he is not able to make good things then he has no power, and if He is able and does not make them, great is His envy. So because He is omnipotent and good He made all things very good.[23]

The context here is God's rest on the seventh day of creation. Augustine does, indeed, state that God rested in order to show that he did not need creation, and so God is not made complete by creation. Yet, as Rogers states, "[A]lthough God does not need creation, it would be inconsistent with His perfect goodness to fail to create . . . . If God is good He will not be envious, He will want to create good things. If He is omnipotent He will be able to create them, and so God could not fail to create."[24]

Given the remarks by Teske and Rogers, it seems plausible to interpret Augustine's view as something very close to Theistic Optimism. In fact, while David Bradshaw claims that such a view is a "repellant view," he nevertheless holds that

> He [i.e., Augustine] asserts frequently that God's will has no external cause and in that sense is unnecessitated. However, it does have an *internal*

necessity, in that for God to create anything less than the best possible world would be a failure of perfect goodness.[25]

According to these commentators, then, Augustine seems to endorse something very close to the idea that God must do the best. Indeed, we might agree with Rogers at this point that "Enough can be said here to show that it is at least reasonable to interpret Augustine as saying that failure to create, and to create this world, would be inconsistent with the divine nature."[26] Again, such statements resonate quite well with Theistic Optimism, and at the very least such statements are clearly against the idea of divine alternativity.

At this point, however, one might object to such an interpretation and claim that there is sufficient textual evidence in Augustine to demonstrate that God exercises divine alternativity, thus claiming that Augustine did not think that God created and created this particular world from an internal necessity. For example, William E. Mann, while contrasting Plato's outlook where "the demiurge created this world and that this world is the best world the demiurge could have created" with that of Augustine's outlook, states the following:

> [T]he thesis that nothing is superior to God's will, precludes God's will from having any cause. For Augustine the explanatory buck stops here. To put it another way, Augustine finds nothing in God's nature that entails that God must create. It is not evident that Augustine thinks that if God decides to create, then God must create the best world that he can. Creation is indeed very good . . . created out of the "fullness of [God's] goodness."[27]

The three most promising texts which could be used (and are, indeed, used by Mann) to support this response can be found in *On Genesis against the Manichees*, *Eighty-Three Different Questions*, and *City of God*.

Since they are quite similar in content, consider first what Augustine says in both *On Genesis against the Manichees* and *Eighty-Three Different Questions*:

> So then, if these people ever say, "Why did it take God's fancy to make heaven and earth?" the answer to be given them is that those who desire to know God's will should first set about learning the force of the human will. You see, they are seeking to know the causes of God's will, when God's will is itself the cause of everything there is. After all, if God's will has a cause, there is something that is there before God's will and takes precedence over it, which it is impious to believe. So then, anyone who says, "Why did God make heaven and earth?" is to be given this answer: "Because he wished to."

It is God's will, you see, that is the cause of heaven and earth, and that is why God's will is greater than heaven and earth. Anyone though who goes on to say, "Why did he wish to make heaven and earth?" is looking for something greater than God's will is; but nothing greater can be found.[28]

And similarly,

To inquire into why God wanted to make the world is to inquire into the cause of God's will. But every cause is productive of some result, everything productive of some result is greater than that which is produced, and nothing is greater than God's will. Therefore [God's will] has no cause to be sought after.[29]

It is noteworthy here that Augustine never endorses divine alternativity. Indeed, he never even mentions it. On the contrary, Augustine is mostly concerned with preserving the superiority of God's will as a regress stopper; he is simply rejecting Manichean metaphysical dualism, where the coeternal could function as a possible external explanation for God's will.

Further, Augustine is emphasizing the idea of *efficient* causality rather than a logically sufficient condition for why God created. Indeed, to even pose the question "What [efficiently] caused the divine will?" is to introduce what Gilbert Ryle would call a "category mistake" where a property is ascribed to something that could not possibly have that property.[30] In other words, asking the question "What [efficiently] caused the divine will?" is like asking the question "How much does the number 7 weigh?" So, according to Augustine, the divine will functions primarily as a regress stopper. Unless one must accept divine alternativity in order to avoid an infinite regress of reasons, there is no reason to think that what Augustine says here is even significant to the present discussion. But do proponents of divine alternativity give us any good reason to think that asserting divine alternativity is the only way to avoid regress problems with respect to God's willing? It would seem not since Theistic Optimism can fully account for God being the ultimate source of His actions, and therefore the regress stopper. For these reasons the two aforementioned texts cannot support the idea that Augustine endorsed divine alternativity.

But what about a specific text from *City of God*? Is there evidence here against Theistic Optimism? For, as Augustine says, "And when it says, God saw that it was good, it signifies clearly enough that God did not make what he made out of any necessity, or out of any need of something useful to himself, but simply out of sheer goodness; that is, he made what he made because it was good."[31] Given that Augustine states "God did not make what he made out of any necessity" this text seems to be in clear opposition to the idea that God, because of His perfect nature, must do the best.

But what exactly does Augustine mean by "necessity" here? According to Rogers, Augustine thinks that necessity is when one is forced to act out of external compulsion. And, if this is what Augustine means by necessity, then it is consistent to affirm an *internal* necessity finding its source from the divine nature. As she says, "Augustine sees no contradiction between saying that God does not create out of any necessity—He is not forced by an external compulsion—and yet holding that there is a cause of creation, that is, God's perfect goodness."[32] Similarly, Teske claims that Augustine, when elaborating on Ps. 135:6, contrasts "being forced, or coerced" with "willing."[33] Accordingly, acting out of necessity is when an agent is forced or coerced to act as he or she does. Teske concludes that "If that is correct . . . it is not clear that he [i.e., Augustine] is ruling out by that phrase an internal necessity grounded in the goodness of God," and thus "to say simply that all necessity is denied may be a bit precipitous."[34] Consequently, God's will has no external cause and in that sense only is it not necessitated. For this reason, then, the aforementioned text in *City of God* is not a good reason to undermine the interpretation that Augustine asserts the idea that God must do the best.[35]

So, with the help of Teske and Rogers, it is plausible to interpret Augustine asserting that the divine will was necessitated by its own perfect goodness, and such a statement rules out divine alternativity. Augustine, then, seems to be more sympathetic to Theistic Optimism and in direct opposition to divine alternativity. Considered as a substantial voice for the Christian tradition, Augustine seems to tip the scales of the Christian tradition toward a non-divine alternativity reading, which harmonizes well with his understanding of necessity as "need," that is, the need of something outside of Himself. Therefore, I think it is safe to say, in agreement with Teske and Rogers, that Augustine wholeheartedly denies divine alternativity.

We now move to Anselm of Canterbury. What might we gather from Anselm as to whether or not divine alternativity is the traditional view? To begin, one might argue that Anselm endorses divine alternativity simply because he claims that God does nothing by necessity. Here is what Anselm says in *Why God Became Man* (*Cur deus homo*):

God does nothing by necessity, since He is in no way compelled to do or prevented from doing anything; and when we say that God does something as if from the necessity of avoiding dishonorableness—which He certainly does not fear—it is rather to be understood that He does this out of the necessity of preserving His honorableness. And this necessity is nothing other than the immutability of His honorableness, which He has from Himself and not from another and which is therefore improperly called necessity.[36]

Because of the influence of contemporary modality it is tempting to assert that in stating that "God does nothing by necessity," Anselm is straightforwardly endorsing divine alternativity. However, upon a closer look, there is no such endorsement. Rather, like his hero Augustine, as we saw earlier, Anselm understands necessity as acting from external compulsion, or what some call "causal necessity." Accordingly, a divine action is necessary if its decisive explanation is external to God. Anselm, then, is motivated to preserve the spontaneity condition of freedom (i.e., that God is the ultimate source of His actions); and divine aseity seems to accomplish this motivation. Consider what Sandra Visser and Thomas Williams say:

Because God's immutable uprightness is "from Himself and not from another," every upright divine action will be self-initiated; and for that very reason Anselm insists that no such action should be called "necessary." Divine aseity in fact guarantees that *every* action God performs is self-initiated. So all of God's actions are free, even if He never has alternative possibilities available to Him.[37]

Divine alternativity, then, is not constitutive of Anselm's understanding of divine action or of divine freedom. Consequently, as Visser and Williams go on to say when commenting on Anselm, "No self-initiated action can ever properly be described as necessary, even if it is not possible for the agent to act otherwise in the relevant circumstances."[38]

Katherin Rogers, like Visser and Williams, offers similar comments regarding Anselm's outlook. Rogers argues that divine aseity is what preserves divine freedom, but divine freedom does not require alternativity. As she says:

[I]f someone [according to Anselm] is forced to render some benefit, they do not deserve gratitude. But, of course, the necessity in question with divine action is not any compulsion or prohibition. "Certainly that necessity is nothing other than the immutability of His honor, which He has from

Himself and not from some other . . . and therefore it is called 'necessity' improperly." Still, Anselm allows the term, "Nevertheless let us say that it is necessary . . . ." . . . As he made clear in talking about created freedom, the key criterion is aseity. The necessity which interferes with freedom is a necessity of which the origin is ultimately something outside the agent, and thus whatever qualified necessity can be properly attributed to God is not the sort that could infringe upon divine freedom.[39]

According to Rogers, then, Anselm denies divine alternativity and a qualified necessity can be applied to His actions. As she further says, "Anselm embraces the view that God simply 'must' do the best, and even allows the use of the term 'necessity' to apply to God's actions."[40]

Still, Rogers further elaborates on Anselm's view by highlighting some statements in his *Monologion*. In Chapters 33 and 34, Anselm is preoccupied with answering the question of whether or not God speaks forth the Word (i.e., the second Person of the Trinity) and the created order with one and the same act. (Undoubtedly, the phrase "one and the same act" gives rise to the doctrine of divine simplicity.) Anselm answers this question in the affirmative by simply concluding, "Therefore, he utters both himself and whatever he made by one and the same Word."[41] Here is Rogers's commentary on the previous quotation from Anselm:

> Of course God does not choose among competing options to speak or not to speak the Word which is the Second Person of the Trinity. If it is by the same act of "speaking" that the Word is begotten and creation is made, then, since God does not have the option not to speak the Word (or to speak some different Word), the plausible conclusion is that in Anselm's view, the creation of our world is "necessary" in the sense that it is the inevitable result of God's perfect goodness.[42]

She concludes from this that what Anselm says here in *Monologion* "might not be conclusive,"[43] but because Anselm's metaphysics of freedom "simply does not find open options to be valuable for God, *the interpretation which sees creation as 'necessary' seems correct.*"[44] Therefore, these texts in *Monologion*, according Rogers, "seem to entail that God could not have failed to create the actual world,"[45] and thus the denial of open options is to be applied to all of God's actions.

In addition to what Anselm says in *Monologion*, Rogers also points to where Anselm "does at one point seem to say that ours is in some sense a 'perfect' or at least ultimately perfectible world."[46] The reason for thinking that our created world is a perfect world is that there is a perfect number of individuals in it who will experience the *visio beatifica* (i.e., the beatific vision). While commenting on what Anselm says in *Cur deus homo* 1.16, Rogers states the following:

> [H]e [i.e., Anselm] notes that God sees that there is a "perfect number" of rational beings who should enjoy everlasting beatitude, such that God "must" see to it that that number is fulfilled. Further, " . . . if the perfection of the world of creatures is to be understood to be not so much in the number of individuals as in the number of natures, then it is necessary that human nature was made either to complete that perfection or else to exceed it, which we dare not say of the nature of the smallest worm."[47]

What this implies, according to Rogers, is that a sort of perfection is possible with respect to the actual world and that our world is perfect in that it alone consists of having the perfect number of created rational beings. She admits that these affirmations of Anselm are "consistent with interpreting Anselm as saying that God 'must' order things properly in our world, but that He might have made other worlds or no world at all."[48] However, in response to this interpretation, Rogers declares that "Anselm does not suggest that the perfection in question is relative to our particular world, as opposed to the other possible worlds, but speaks rather of '*the* world of creatures.'"[49]

Rogers concludes, then, given what Anselm says in *Monologion*—where speaking forth the second Person of the trinity and creation in one and the same act implies creation as necessary—and what Anselm says with respect to our world consisting of a perfect number of rational beings, we thus have good reason to think that the denial of open options is to be applied to *all* of God's actions, not merely to actions which are subject to a specific world. As she states, "we have good reason to take it that Anselm's point in *Cur deus homo* that God's freedom does not require choosing between open options is intended to apply to any divine act, not just actions relative to a given world."[50] Consequently, Rogers concludes that "divine freedom is entirely consistent with God doing the best as an inevitability of His nature."[51]

We finally come to the American philosophical theologian, Jonathan Edwards. Does Edwards carry the same torch of Augustine and Anselm? Or is he more sympathetic to the outlook of divine alternativity? Here we will look at "Part III: Section 7. Concerning the Necessity of the Divine Will," in

Edwards's work, *Freedom of the Will*.[52] It is in this section that Edwards speaks most clearly of the divine will.[53]

In "Concerning the Necessity of the Divine Will," Edwards first considers the possible objection that if the will, whether it is human or divine, acts necessarily because of some superior motive, then "the will of *God himself* is necessary in all its determinations."[54] That is, if God must do "what he sees *fittest* and *best*," then such an action violates alternativity, and thus the liberty of choice.[55] To better understand this objection, consider Edwards's chief polemical partner, Isaac Watts, in his *Essay on the Freedom of the Will in God and in the Creature* when he argues against Edwards:

> What strange doctrine is this, contrary to all our ideas of the dominion of God? Does it not destroy the glory of his liberty of choice, and take away from the creator and governor and benefactor of the world, that most free and sovereign agent, all the glory of this sort of freedom? Does it not seem to make him a kind of mechanical medium of fate, and introduce Mr. Hobbes's doctrine of fatality and necessity, into all things that God hath to do with? . . . In short, it seems to make the blessed God a sort of almighty minister of fate, under its universal and supreme influence; as it was the professed sentiment of some of the ancients, that fate was above the gods.[56]

From these statements it appears that Watts is clearly antithetical toward any view that denies alternativity to the divine will. By extension, in other words, we might say that what Watts argues here is that Theistic Optimism is a repugnant view of God's will, and therefore needs to be jettisoned.

Now in responding to this type of objection, Edwards (perhaps borrowing from Leibniz) makes a strong appeal to what he calls the "moral necessity" of the divine will, where there is something about the perfect moral nature of God which precludes Him from being able to choose otherwise. Consequently, to choose according to moral necessity does not result in "imperfection" or "inferiority."[57] Here is what Edwards says:

> That all the seeming force of such objections and exclamations [from Watts] must arise from an imagination, that there is some sort of privilege or dignity in being without such a moral necessity, *as will make it impossible to do any other, than always choose what is wisest and best*; as though there were some disadvantage, meanness and subjection, in such a necessity; a thing by which the will was confined, kept under and held in servitude by something, which, as it were, maintained a strong and invincible power

and dominion over it, by bonds that held him fast, and that he could by no means deliver himself from. Whereas, this must be all mere imagination and delusion. Tis no disadvantage or dishonor to a being, necessarily to act in the most excellent and happy manner, from the necessary perfection of his own nature.[58]

What we see here, according to Edwards, is a commitment to the idea that God always chooses what is wisest and best because of the perfection of God's nature. That is, there is something about the moral makeup of God which precludes Him from being able to do otherwise than that which is wisest and best.

It is noteworthy, however, that the idea of moral necessity was not original to Edwards but was, rather, a significant part of the philosophical discourse prior to and during the Enlightenment period.[59] We can see this, for example, from the philosopher, Samuel Clarke, (whom Edwards, in *Freedom of the Will*, quotes authoritatively) as he similarly applies the notion of moral necessity to the divine will. It is in these statements from Clarke that we can glean a better understanding of Edwards's outlook on God's freedom with respect to creating. Here is what Clarke says:

> The supreme cause, therefore, and author of all things, since . . . he must of necessity have infinite knowledge and the perfection of wisdom . . . and since he is likewise self-existent, absolutely independent and all-powerful . . . it is evident he must of necessity (meaning not a necessity of fate, but such a moral necessity as I before said was consistent with the most perfect liberty) do always what he knows to be fittest to be done. That is, he must act always according to the strictest rules of infinite goodness, justice, and truth, and all other moral perfections.[60]

And more explicitly,

> [T]hough God is a most perfectly free agent, yet *he cannot but do always what is best and wisest in the whole.* The reason is evident, because perfect wisdom and goodness are steady and certain principles of action as necessity itself. And an infinitely wise and good being endowed with the most perfect liberty can no more choose to act in contradiction to wisdom and goodness, than a necessary agent can act contrary to the necessity by which it is acted, it being as great an absurdity and impossibility in choice for infinite wisdom to choose to act unwisely, or infinite goodness to choose what is not good, as it would be in nature for absolute necessity to fail of producing its necessary effect.[61]

Despite these affirmations, whether or not Edwards was dependent on Clarke is beside the point—Edwards's idea of moral necessity, like that of Clarke's (and Leibniz's), seems to rule out divine alternativity.

It is also worth emphasizing at this point that it would not be off the mark, in the case of Clarke and Edwards, to state the Leibnizian idea that what does the necessitating is the *wisdom* of God. If so, then the wisdom of God is what corresponds to the idea of "moral" in moral necessity.[62] The divine attribute of wisdom, in other words, results in the fact that God performs that specific act which is wisest and best. Further, to think that God could perform that which is not the best would be to implicitly affirm an unwise and imperfect being. So, to be clear, it is divine wisdom that is primarily operative and functioning when God "must" do the best. To see this point more clearly, here are some final remarks from Edwards on divine wisdom and how it correlates with God doing the best:

> If God's will is steadily and surely determined in everything by *supreme* wisdom, then it is in everything necessarily determined to that which is *most* wise. And certainly it would be a disadvantage and indignity, to be otherwise. For if the divine will was not necessarily determined to that which in every case is wisest and best, it must be subject to some degree of undesigning contingence; and so in the same degree be liable to evil. To suppose the divine will liable to be carried hither and thither at random, by the uncertain wind of blind contingence, which is guided by no wisdom, no motive, no intelligent dictate whatsoever . . . would certainly argue a great degree of imperfection and meanness, infinitely unworthy of the deity. If it be a disadvantage, for the divine will to be attended with this moral necessity, then the more free from it, and the more left at random, the greater dignity and advantage.[63]

In summary, Edwards, like his predecessors Augustine and Anselm, is quite comfortable asserting that God must do what is best since the "must" finds its source in God's perfect nature. Perhaps the comments of William Wainwright on Edwards are instructive at this point:

> Edwards . . . appears committed to the claim that God necessarily creates *this* world (call it w^*). God necessarily does what is "fittest and best." It is thus necessarily true that God creates the best possible world. Now God has created w^*. Hence, w^* is the best possible world. "Being the best possible world" is an essential property of whatever world has it, however. It is

therefore necessarily true that w^* is the best possible world. It follows that it is necessarily true that God creates w^*.[64]

So, although Augustine and Anselm do not explicitly appeal to the idea of moral necessity, such an idea is consistent with their understanding of God and creation. Further, Edwards clearly denies divine alternativity. Indeed, if God is a perfect being, then God must do that which is wisest and best. To propose otherwise would simply reduce God to a deficient, imperfect being since it is "no disadvantage or dishonor to a being, necessarily to act in the most excellent and happy manner, from the necessary perfection of his own nature."[65]

In this section I have looked at what can be gleaned from significant theological figures with respect to Theistic Optimism. I argued that it is plausible to interpret Augustine as asserting the idea that God must do what is best, so long as the "must" is internal to the divine nature. If this is a reasonable understanding of Augustine, then Augustine seems to be more sympathetic to Theistic Optimism than to divine alternativity. Further, given Visser and Williams's along with Rogers's interpretations of Anselm, we can conclude that Anselm, like his hero Augustine, also seems comfortable denying divine alternativity. Finally, I argued that Jonathan Edwards continues to carry the torch of Anselm and Augustine, thus holding that God must do what is wisest and best so long as the "must" in question finds its ultimate source within God's nature. The conclusion thus far, then, is that given Augustine, Anselm, and Edwards as significant theological representatives, it is not the case that divine alternativity is the traditional view.

7.5 What about the First Vatican General Council of 1870?

Thus far I have argued that Theistic Optimism is consistent with authoritative writings, namely, Scripture and the Ecumenical Creeds. I further argued that Augustine, Anselm, and Edwards seem to be advocates of the idea that God must do the best; at the very least they deny divine alternativity. If this holds true, then Theistic Optimism begins to have a significant voice within the Christian tradition. However, a potential objection may arise at this point and can be stated as follows: Sure, while Theistic Optimism is consistent with Scripture and the Ecumenical Creeds, along with being represented by such significant theological figures as Augustine, Anselm, and Edwards, such a view is nevertheless clearly at odds with the statements found in the Roman Catholic First Vatican General Council of 1870. For, in Canons 1.5 entitled "God the creator of all things" the Council reads:

> If anyone . . . says that God created, not by an act of will free from all necessity, but with the same necessity by which he necessarily loves himself . . . let him be anathema.[66]

From these strong statements one might argue that the Vatican Council speaks straightforwardly of divine alternativity since it states that God is "free from *all* necessity." Moreover, if we take the quantifier "all" in its broadest sense to rule out a divine internal necessity (which Theistic Optimism affirms), then surely the Council would at least rule out the idea that God must do the best.

By way of response to this objection, one might first declare that the Roman Catholic First Vatican General Council of 1870 is not binding on one's theological belief system. In other words, a non-Catholic thinker might concede the point that the General Council is, indeed, inconsistent with Theistic Optimism, but highlight the fact that he or she need not be committed to what the General Council concludes. A second line of response could draw attention to two good reasons to think that Theistic Optimism is consistent with the First Vatican Council, and thus the Council could be interpreted in less than its broadest sense. First, it could be argued that, given Theistic Optimism, it is not the case that God created necessarily with the *same* necessity as He necessarily loves Himself.[67] For, it is noticeable how the Council contrasts God's freedom in the latter part of the passage with the absolute necessity of His loving Himself. What the Council is basically stating here is that the willing activity of God to create cannot be exactly the same as God's willing activity to love Himself. So, one might make the required distinction at this point, maintaining that God's necessary love for Himself is a different sort of activity than would be His necessary act of creating. That is, the divine will to create necessarily is not identical to the necessity of the divine will to love itself.

To elucidate further, it is plausible to think that the willing activity of God to create is *specifically intentional*, where God plans and designs to bring about some specific purpose. We might call this necessity, *creational necessity*. God's willing activity to love Himself, on the other hand, could be characterized by joint (supposing the Trinity) *desire* and affirmation. We might call this necessity, *constitutive necessity*. This is not to say, however, that God does not desire what He intends to bring about. Rather, this is to highlight that God's love for Himself (i.e., constitutive necessity) does not have an intending aspect to it—God does not plan and design to love Himself in a manner like that of creating. Therefore, given this subtle difference between constitutive necessity (i.e., the necessity by which God's loves Himself) and creational necessity (i.e., the necessity by which He creates), Theistic Optimism could agree with the Council that God did not create with the *same* necessity by which He necessarily loves Himself. To put it simply, then, the first reason why Theistic Optimism is consistent with the Council is that the necessity to create is *ad extra*, while the necessity for God to love Himself is *ad intra*.

The second reason for thinking that Theistic Optimism is consistent with the First Vatican Council is that the First Vatican Council is specifically rejecting particular worldviews, and in this specific case, the worldview seems to be pantheism. To see that pantheism is in view, Pope Pius IX, on June 29, 1868, convoked the First Vatican General Council to consider the rising influence of the methods of rationalism and naturalism applied to Christian doctrine. Accordingly, if these methods were to be utilized by the church, then these methods would inevitably reduce to heterodox theological positions (e.g., pantheism). In the preface to *Dei Filius*, Pope Pius IX states:

> Indeed even the holy Bible itself, which they at one time claimed to be the sole source and judge of the christian faith, is no longer held to be divine . . . . Thereupon there came into being and spread far and wide throughout the world that doctrine of rationalism and naturalism, utterly opposed to the christian religion . . . . Thus they would establish what they call the rule of simple reason or nature. The abandonment and rejection of the christian religion, and the denial of God and his Christ, has plunged the minds of many into the abyss of pantheism, materialism and atheism, and the consequence is that they strive to destroy rational nature itself . . .[68]

Consequently, for Pope Pius IX, if an anti-scriptural, rationalistic methodology is employed, then one of the heterodox theological positions that would follow is *pantheism*.

We can similarly see that pantheism is being rejected according to the commentary of the revered "Denzinger" text on Canons 1.5 "God the Creator of all things" when it reads that the Council is

(a) Against the pantheists and materialists; (b) against the followers of [Anton] Gunther; (c) against the followers of Gunther and [Georg] Hermes.[69]

Additionally, recent studies have shown that Hermes was under the influence of Fichte, while Gunther was under the influence of Hegel, both of whom were arguably pantheists.[70] We can conclude, then, from Pope Pius IX and "Denzinger" that what is explicitly being condemned by the Council in Canons 1.5 "God the creator of all things" is the heterodox view of *pantheism*.

Now one might further object and argue that while the Council is, indeed, rejecting pantheism in Canons 1.5, nevertheless the affirmation of Theistic Optimism implies pantheism, and so Theistic Optimism would be inconsistent with the Council by way of implication. However, this objection was already laid to rest in Chapter 5, where I argued that the idea that God must do the best (i.e., Theistic Optimism) implies neither panentheism nor pantheism. In short, I argued that even if Theistic Optimism holds true, then the relationship between God and world in all other regards could affirm the absolute Creator-creature distinction of traditional theism, which denies that the created order is ontologically identical to God or ontologically a participant in the divine nature. Therefore, because (1) Theistic Optimism does not entail that God created with the same necessity as He necessarily loves Himself, and because (2) Theistic Optimism does not reduce to a pantheistic metaphysical monism, I conclude that the idea that God must do the best is consistent with the First Vatican General Council. It follows, then, that divine alternativity is not necessarily demanded from this later church council.

7.6 Conclusion

In this chapter I began by examining the claims from Morris, Hasker, Copan, and Craig, along with Menssen and Sullivan, that divine alternativity is the traditional view. I first explored what can be found within authoritative writings and concluded that the testimony from Holy Scripture and two Ecumenical Creeds (the Apostles' Creed and Nicene Creed) do not demand divine alternativity. Although divine alternativity is consistent with both these forms of authoritative writings, nevertheless it is not demanded by either of them. I further argued, and concluded, that Theistic Optimism is consistent with both these expressions of authoritative writings.

I next looked at what could be gleaned by consulting significant theological figures. Looking to Augustine, Anselm, and Edwards as sufficient representatives of the Christian tradition, I pointed out that these theological figures are clearly opposed to divine alternativity, and thus readily affirm something akin to Theistic Optimism. The overarching conclusion of this chapter, then, is that the idea that God must do the best is consistent with the claims of the Christian tradition, and thus divine alternativity is not necessarily the traditional view. Although I have not examined the Christian tradition exhaustively, but merely sampled it, what I have sampled is, indeed, sufficient to claim that Theistic Optimism is anything but a deviation from the Christian tradition. In fact, given Augustine, Anselm, and Edwards, Theistic Optimism seems to be demanded by it. Therefore, what I have shown in this chapter is that divine alternativity is at best only one option within the Christian tradition and that Theistic Optimism is another alternative option. We might do well at this point to echo the statement made by Rogers that "it is impossible that the God of traditional, classical theism could sin, or even do less than the best."[71]

Theistic Optimism and Theistic Compatibilism

8.1 Introduction

So far I have endeavored to provide plausible solutions to a number of contemporary objections leveled against Theistic Optimism. In this final chapter I argue that a certain variation of theism, which I call Theistic Compatibilism (to be explained in what follows), cannot hold to divine alternativity, and thus Theistic Optimism ought to be the preferred option for Theistic Compatibilism in the Christian tradition. More specifically, I consider whether the Theistic Compatibilist's typical understanding of an intelligible, nonarbitrary free choice is consistent with the affirmation that God is free in an alternativity sense, particularly with His freedom to create or not to create. The crux of the problem is this: the Theistic Compatibilist's typical assertion that an intelligible, nonarbitrary free choice demands a *full* explanation seems to entail that God cannot be free in an alternativity sense. However, if this is the case, then God must create, and thus on the face of things it seems that the most convincing strategy for the Theistic Compatibilist is to affirm Theistic Optimism. This chapter will show why this is so.

In Section 8.2 I will sketch the general structure of the objection against Theistic Compatibilism. Then, after highlighting the general structure of the objection, in Section 8.3 I will consider how some contemporary Theistic Compatibilists typically account for an intelligible, nonarbitrary free choice. After arguing in Section 8.4 that this account fails to be in harmony with divine alternativity, I will consider in Section 8.5 various responses open to Theistic Compatibilists concerning this objection, and conclude that Theistic Optimism ought to be the best option to preserve God's freedom.

8.2 The Inconsistency Between Theistic Compatibilism and Divine Alternativity

Recall that while many would agree that the spontaneity condition (i.e., that God is the ultimate source of His actions) is a necessary constituent of God's freedom, they also maintain that such a condition is not sufficient. God, it is said, must also be able to choose otherwise if He is to be free. For example, God has the freedom to create this particular world only if He could have created a different world instead or even refrained from creating at all. These characteristics underscore what we have called *divine alternativity*.[1] Consider the contemporary Theistic Compatibilist, John Frame:

> [T]he whole world is, we say, a free creation of God, not one in which he was constrained, even by his own nature. The same may be said of providence and especially redemption, for the very idea of grace seems to imply that *God might have chosen to do otherwise*. God's nature, it seems, does not force him to create or to redeem. For if he must create or redeem, even if the necessity comes from his own nature, it would seem that he owes something to the creation, that the creation has a claim on him.[2]

Consequently, for Frame, divine alternativity is employed in order to preclude the thought that God must create. God is, therefore, equally as free not to create as He is/was free to create.[3] Of course, the "might have chosen otherwise" here is not merely to be understood in a subjunctive or conditional sense, where God might have chosen otherwise *if* some condition C had been fulfilled. Rather, since nothing in God's nature prevents Him from choosing otherwise, then surely choosing otherwise is just as free as what was actually chosen. This is a case of divine alternativity, as is clear from what Frame further states, "I know of nothing in God's nature that prevented him from not creating or not redeeming . . . there is nothing in God's nature that required him to create and redeem."[4]

Given this conception of divine freedom (i.e., divine alternativity), the central question at hand is as follows: If nothing prevented God from not creating, and nothing in God's nature necessitates Him to create, then why did God choose to create rather than not create? What sort of *explanation* can be given for His choice to create in order to avoid sheer arbitrariness? My argument is that there is an incompatibility between divine alternativity outlined above and the typical Theistic Compatibilist account of an intelligible, nonarbitrary free choice that I have drawn attention to. Affirming the latter seems to require the denial of, or perhaps a modification of, the former. The reasoning for such a conclusion is as follows: if an intelligible, nonarbitrary free choice is one that must be *fully* explained, then it seems that God was not free not to create. It stands to reason, then, that if a Theistic Compatibilist's conception of divine freedom requires alternativity, then the typical Theistic Compatibilist understanding of an intelligible, nonarbitrary free choice is called into question.

Before I develop this inconsistency, however, I need to make it clear what I am not arguing. First, there is no inconsistency between divine alternativity and Theistic Compatibilism per se. One can affirm the essentials of Theistic Compatibilism (whatever they may be) and consistently hold to alternativity with respect to God's freedom. Therefore, my argument should not be understood as a refutation of Theistic Compatibilism but, rather, as one variety of it. Second, there is no inconsistency between what God's freedom is like and the nature of *human* freedom. One can consistently hold to different or similar views with respect to divine and human freedom. The inconsistency, rather, arises between divine alternativity and *a particular argument* against this certain type of freedom. So, the inconsistency arises between divine alternativity and the Theistic Compatibilist understanding that alternativity freedom results in an unintelligible, arbitrary free choice.

Let me summarize the argument in the form of *modus tollens*, thus having a more succinct goal in mind.

(1) If an intelligible, nonarbitrary free choice must be fully explained, then it is not the case that God is free in an alternativity sense.

(2) God is free in an alternativity sense.

(3) Therefore, it is not the case that an intelligible, nonarbitrary free choice must be fully explained.

Because it is my intention to assert (2), that God is free in an alternativity sense, it will be supposed throughout the rest of this chapter. I therefore will focus my attention not only on exploring the truth of premise (1) but also on its consequences for Theistic Compatibilism.

Before engaging with the argument, however, I must pause to acknowledge that up to this point I have been speaking quite loosely of Theistic Compatibilism. Unsurprisingly, Theistic Compatibilism is the conjunct of

Theism and Compatibilism, where the latter asserts that human freedom and moral responsibility are compatible with determinism. The theistic aspect, on the other hand, highlights a certain variation of theism where the focus is on the exhaustive, meticulous sovereignty of God above all else. On this account of sovereignty, God plans, decrees, ordains, or determines *all* things to come to pass, from the least of things to the greatest. Theistic Compatibilists frequently align themselves with the *Westminster Confession of Faith* as it says, "God from all eternity, did, by the most wise and holy counsel of His own will, freely, and unchangeably ordain whatsoever comes to pass."[5] So we might say, then, that *Theistic* Compatibilism holds that human freedom and moral responsibility are consistent with *God's* exhaustive and meticulous determinism. That is, God is the ultimate determiner of human choices, but human beings are nonetheless free and morally responsible for their choices.

However, it will be important for our discussion to briefly differentiate Theistic Compatibilism from another form of compatibilism which I will call "Motive Compatibilism." Motive Compatibilism is the view that human free choices are the necessary byproduct of what the human intellect judges to be most desirable or is most inclined to choose. I take my cue from Jonathan Edwards in *Freedom of the Will*, as he says, "With respect to that grand inquiry, What determines the will? . . . It is sufficient to my present purpose to say, It is that motive which, as it stands in the view of the mind, is the strongest, that determines the will."[6] Further, by "strongest motive" Edwards means "that which appears most inviting . . . the greatest degree of previous tendency to excite and induce the choice."[7] Or, as he later puts it, "the will always is as the greatest apparent good is."[8] Therefore, on Motive Compatibilism, it is an agent's highest desire or strongest inclination which determines the choice, thus precluding the agent from exercising alternativity.[9] In short, an agent is simply free to choose what he or she most wants to choose.

Now the reason for this important distinction between Theistic Compatibilism and Motive Compatibilism is that, as we will shortly see, it is typical of Theistic Compatibilists to also affirm Motive Compatibilism. Parsing this out in Thomistic fashion, we might say, then, that compatibilism functions both at the *primary* level of causation (where God is the cause of human choices) and at the *secondary* level of causation (where a human's strongest desire is the cause of human choices). So, regardless of whether or not the emphasis is put on the primary or secondary level of causation, an agent could not have chosen otherwise—human freedom and moral responsibility are compatible with determinism on both levels. We can see how the Thomistic distinction between primary and secondary causation functions in the work of Frame, when he states the following:

> In a well-wrought story, there is a causal nexus within the world that the author creates. Events can be explained, not only by the author's intention, but also by the structure of "secondary causes" within the world of the story . . . . In Shakespeare's play *Macbeth*, Macbeth kills King Duncan for his own reasons, using resources that are available to him. Duncan's death can be described entirely by the causes and effects within the world of the play. But the author, Shakespeare, is the ultimate cause of everything. Furthermore, although Duncan's death can be explained by causes within the drama, the author is not just the "primary cause" who sets in motion a chain of causes and effects that unfold without his further involvement. Rather, he writes every detail of the narrative and dialogue; as author, he is involved in everything that happens. So there are two complete causal chains. Every event in *Macbeth* has two causes, two sets of necessary and sufficient conditions: the causes within the play itself, and the intentions of Shakespeare.[10]

Theistic Compatibilist Bruce Ware speaks similarly when elaborating on God's asymmetrical relation to good and evil. With respect to God causing good in the world, he says the following:

> Perhaps we should speak, then, of God's relation to goodness as being through a kind of *direct and immediate divine agency* in which there is a necessary correspondence between the character and agency of God and the goodness that is produced in the world. We might call this kind of divine agency "direct-causative" divine action, since it is strictly impossible for any goodness to come to expression apart from God's direct causation and as the outgrowth of his own infinitely good nature. Goodness, then, is controlled by God as he controls the very manifestation and expression of his own nature, causing all the various expressions of goodness to be brought into our world, whether goodness in nature or goodness revealed through human (secondary) agency.[11]

According to Frame and Ware, then, the primary/secondary distinction allows the Theistic Compatibilist to affirm determinism at both the primary level (where God is the cause of human choices) and the secondary level (where human reasons, motives, or desires are the cause of human choices). The motivation is clear: affirming compatibilism at both the primary and secondary levels preserves the exhaustive and meticulous sovereignty of God—God determines *all* things. To be clear, then, according to Theistic Compatibilists (such as Frame and Ware), human free choices are similarly necessitated in terms of primary causation *and* in terms of secondary causation.[12] I now investigate the writings of these contemporary Theistic Compatibilist theologians on what according to them it means for an agent to exercise an intelligible, nonarbitrary free choice given the exhaustive and meticulous determinism of God.

8.3 Theistic Compatibilists on the Intelligibility of a Free Choice

While articulating their account of an intelligible, nonarbitrary free choice, Theistic Compatibilists typically propound what is called the *intelligibility problem*, arguing that undetermined choices, that is, choices that result from alternativity freedom, inevitably reduce to random, irrational, arbitrary, nonsensical, chance events—that is, they are unintelligible.[13] The problem that Theistic Compatibilists seem to be addressing can be summarized as follows: if alternativity is a necessary condition for freedom, then there does not seem to be an adequate explanation of any sort for why one choice was made over another, and thus any choice which was alternativity free results in sheer randomness. What exactly is the Theistic Compatibilist's solution for avoiding the intelligibility problem? The Theistic Compatibilists seem to focus on two metaphysical claims which begin to formulate their understanding of an intelligible free choice: (1) an intelligible, nonarbitrary free choice must have a choice-specific explanation, and (2) an intelligible, nonarbitrary free choice must be chosen in accordance with one's highest desire. Let us now look at these two metaphysical claims.

First, such Theistic Compatibilists argue that an intelligible, nonarbitrary free choice is one that must have a choice-specific reason, or set of reasons. That is, the explanation for why one particular choice was made could not possibly be the same explanation as that for a contrary choice. There is a one-to-one correspondence, in other words, between the explanation and the choice that was made. Consider Ware, when he appeals to the intelligibility problem in arguing against the coherence of alternativity freedom:

[I]f at the moment that an agent chooses A, with all things being just what they are when the choice is made, he could have chosen B, or not-A, then it follows that any reason or set of reasons for why the agent chooses A would be the *identical reason or set of reasons* for why instead the agent might have chosen B, or not-A. That is, since at the moment of choice, all factors contributing to why a choice is made are present and true regardless of which choice is made (i.e., recall that the agent has the power of *contrary* choice), this means that the factors that lead to one choice being made must, by necessity, also be able to lead just as well to the opposite choice. But the effect of this is to say that there can be *no choice-specific reason or set of reasons* for why the agent chose A *instead of* B, or not-A. It, rather, is the case . . . that every reason or set of reasons must be *equally explanatory* for why the agent might choose A, *or* B, *or* not-A. As a result, our choosing reduces, strictly speaking, to arbitrariness. We can give no reason or set of reasons for why we make the choices we make that wouldn't be the identical reason or set of reasons we would invoke had we made the opposite choice! Hence, our choosing A over its opposite is arbitrary.[14]

In summary, the first step in the Theistic Compatibilist's argument is to assert that an intelligible, nonarbitrary free choice must be one that consists of a choice-specific explanation. To think that the same explanation could be given for two possible choices is simply to succumb to the intelligibility problem. So, to reiterate, a choice-specific explanation is a necessary condition for an intelligible, nonarbitrary free choice.

The second line of argument in accounting for an intelligible, nonarbitrary free choice is to claim that an intelligible, nonarbitrary free choice is one that is chosen based only upon one's highest desire. Agents, accordingly, always choose what they most want to choose. Theistic Compatibilists, when explaining why one choice was made over another, frequently echo the sentiments of Jonathan Edwards and speak of one's "strongest desires" and "character traits."[15] Here we have a straightforward appeal to what I earlier called Motive Compatibilism. As Frame says:

We act and speak, then, according to our character. We follow the deepest desires of our heart . . . . In everyday life, we regularly think of freedom as doing what we want to do. When we don't do what we want, we are either acting irrationally or being forced to act against our will by someone or something outside ourselves. This kind of freedom is sometimes called compatibilism, because it is compatible with determinism.[16]

And again, Ware adds:

> We are free when we choose and act and behave in accordance with our strongest desires, since those desires are the expressions of our hearts and characters. In a word, we are free when we choose to do what we want. But it stands to reason that if we choose to do what we want, then at the moment of that choice, we are not "free" to do otherwise. That is, if I want an apple, not an orange, and if my freedom consists in choosing to do what I want, then I'm free to choose the apple but I'm not free to choose the orange. Freedom, then, is not freedom of contrary of choice but freedom to choose and act in accordance with what I most want.[17]

Therefore, acting in accordance with one's highest desire rules out alternativity. An agent's freedom is simply the freedom to choose whatever he or she most wants to have, to do, to possess, or to achieve. The possibility that one could have chosen otherwise in this situation is not a necessary condition in order for one to be considered free. Accordingly, choosing upon one's highest desire is a necessary condition to account for an intelligible, nonarbitrary free choice.

Now before considering the problematic implications of this account of an intelligible, nonarbitrary choice, we need to notice that there seems to be an oddity at work in how these Theistic Compatibilists explain the consistency between God's exhaustive, meticulous determinism and human freedom. Notice, earlier, how both Frame and Ware appeal to a human's highest desire when accounting for compatibility between determinism and human freedom—that is, they appeal to Motive Compatibilism. Apparently, the highest desire is what necessitates the human choice, and thus rules out alternativity. But how does an appeal to Motive Compatibilism, that is, a *human's* highest desire, even begin to clarify how human freedom is compatible with *God's* exhaustive and meticulous determinism? There seems to be a shift of emphasis by Frame and Ware in respect of what does the necessitating from God to human desires, that is, from the primary to the secondary cause. It seems reasonable to think, for example, that a non-theist could also appeal to Motive Compatibilism in order to account for compatibility between, say, (physical) determinism and human freedom. If such a nontheist could do so, then the appeal to Motive Compatibilism by Frame and Ware to account for the compatibility between God determining all things and human choices loses credibility. So, given God's exhaustive and meticulous determinism, it seems odd to explain the compatibility between determinism and human freedom by appealing to a *human's* highest desire since such an appeal puts all the weight on (or perhaps collapses into) secondary causation.[18]

Nevertheless, despite this oddity it is clear that what these Theistic Compatibilists deny with respect to human choice (i.e., alternativity), they seem to also require of God if He is to be free. But how could this be so given their understanding of an intelligible, nonarbitrary free choice? Can one consistently employ the intelligibility problem with respect to human free choices and at the same time assert and uphold alternativity with respect to *God's* freedom? It will be the focus of the next section to consider these questions.

8.4 Does an Intelligible Free Choice Undermine Divine Alternativity?

As we have seen, it is without question that Theistic Compatibilists such as Frame and Ware frequently propound the intelligibility problem in order to account for their understanding of the compatibility between human freedom and God's exhaustive, meticulous determinism. However, is this position consistent? I will now argue that it is not. The problem with the Theistic Compatibilist's defense of an intelligible nonarbitrary free choice can be seen by considering two problematic implications which undermine God's alternativity freedom.

The first problematic implication of the Theistic Compatibilist's reasoning can be recognized by examining the nature of explanation more closely. Just what sort of explanation does the Theistic Compatibilist have in mind when speaking of a *choice-specific* explanation? It is typical within the metaphysics of explanation to distinguish between what is called a "full explanation" and a "partial explanation," or between a "complete explanation" and an "incomplete explanation." Richard Swinburne puts the distinction this way:

> [I]f there is a full cause C of [event] E and a reason R that guarantees C's efficacy, there will be what I shall call a *full explanation* of E. For, given R and C, there will be nothing unexplained about the occurrence of E. In this case, the "what" and "why" together will deductively entail the occurrence of E. But, if there is no full cause of E . . . or no reason that ensured that the cause would have the effect that it did, there will be at most what I shall call a partial explanation.[19]

Given this distinction, I think it is safe to say that what the Theistic Compatibilist has in mind with regard to an intelligible, nonarbitrary free choice is a *full* explanation, since, as Ware states, a choice-specific explanation "can and does account *fully* for why we make the choices we make."[20] There is simply nothing whatever left unexplained. Therefore, to apply Swinburne's reasoning, we might say that the agent (i.e., the "what") in conjunction with the highest desire (i.e., the "why") entails the occurrence of some particular event, that is, the choice. To think otherwise would inevitably reduce a choice to an unintelligible, arbitrary decision.

This is not to confuse an epistemic issue with a metaphysical issue. The Theistic Compatibilist is making a metaphysical claim about what an intelligible free choice amounts to, namely, that there needs to be a full explanation in order for it to be nonarbitrary. Nevertheless, this metaphysical assertion is perfectly consistent with the claim that we do not know the explanation in its entirety—that is, all the conditions at hand which entail the choice. With that caveat in mind, the first implication for the Theistic Compatibilist is that a full explanation is a necessary condition for an intelligible, nonarbitrary free choice.

The second problematic implication of the Theistic Compatibilist's argument is associated with the claim that an agent chooses based upon his or her highest desire. In virtue of one's highest desire, "we always do what we most want to do, and hence there always is an explanation (i.e., a choice-specific explanation) for the particular choices."[21] We might say, then, that the highest desire here functions as the full explanation. That is, when one chooses what he or she most wants to choose, there not only is an explanation, but there is also a full explanation—one that fully accounts for why one choice was made over the other. The highest desire, in other words, entails the particular choice.[22]

However, if one's highest desire functions as the full explanation, then there is no possible way in which one could have chosen otherwise, given that particular highest desire. The highest desire fully explains why on this occasion one choice was made over another, and thus why, when one chooses, one *must* choose. Therefore, a full explanation on this understanding necessitates the choice. As Swinburne further says, "An explanation of E by F is a full one if F includes both a cause, C, and a reason, R, which together *necessitated* the occurrence of E."[23] Therefore, the second problematic implication is that a necessitated choice is a necessary condition for an intelligible, nonarbitrary free choice.

Here is a summary of the argument so far. The burden of the Theistic Compatibilist is to try and harmonize his or her account of an intelligible, nonarbitrary free choice with:

(i) Divine alternativity.

The implications of his account are as follows:

(ii) An intelligible free choice has a full explanation.
(iii) A choice that has a full explanation is a necessitated choice.

The Theistic Compatibilist's ability to hold together divine alternativity and his or her account of an intelligible, nonarbitrary free choice, therefore, depends on the consistency of (i), (ii), and (iii). But how could this be? How can the Theistic Compatibilist successfully hold together divine alternativity and his or her account of an intelligible, nonarbitrary free choice? If the Theistic Compatibilist asserts that God is free in the alternativity sense, then this results in an unintelligible, arbitrary free choice, based on the Theistic Compatibilist's account of explanation. Furthermore, if the Theistic Compatibilist tries to retain his or her account of an intelligible, nonarbitrary free choice, then God is not free to create in the alternativity sense. That is, God's choice must be necessitated if it is to have the explanatory force and thus count as an intelligible choice. Therefore, the Theistic Compatibilist is caught in a dilemma: either God is free in the alternativity sense or God exercises an intelligible, nonarbitrary free choice such that the choice was fully explained and hence necessitated.[24]

In summary, if only a full explanation necessitates a choice and a full explanation is required for an intelligible free choice, then it follows that to have a full explanation, that is, according to the Theistic Compatibilist, to have an intelligible free choice, it follows that God must create.[25]

8.5 Possible Responses for the Theistic Compatibilist

Let us suppose that what I have argued for is essentially correct, namely, that the Theistic Compatibilist's typical understanding of what amounts to an intelligible, nonarbitrary free choice undermines divine alternativity. Must all Theistic Compatibilists, however, go down such a trail? Perhaps it is possible for the Theistic Compatibilists to think that some of their brethren start off on the wrong foot, and their stance consequently needs to be amended. In other words, one might assert that this variation of Theistic Compatibilism under scrutiny is a problem not because of Theistic Compatibilism *per se* but, rather, because of certain metaphysical commitments with respect to either explanation or divine freedom.

What, then, are the possible responses which are available to the Theistic Compatibilist? There seem to be, as far as I can see, at least five general avenues of response. *First*, one might simply admit that God's alternativity free choices are, indeed, arbitrary. *Second*, it could be argued that the intelligibility problem can be applied only to human and not divine freedom with respect to choosing otherwise. *Third*, one might simply say that we do not know how to account for a divine intelligible, nonarbitrary free choice. God's freedom is utterly mysterious. *Fourth*, one could argue, *contra* Frame and Ware, that alternativity free choices are, indeed, intelligible, but realize that such an assertion does not commit one to the truth of *human* alternativity free choices. *Lastly*, one might deny that alternativity is a necessary part of the metaphysical makeup of divine freedom. Perhaps there is some other sense in which God's freedom is to be construed, a sense offered in Chapter 3. Let us look at each of these possible responses.

A first line of response could be to *concede the point* and admit that even God's free choices are, indeed, unintelligible. That is, His choices are random and arbitrary given divine alternativity. According to this response, the Theistic Compatibilist would be unwilling to relinquish his or her understanding of an intelligible, nonarbitrary free choice while holding to alternativity with respect to God's freedom. Although I know of no Theistic Compatibilist who affirms that God's choices are random, such a position is not unheard of in contemporary philosophy of religion. Daniel and Frances Howard-Snyder, however, think that divine alternativity can be preserved by claiming that there is possibly an infinite hierarchy of better choices (i.e., worlds) for God from which He can choose.[26] God, then, chooses arbitrarily from the hierarchy. Here is their thought experiment:

> Imagine that there exists a good, essentially omniscient and omnipotent being named Jove, and that there exists nothing else. No possible being

is more powerful or knowledgeable. Out of his goodness, Jove decides to create. . . . [H]e holds before his mind a host of worlds, Jove sees that for each there is a better one. Although he can create any of them, he can't create the best of them because there is no best. . . . [Jove] creates a very intricate device that, at the push of a button, will randomly select a number and produce the corresponding world. Jove pushes the button; the device hums and whirs and, finally, its digital display reads "777": world no. 777 comes into being.[27]

Accordingly, God does not need to have a full explanation for choosing as He did—God chooses randomly. Others, similarly, appeal to the idea in economic theory known as satisficing. According to this view, there is an infinite number of good choices (or perhaps many unsurpassable good choices) for God to select from, and God made a choice that will secure an outcome that is *good enough*.[28] The problem with this response is that there is a strong consensus within the Theistic Compatibilist tradition to hold that God does not make choices arbitrarily, especially in light of a soteriology where God unconditionally elects individuals to be saved. Would the Theistic Compatibilist appeal to a conception of God, where God blindly elects a people for himself? Apparently not, since, as Frame claims, God's "decisions [e.g., electing and creating] are not libertarian random accidents."[29] So, while this is a possible response, it is not likely to be warmly embraced by the Theistic Compatibilist.

A second possible response could be to say that while the intelligibility problem holds true for human choices, *it cannot be applied to divine choices.* In other words, there is something about human choices that renders them unintelligible when alternativity is a necessary condition. When God's choices are brought into the picture, however, the intelligibility problem quickly vanishes. I think the obvious problem with this response is that the distinction between human and divine choices introduces an ad hoc selectivity with respect to what free choices are intelligible and what are not. In order to avoid this contrived hypothesis, the Theistic Compatibilist would have to come up with some good reason for why the intelligibility problem cannot apply to God (i.e., divine alternativity) but only to human choices. However, what sort of reason could that be? One might appeal to the Thomistic doctrine of analogical predication, arguing that the intelligibility problem cannot apply to God since God's freedom is not much like ours.[30] Admittedly, as far I can tell, Ware is silent on how one ought to predicate attributes on God. Frame, however, is quite critical of analogical predication, claiming it to be "inconsistent," thus opting, instead, for univocal predication. Here is what he says:

> [I]f *goodness* applies to God analogously by a causal relation, what about the word *cause*? Does that require another analogous relation, and another, *ad infinitum*? Somewhere, it would seem, we must be able to say something about God univocally, for there must be some univocal attribute on which to hang the analogies, whether that be *cause*, *being*, or something else. But if *cause* can be univocal, why can't *goodness* be? This inconsistency can be pressed either toward global agnosticism or toward some level of literal knowledge about God.[31]

Frame concludes by opting for the second horn of the dilemma:

> We need not be afraid of saying that some of our language about God is univocal or literal. God has given us language that literally applies to him. When one says negatively that "God is not a liar," no word in that sentence is analogous or figurative. The sentence distinguishes God from literal liars, not analogous ones. Similarly, the statement that "God is good" uses the term *good* univocally.[32]

Accordingly, because of Frame's insistence upon univocity, the appeal to analogical predication is not a good reason (for him) to avoid the *ad hoc-ness* of the intelligibility problem applying only to God. Therefore, this is not a response that the Theistic Compatibilist should look to embrace.

Another line of response could be to claim that while God does, indeed, exercise alternativity freedom, *it is simply beyond our ken to understand or know* just how God's choice is to be intelligible and nonarbitrary. That is, although God's alternativity free choices are not unintelligible, one simply does not know how to account for their intelligibility. This sort of agnosticism response is, indeed, what Frame appeals to when he elaborates on divine alternativity. He begins by asking, "[I]f God's free decisions are not determined by any of his attributes, then where do they come from? If these decisions are not libertarian random accidents, then what accounts for them?" He concludes by answering, "I can only reply, with [the apostle] Paul, 'Oh the depth of the riches of wisdom and knowledge of God! How unsearchable his judgments, and his paths beyond tracing out!' (Rom. 11.33)."[33]

Given the application of this biblical text to God's freedom, accounting for a divine intelligible, nonarbitrary free choice is, according to Frame, "unsearchable" and "beyond tracing out."[34] The problem with this response, however, is that it does not seem to be any different from the typical response to the intelligibility problem as regards *human* free choices. Is it not the case that some of those who hold to alternativity with respect to human freedom also frequently appeal to agnosticism and "mystery" when accounting for intelligibility?[35] If the Theistic Compatibilist wants to sustain this agnosticism response, then he or she will have to concede that the agnosticism response with respect to human choices is just as plausible. Further, if the agnosticism response is, indeed, just as plausible, then the initial employment by the Theistic Compatibilist of the intelligibility problem loses its force. In addition to this, if the Theistic Compatibilist thinks that the agnosticism response can be applied only to the intelligibility of divine choices and not to that of human choices, then the ad hoc problem rears its head once again. For these reasons, the agnosticism response is not something the Theistic Compatibilist should embrace.

Another possible response available to the Theistic Compatibilist is to *jettison the intelligibility problem* from his arsenal of arguments for why he thinks alternativity freedom is false, or at least implausible. In other words, the Theistic Compatibilist, *contra* Frame and Ware, simply needs to admit the intelligibility of human alternativity free choices. Perhaps one could endorse the work by Robert Kane with respect to the intelligibility problem where he illustrates the example of a businesswoman confronting an assault taking place in an alley on her way to a meeting. Here, there is a struggle between her conscience and her career ambitions—the former tells her to stop and call for help, while the latter tells her she cannot miss the meeting. Such a struggle, Kane argues, does not result in an unintelligible, arbitrary choice once the choice is made. Here is what he says:

> [U]nder such conditions, the choice the woman might make either way will not be "inadvertent," "accidental," "capricious," or "merely random" (as critics of indeterminism say) because the choice will be *willed* by the woman either way when it is made, and it will be done for *reasons* either way—reasons that she then and there *endorses*. . . . So when she decides, she endorses one set of competing reasons over the other as the one she will act on. But *willing* what you do in this way, and doing it for *reasons* that you endorse, are conditions usually required to say something is done "on purpose," rather than accidentally, capriciously, or merely by chance.[36]

Similarly, Alexander Pruss seeks to avoid the intelligibility problem by defending the position "that a choice of *A* can be explained in terms of a state that was compatible with choosing B."[37] Pruss begins his defense by offering a hypothesis about how human freedom may plausibly work, where "free choices are made on the basis of reasons that one is 'impressed by,' that is, that one takes into consideration in making the decision."[38] The following is the essence of his hypothesis:

> [S]uppose that when the agent x chooses A, there is a subset S of reasons that favor A over B that the agent is impressed by, such that x freely chooses A on account of S. My explanatory hypothesis, then, is that x freely chooses A because x is making a free choice between A and B while impressed by the reasons in S. On my hypothesis, further, had the agent chosen B, the agent would still have been impressed by the reasons in S, but the choice of B would have been explained by x's freely choosing between A and B while impressed by the reasons in T, where T is a set of reasons that favor B over A. Moreover, in the actual world where A is chosen, the agent is also impressed by T. However, in the actual world, the agent does not act on the impressive reasons in T, but on the reasons in S.[39]

What we see from both Kane and Pruss is that the fundamental motivation to avoid the intelligibility problem, and thus preserve the coherence of alternativity freedom, is to try to provide a *sufficient* explanation without that explanation being interpreted as a logically sufficient explanation. In other words, the *explanans* (i.e., that which does the explaining) is sufficient but does not *entail* the *explanandum* (i.e., that which is explained). So, to be clear, neither thinker is claiming that the same thing would possibly explain one particular choice over a contrary choice.

Nevertheless, whether or not one is convinced of Kane's or Pruss's answer to the intelligibility problem, does abandoning this argument (i.e., the intelligibility problem) commit the Theistic Compatibilist to asserting that alternativity with respect to *human* freedom is, indeed, true? Certainly not. The reason is that the Theistic Compatibilist can argue for the falsity of alternativity for *other* reasons unrelated to intelligibility. For instance, supposing that God's exhaustive and meticulous determinism entails human compatibilistic freedom, it could be argued *exegetically* that the sort of divine sovereignty that Frame and Ware affirm is to be found in the Bible.[40] Therefore, if that sort of divine sovereignty is to be found in the Bible, then it would follow, on our supposition, that alternativity freedom is, indeed, false.[41] Second, one could argue that if the *saints in heaven* exercise human compatibilistic freedom, then it would not seem any less implausible for humans on this side of death to do the same as well.[42] Lastly, one could argue for the falsity of alternativity freedom given a certain understanding of *divine biblical inspiration*, that is, verbal plenary inspiration.[43] Here it could be thought that the only plausible way to account for every word and every grammatical construction as divinely inspired while also being written by human beings is to appeal to human compatibilistic freedom. It would seem utterly unreasonable to some that God could inspire exactly what He wanted the biblical authors to write if the authors could have chosen different words and grammatical constructions than they actually did. So, given divine verbal plenary inspiration, alternativity freedom is false.

Therefore, if these other reasons for why alternativity freedom is false are found reasonable, then it is perfectly consistent for the Theistic Compatibilist to claim that alternativity free choices are, indeed, intelligible, but that this type of human freedom is still false or at least less plausible than its rivals. What this consistency shows, consequently, is that the door is open for the Theistic Compatibilist to retain alternativity with respect to divine freedom while at the same time asserting that alternativity is not necessary with respect to human freedom. This type of response, however, comes with a stiff cost, namely, abandoning a strong argument against alternativity freedom.

Perhaps there is one final response available to the Theistic Compatibilist. Why should we think that alternativity is necessary in order for God to be free? Perhaps the Leibnizian-inspired account of divine freedom offered in Chapter 3 can provide some headway. I think that this is the most promising response for the Theistic Compatibilist to make in order to retain his or her account of an intelligible, nonarbitrary free choice. Indeed, this is exactly what some thinkers have done. For example, Paul Helm, when critiquing Thomas Aquinas's model of creation participating in God's perfection in an infinite number of possible ways, states:

> The problem with such a position is that . . . it is hard to see how divine caprice can be avoided. For God is portrayed as actualizing one of a number of co-optimific goals. If we suppose this makes sense, on what grounds could God decide in favour of one rather than another?[44]

According to Helm, there simply are no grounds for why God chose as he did, and thus the choice is a result of "pure whimsy."[45]

Similarly, Katherin Rogers claims:

But if God has freedom of indifference with regard to creation, then this is no explanation at all, since there is absolutely no reason why God chose our world over some other creation or over none at all. His wisdom and love might equally have issued in a creation containing only well-ordered cosmic dust, or in no creation at all. . . . Ascribing freedom of indifference to God posits radical arbitrariness at the heart of creation such that there is no ultimate meaning or purpose to the world—at least no meaning or purpose that would not be equally fulfilled by a creation of cosmic dust or a lack of any creation at all.[46]

What we see here from both Helm and Rogers are echoes of the intelligibility problem applied to God's freedom. However, in remaining consistent, they both affirm that alternativity is not necessary in order for God to be free. Helm and Rogers, we might say, claim that there is something about God's essential perfection that precludes Him from being able to choose otherwise. Accordingly, divine freedom is primarily a function of God being the ultimate source of His choices. He freely chooses if nothing metaphysically outside of Him is the ultimate explanation for why He chooses one thing over another.[47] While such a position is consistent, it does not seem to be a position that Theistic Compatibilists such as Frame and Ware would want to adopt given their commitment to alternativity with respect to God's freedom.[48] Nevertheless, this final response, I suggest, is the way forward for the Theistic Compatibilist.

8.6 Conclusion

The Theistic Compatibilist's employment of the intelligibility problem has been influential in theological and philosophical writings, thus arguing against the coherence of alternativity freedom. Nevertheless, I have argued that the typical Theistic Compatibilist position is problematic because it implies the denial of divine alternativity. What I have suggested in light of this problem is that the Theistic Compatibilists affirm Theistic Optimism given their metaphysical commitments to both human freedom and explanation.

Conclusion

9.1 Two Peripheral Issues

In this book I have argued that Theistic Optimism, the view that God must do the best, does not fall prey to the charges typically leveled against it. More specifically, I have argued that the idea that God must do the best is consistent with divine freedom, His aseity, and that He may be able to be praiseworthy and thankworthy, along with deserving a respectable place at the table of the Christian tradition. In addition, it has been argued that if one concedes the point that the best possible world is the only possible world, then it is plausible to understand other worlds as conceivable worlds (but not as possible worlds). Finally, I argued that the outlook that I called Theistic Compatibilism ought to embrace Theistic Optimism, given their commitment to the intelligibility problem, that is, given their commitment to the notion that alternativity freedom results in random, arbitrary choices.

At this point, however, one might wonder why certain issues were not mentioned and thus have some remaining questions. The immediate response is to say that space is limited and the research was focused on the primary issues within the literature. Because of this, peripheral issues and questions were left aside for further discussion. Nevertheless, I intend in this conclusion to highlight two of those peripheral issues and offer a few brief concluding comments on how the discussion might proceed with respect to Theistic Optimism.

9.2 God's Essential Properties

First, a reader might note that, according to Leibniz and those who follow him, God's wisdom and goodness are stipulated as *essential* properties. That is, these properties are set forth such that the being who is God cannot cease to be wise and good or cannot cease to possess wisdom and goodness.[1] But why, it might be asked, ought we to think with Leibniz that God's wisdom and goodness are essential properties? Perhaps, instead, these particular properties ought to be understood as nonessential properties. Employing possible world semantics, one might say that God possesses wisdom and goodness in the actual world, but hold that there are worlds in which He does not possess those properties. So, while God can and, indeed, does possess wisdom and goodness in the actual world, He nevertheless possesses wisdom and goodness in a contingent manner. Moreover, the relevancy concerning the issue of God's essential properties versus contingent properties as it relates to Theistic Optimism can be put as follows: if God's wisdom and goodness are contingent properties (i.e., not essential properties), then divine alternativity ensues, and consequently it is not the case that God must do the best. In fact, God may exercise alternativity in order to do evil. Therefore, advancing the idea that wisdom and goodness are contingent properties could undermine Theistic Optimism from the outset since alternativity is now applied to God's properties.

There are two lines of argumentation that one could advance in responding to the notion that God's wisdom and goodness are contingent properties. First, it could be argued that a being who is wise and good in all worlds is better (or greater) than a being who is wise and good in at least one world. With respect to other perfections, then, God not only has, say, the perfection of omnipotence and omniscience but also has omnipotence and omniscience *necessarily*. Katherin Rogers puts the argument this way as it applies to God's goodness:

> It seems intuitively obvious that "that than which a greater cannot be conceived" could not lack the attribute of goodness, and that it is greater to possess it necessarily than contingently. A being that might cease to be good is corruptible even if not now corrupted, and so is not as good as a being that is intrinsically incorruptible.[2]

Accordingly, wisdom and goodness are not only perfections, but possessing them necessarily is a perfection as well.

A second way of casting doubt on the idea that God's wisdom and goodness are contingent is to advance an argument from God's essential omniscience and essential omnipotence. Laura Garcia argues that because God is essentially omniscient and essentially omnipotent the traditional theist ought to reject the following proposition:

> There is some possible world W such that in W, God allows a contingent state of affairs S to obtain and God is morally blameworthy for allowing S to obtain.[3]

However, while rejecting such a proposition, it follows that

> There is no possible world W such that in W, God allows a contingent state of affairs S to obtain and God is morally blameworthy for allowing S to obtain.[4]

According to Garcia, then, in every possible world W, God is morally perfect in W.

So, while there is no doubt further discussion to be had with respect to God's essential properties, there are some plausible reasons motivated from the idea that God is a perfect being to conclude that God not only possesses wisdom and goodness but also possesses them necessarily. To claim otherwise and thus embrace the notion that God possesses those properties contingently is to call into question God's ontological perfection.

9.3 Petitionary Prayer

A second question that one might ask is how Theistic Optimism squares with the idea of petitionary prayer. While prayers can get expressed in a number of different ways (e.g., giving thanks), petitionary prayer is the idea that a petitioner is *requesting* something from God. However, are one's requests that are laid before God simply meaningless and utterly insignificant, supposing that Theistic Optimism holds true? To put differently, are one's requests effective in the sense that the prayers influence God were the prayers not offered, then the requests would not have transpired?

How this issue relates to Theistic Optimism is expressed by Scott Davison when he begins by stating, "Instead of supposing that God is free both to bring about E in response to S's request and not to bring about E despite S's request . . . let us suppose that there is no alternative sequence in which God decides not to bring about E."[5] Given this supposition (i.e., the denial of divine alternativity), which resonates with Theistic Optimism, Davison goes on to highlight an alleged problem:

> [F]rom a practical point of view, the no choice challenge might undercut some of the motivation that people take themselves to have for offering petitionary prayers . . . . [T]hey could reason as follows . . . "Since I have no idea whether God's reasons line up with what I might request in this case, I have no idea whether my petitionary prayer could play any role in God's action, so I will take the trouble to pray only when I am desperate and the stakes are high."[6]

Accordingly, given Theistic Optimism one is simply ignorant regarding God's reasons lining up with what he or she might request. In addition, if one is simply ignorant regarding God's reasons lining up with what he or she might request, then he or she will lack motivation for offering petitionary prayers. Therefore, if Theistic Optimism holds true, then, according to Davison, a petitioner will lack motivation for offering petitionary prayers.

What can be said in response to the problem that Theistic Optimism undercuts motivation to offer petitionary prayer? First, it is worth mentioning that the ignorance of God's reasons lining up with what is requested does not apply only to a Theistic Optimism outlook. That is, the petitioner would certainly be ignorant of God's reasons lining up with what he or she requested in a non-Theistic Optimism metaphysic as well. In addition, if the ignorance holds true in a non-Theistic Optimism metaphysic, then the petitioner would again lack motivation for offering such prayers. Therefore, this objection is a double-edged sword and thus does not gain any traction against Theistic Optimism.

Second, one might respond to the problem of petitionary prayer by stating that it is a mistake to isolate and abstract the action of praying from the rest of the actions and events which constitute a world. In other words, it is wrongheaded to ask, "If person P had not prayed, then would event E have occurred?" since the question assumes that the human action of praying is causally sufficient for the result to occur. Consider these remarks from Paul Helm:

> Why are such attempts at prising apart one or other action, whether it is praying or some other action, from the matrix of events and actions to be resisted? We should resist them because, if it is supposed that A had not

prayed, then the total matrix of events and actions is thereby changed. A
different matrix is introduced since the original situation *did* involve praying.
Whether the question "If A had not prayed, what would have happened?" is
worth discussing very largely depends upon how much *general* information
there is about such cases, and therefore in how warranted we are in making
generalizations about them.[7]

What I take Helm to be cautioning here is that we often do not have sufficient
information to adjudicate the truth of conditional propositions such as, "If
person P did not pray for X, then X would not have happened." Consequently,
to limit the efficacy of the praying to the petitioner is unacceptable since actions
and events within a world are intimately connected, and especially so given
Theistic Optimism. In fact, highlighting the connectedness of actions and events
as it relates to prayer is something that Leibniz is sympathetic to. As he says:

> [I]t must be known that all things are *connected* in each one of the possible
> worlds: the universe, whatever it may be, is all of one piece, like an ocean:
> the least movement extends its effect there to any distance whatsoever, even
> though this effect become less perceptible in proportion to the distance.
> Therein God has ordered all things beforehand once for all, having foreseen
> prayers, good and bad actions, and all the rest; and each thing *as an idea* has
> contributed, before its existence, to the resolution that has been made upon
> the existence of all things; so that nothing can be changed in the universe . .
> . save its essence or, if you will, save its *numerical individuality*. Thus, if the
> smallest evil [or petitionary prayer] that comes to pass in the world were
> missing it, it would no longer be this world; which, with nothing omitted
> and all allowance made, was found the best by the Creator who chose.[8]

So, it appears that Helm and Leibniz are advising that we ought not to isolate
actions of, say, praying from the rest of the matrix of events and actions,
especially given Theistic Optimism. To do so is to omit an action and thus
introduce an entirely different world or matrix of events.

9.4 The Final Conclusion

Now by drawing attention to these two issues (i.e., God's essential properties
and petitionary prayer) I am not claiming that the arguments in response
to these issues are decisive and conclusive. Rather, as already mentioned,

by highlighting how one might respond to some of these peripheral issues, I offered some brief comments on how the discussion might proceed with respect to Theistic Optimism. So, there appears to be further discussion to be had here; there typically is. Nevertheless, I have argued in this book that the problems and objections typically leveled against Theistic Optimism are not good objections. Accordingly, I have offered a fresh philosophical defense of Theistic Optimism, namely, that if Theistic Optimism holds true, then the charges leveled against it are found wanting.

Notes

Chapter 2

1 Gottfried Wilhelm Leibniz, *Theodicy: Essays on the Goodness of God, the Freedom of Man, and the Origin of Evil*, ed. by Austin Farrer and trans. by E. M. Huggard (London: Routledge and Kegan Paul, 1952), paragraph 44, 98. Emphases original.
2 Leibniz, *Theodicy*, paragraph 196, 249.
3 Gottfried Leibniz, "A Vindication of God's Justice Reconciled with His Other Perfections and All His Actions," in *Monadology and Other Philosophical Essays*, trans. by Paul Schrecker and Anne Martin Schrecker (Indianapolis: The Bobbs-Merrill Company, Inc.), paragraph 79, 131.
4 Leibniz, "A Vindication of God's Justice Reconciled with His Other Perfections and All His Actions," paragraph 67, 128.
5 Leibniz, *Theodicy*, paragraph 117, 188.
6 Leibniz, *Theodicy*, paragraph 52, 151.
7 While, as far I as can tell, Leibniz does not offer a definition or conceptual analysis of what amounts to a universe, a series, or a plan, he nevertheless states that a "world" is "the whole succession and the whole agglomeration of all existent things." *Theodicy*, paragraph 8, 128.
8 See, for instance, William L. Rowe, *Can God be Free?* (Oxford: Oxford University Press, 2004).
9 Leibniz, *Theodicy*, paragraph 8, 128.
10 Leibniz, *Theodicy*, paragraph 201, 253.
11 Leibniz, *Theodicy*, paragraph 117, 187.
12 Leibniz, *Theodicy*, paragraph 117, 187.
13 Leibniz, *Theodicy*, paragraph 117, 187. Emphasis original.
14 Leibniz, *Theodicy*, paragraph 201, 253.
15 Michael J. Murray argues that Leibniz uses moral necessity in two different senses, namely, a deontic sense (i.e., relating to duty and obligation) and an action theoretic sense (i.e., relating to the course of action which the practical intellect judges as best). Given these two different senses of moral necessity, it is the latter that is our primary concern. Michael J. Murray, "Pre-Leibnizian Moral Necessity," *The Leibniz Review*, 14 (2004): 1–28. For further discussion on

Leibniz and moral necessity, see Michael J. Murray, "Spontaneity and Freedom in Leibniz," in *Leibniz: Nature and Freedom*, ed. by Donald Rutherford and J. A. Cover (Oxford: Oxford University Press, 2005), 194–216.

16 Leibniz, *Theodicy*, paragraph 132, 203. Emphasis original.

17 Leibniz, *Theodicy*, paragraph 230, 270.

18 "Reflexions on the Work of Mr. Hobbes Published in English on 'Freedom, Necessity, and Chance,'" in *Theodicy*, paragraph 3, 395.

19 Robert Adams, "Moral Necessity," in *Leibniz: Nature and Freedom*, ed. by Donald Rutherford and J. A. Cover (Oxford: Oxford University Press, 2005), 183. Emphasis original.

20 Gottfried Leibniz, *Correspondence*, ed. by Roger Ariew (Indianapolis: Hackett Publishing), 36.

21 Gottfried Leibniz, "On Freedom and Possibility," in *Philosophical Essays*, ed. and trans. by Roger Ariew and Daniel Garber (Indianapolis: Hackett Publishing, 1989), 21.

22 Leibniz, *Theodicy*, paragraph 8, 128.

23 Leibniz, *Theodicy*, paragraph 8, 128.

24 Leibniz, *Theodicy*, paragraph 225, 267–8.

25 Leibniz, *Theodicy*, paragraph 226, 268.

26 Gottfried Leibniz, "Monadology," in *Philosophical Essays*, ed. and trans. by Roger Ariew and Daniel Garber (Indianapolis: Hackett Publishing, 1989), paragraph 43, 218.

27 Leibniz, "Monadology," in *Philosophical Essays*, paragraph 44, 218.

28 Leibniz, "Monadology," in *Philosophical Essays*, paragraph 43, 218. Emphasis added.

29 Leibniz, *Theodicy*, paragraph 189, 246.

30 Leibniz, *Theodicy*, paragraph 20, 135.

31 Leibniz, "Monadology," in *Philosophical Essays*, paragraph 46, 218–19.

32 Leibniz, "Monadology," in *Philosophical Essays*, paragraph 46, 219.

33 For discussion, see *Beyond the Control of God?: Six Views on the Problem of God and Abstract Objects* (London: Bloomsbury Academic, 2014).

34 Roger Woolhouse, *Starting with Leibniz* (London: Continuum International Publishing, 2010), 113–14. Emphases original. Similarly, Franklin Perkins adds: "Leibniz's account of God's understanding plays a central role in his philosophy, not only because it explains the creation of this particular world, but also because it is the foundation for the status of necessary truths and is the model for human understanding, which he says mirrors or expresses that of God. What is this understanding that God has? What does it contain? All possibilities in

all possible combinations, that is, everything which can be conceived." Franklin Perkins, *Leibniz: A Guide for the Perplexed* (London: Continuum International Publishing, 2007), 33.

35 Gottfried Leibniz, "Discourse on Metaphysics," in *Philosophical Essays*, ed. and trans. by Roger Ariew and Daniel Garber (Indianapolis: Hackett Publishing, 1989), section 3, 37.

36 Leibniz, "Discourse on Metaphysics," in *Philosophical Essays*, section 3, 37.

37 Leibniz, "Discourse on Metaphysics," in *Philosophical Essays*, section 4, 37.

38 Leibniz, "Discourse on Metaphysics," in *Philosophical Essays*, section 4, 37. Emphasis added.

39 Leibniz, "Discourse on Metaphysics," in *Philosophical Essays*, section 4, 37.

40 Leibniz, "Discourse on Metaphysics," in *Philosophical Essays*, section 5, 38.

41 Leibniz, "Discourse on Metaphysics," in *Philosophical Essays*, section 4, 37.

42 See Voltaire, *Candide, or, Optimism: A New translation, Backgrounds, Criticism*, ed. Robert Martin Adams (New York: Norton, 1966).

43 Leibniz, "Discourse on Metaphysics," in *Philosophical Essays*, section 1, 35.

44 Leibniz, "Monadology," in *Philosophical Essays*, paragraph 41, 218. Emphasis original.

45 Leibniz, "Discourse on Metaphysics," in *Philosophical Essays*, section 1, 35.

46 Leibniz, "Discourse on Metaphysics," in *Philosophical Essays*, section 1, 35.

47 Leibniz, "Discourse on Metaphysics," in *Philosophical Essays*, section 1, 35.

48 Leibniz, "Discourse on Metaphysics," in *Philosophical Essays*, section 1, 35. Emphasis added.

49 Gottfried Leibniz, "Principles of Nature and Grace, Based on Reason," in *Philosophical Essays*, ed. and trans. by Roger Ariew and Daniel Garber (Indianapolis: Hackett Publishing, 1989), section 10, 210.

50 Leibniz, *Theodicy*, paragraph 201, 252.

51 Lloyd Strickland, "On the Necessity of the Best (Possible) World," *Ars Disputandi*, 5 (2005): 1.

52 Leibniz, "Monadology," in *Philosophical Essays*, paragraphs 31 and 32, 217. Emphases original.

53 Leibniz, "Principles of Nature and Grace, Based on Reason," in *Philosophical Essays*, section 7, 210.

54 Gottfried Leibniz, *Correspondence*, ed. by Roger Ariew (Indianapolis: Hackett Publishing), 7.

55 For further discussion, see Gonzalo Rodriguez-Pereyra, "The Principles of Contradiction, Sufficient Reason, and the Identity of Indiscernibles," in *The Oxford Handbook of Leibniz* (Oxford: Oxford University Press, 2018), 48–9.

56 Alexander R. Pruss, *The Principle of Sufficient Reason: A Reassessment* (Cambridge: Cambridge University Press, 2006), 103–4. Emphasis original.

57 The reason why Pruss's interpretation of Leibniz is important is that one may disagree with Leibniz and thus offer a softer understanding of the PSR. Accordingly, one might argue that a sufficient reason, while sufficiently explaining the explanandum, does not entail the explanandum.

58 Perkins, *Leibniz: A Guide for the Perplexed*, 16.

59 Leibniz, "Principles of Nature and Grace, Based on Reason," in *Philosophical Essays*, section 7, 210.

60 Leibniz, "Monadology," in *Philosophical Essays*, section 53–5, 220.

61 Brandon C. Look, "Gottfried Wilhelm Leibniz," *The Stanford Encyclopedia of Philosophy* (Summer 2017 Edition), Edward N. Zalta (ed.), URL = https://pl ato.stanford.edu/archives/sum2017/entries/leibniz/. Similarly, see Woolhouse, *Starting with Leibniz*, 102.

62 Gottfried Leibniz, "2a. The Principle of Sufficient Reason," in *Leibniz: Selections*, ed. by Philip P. Wiener (Charles Scribner's Sons: New York, 1951), 95.

63 Leibniz, "Discourse on Metaphysics," in *Philosophical Essays*, section 3, 37.

64 Gottfried Leibniz, "On Scripture, the Church and the Trinity," in *Leibniz on God and Religion: A Reader*, ed. by Lloyd Strickland (London: Bloomsbury Academic, 2016), 227.

65 Leibniz, "Discourse on Metaphysics," in *Philosophical Essays*, section 3, 37.

66 *JPS Hebrew-English TANAKH: The Traditional Hebrew Text and the New JPS Translation*, 2nd edition (Philadelphia: The Jewish Publication Society, 1999), 445.

67 *JPS Hebrew-English TANAKH*, 697.

68 *The Greek-English New Testament, Nestle-Aland 28th Edition and English Standard Version* (Wheaton: Crossway, 2012), 27.

69 Leibniz, "Discourse on Metaphysics," in *Philosophical Essays*, section 3, 37.

70 While Leibniz does not explicitly refer to any specific biblical text in order to support his Theistic Optimism, Lloyd Strickland has recently drawn attention to the fact that Georg Christian Knoerr (1691–1762) and Johann Franz Budde (1667–1729) endeavor to establish Theistic Optimism from Genesis 1:31. Strickland states, "Alluding to Genesis 1.31, which states that after creating the world and everything in it 'God saw all that he had made, and it was very good', Knoerr and Budde . . . insist that a lexical analysis of the final two Hebrew words of this passage . . . reveals that the word often translated as 'very' . . . is in fact a superlative modifier, making the two-word combination equivalent to the Latin 'optimum' (best)." Lloyd Strickland, "Staying Optimistic: The Trials and Tribulations of Leibnizian Optimism," *Journal of Modern Philosophy*, 1 (2019): 4.

Chapter 3

1 Nicholas Jolley, *Leibniz*, 2nd edition (New York: Routledge, 2020), 153.

2 Jolley, *Leibniz*, 153.

3 William L. Rowe, *Can God be Free?* (Oxford: Oxford University Press, 2004), 16.

4 Rowe, *Can God be Free?*, 18.

5 Jolley, *Leibniz*, 153.

6 Jolley, *Leibniz*, 152–3. Emphasis added.

7 Rowe, *Can God be Free?*, 17. Emphasis added.

8 Jolley, *Leibniz*, 161.

9 Rowe, *Can God be Free?*, 2.

10 Rowe, *Can God be Free?*, 13. Emphasis original.

11 I assume I have made it sufficiently clear that Jolley and Rowe have the alternative possibilities condition in mind (i.e., divine alternativity) with respect to God's freedom, so I hereafter drop the qualify "in the sense that requires alternativity."

12 Jolley, *Leibniz*, 125.

13 Gottfried Wilhelm Leibniz, *Theodicy: Essays on the Goodness of God, the Freedom Man, and the Origin of Evil*, ed. by Austin Farrer and trans. by E. M. Huggard (London: Routledge and Kegan Paul, 1952), paragraph 301, 309–10.

14 Roger Woolhouse, *Starting with Leibniz* (London: Continuum International Publishing, 2011), 121.

15 Leibniz, *Theodicy*, paragraph 290, 303.

16 Leibniz, *Theodicy*, paragraph 288, 303.

17 Leibniz, *Theodicy*, paragraph 288, 303.

18 Leibniz, *Theodicy*, paragraph 289, 303. Emphasis original.

19 Gottfried Leibniz, "Principles of Nature and Grace, Based on Reason," in *Philosophical Essays*, ed. and trans. by Roger Ariew and Daniel Garber (Indianapolis: Hackett Publishing, 1989), 211.

20 Leibniz, *Theodicy*, paragraph 301, 310. Emphases original.

21 Julia Jorati, "Gottfried Leibniz: Philosophy of Mind," *The Internet Encyclopedia of Philosophy*, ISSN 2161-0002, https://www.iep.utm.edu/, February 19, 2020.

22 Leibniz, *Theodicy*, paragraph 310, 313.

23 Leibniz, *Theodicy*, paragraph 288, 303.

24 Leibniz, *Theodicy*, paragraph 116, p. 187. Emphases original.

25 Edward Wierenga, "The Freedom of God," *Faith and Philosophy*, 19 (2002): 425.

26　Gottfried Leibniz, "The Principles of Philosophy, or, The Monadology,"
　　in *Philosophical Essays*, ed. and trans. by Roger Ariew and Daniel Garber
　　(Indianapolis: Hackett Publishing, 1989), 220.

27　Wierenga, "The Freedom of God," 426.

28　Wierenga, "The Freedom of God," 433. Emphases original.

29　Wierenga, "The Freedom of God," 434. Emphasis original.

30　Thomas D. Senor, "Defending Divine Freedom," in *Oxford Studies in Philosophy of
　　Religion*, vol. 1, ed. Jonathan Kvanvig (Oxford: Oxford University Press, 2008), 182.

31　Senor, "Defending Divine Freedom," 182.

32　Senor, "Defending Divine Freedom," 182.

33　Senor, "Defending Divine Freedom," 183.

34　Senor, "Defending Divine Freedom," 183.

35　Senor, "Defending Divine Freedom," 183.

36　Senor, "Defending Divine Freedom," 184.

37　Senor, "Defending Divine Freedom," 184.

38　Gottfried Leibniz, "On Freedom and Possibility," in *Philosophical Essays*, ed. and
　　trans. by Roger Ariew and Daniel Garber (Indianapolis: Hackett Publishing,
　　1989), 21. Emphasis added.

39　Kevin Timpe, *Free Will in Philosophical Theology* (New York: Bloomsbury
　　Academic, 2014), 22.

40　Timpe, *Free Will in Philosophical Theology*, 22.

41　Timpe, *Free Will in Philosophical Theology*, 22.

42　Timpe, *Free Will in Philosophical Theology*, 22.

43　Timpe, *Free Will in Philosophical Theology*, 22.

44　Timpe, *Free Will in Philosophical Theology*, 23.

45　Timpe, *Free Will in Philosophical Theology*, 23.

46　For an example of one who denies this rationality condition, see Laura Garcia
　　"Moral Perfection," in *The Oxford Handbook of Philosophical Theology*, eds.
　　Thomas P. Flint and Michael C. Rea (Oxford: Oxford University Press, 2011), 220.

47　Timpe, *Free Will in Philosophical Theology*, 109–10. Emphasis added.

48　Gottfried Leibniz, "Discourse on Metaphysics," in *Philosophical Essays*, ed. and
　　trans. by Roger Ariew and Daniel Garber (Indianapolis: Hackett Publishing,
　　1989), 21.

49　Timpe, *Free Will in Philosophical Theology*, 116.

50　Senor, "Defending Divine Freedom," 184.

51　Thomas Talbott, "God, Freedom, and Human Agency," *Faith and Philosophy*, 26
　　(2009): 380. Emphasis original.

52　Talbott, "God, Freedom, and Human Agency," 381–2.

Chapter 4

1 Gottfried Leibniz, "Discourse on Metaphysics," in *Philosophical Essays*, ed. and trans. by Roger Ariew and Daniel Garber (Indianapolis: Hackett Publishing, 1989), 37.

2 Richard Swinburne, *The Coherence of Theism*, revised edition (Oxford: Oxford University Press, 1993), 292.

3 W. Paul Franks, "Divine Freedom and Free Will Defenses," *Heythrop Journal*, 56 (2015): 108.

4 Thomas D. Senor, "Defending Divine Freedom," in *Oxford Studies in Philosophy of Religion*, vol. 1, ed. Jonathan Kvanvig (Oxford: Oxford University Press, 2008), 185. Emphases original.

5 *JPS Hebrew-English TANAKH: The Traditional Hebrew Text and the New JPS Translation*, 2nd edition (Philadelphia: The Jewish Publication Society, 1999), 1542.

6 *Catechism of the Catholic Church*, "V. Prayer of Praise," 2639.

7 Robert M. Adams, "Must God Create the Best?" *Philosophical Review*, 81 (1972): 325.

8 Laura Garcia, "Divine Freedom and Creation," *The Philosophical Quarterly*, 42 (1992): 192.

9 William Rowe, "Divine Power, Goodness, and Knowledge," in *The Oxford Handbook of Philosophy of Religion*, ed. William Wainwright (Oxford: Oxford University Press, 2007), 23.

10 William Rowe, "Response to: Divine Responsibility without Divine Freedom," *International Journal for Philosophy of Religion*, 67 (2010): 47–8.

11 Daniel Howard-Snyder, "The Puzzle of Prayers of Thanksgiving and Praise," in *New Waves in Philosophy of Religion*, ed. Yujin Nagasawa and Erik J. Wielenberg (Palgrave Macmillan, 2008), 127.

12 Howard-Snyder, "The Puzzle of Prayers of Thanksgiving and Praise," 127. Emphasis original.

13 Howard-Snyder, "The Puzzle of Prayers of Thanksgiving and Praise," 127.

14 Katherin A. Rogers, *Anselm on Freedom* (Oxford: Oxford University Press, 2008), 195.

15 Rogers, *Anselm on Freedom*, 195–6. Emphasis original.

16 Rogers, *Anselm on Freedom*, 196.

17 Rogers, *Anselm on Freedom*, 195–6. Emphasis original.

18 Rogers, *Anselm on Freedom*, 195–6.

19 *JPS Hebrew-English TANAKH: The Traditional Hebrew Text and the New JPS Translation*, 2nd edition (Philadelphia: The Jewish Publication Society, 1999), 188.

20 *JPS Hebrew-English TANAKH: The Traditional Hebrew Text and the New JPS Translation*, 2nd edition (Philadelphia: The Jewish Publication Society, 1999), 1592.

21 *The Greek-English New Testament, Nestle-Aland 28th Edition and English Standard Version* (Wheaton: Crossway, 2012), 1413, 1415.

22 Leibniz, "Discourse on Metaphysics," 38.

23 *JPS Hebrew-English TANAKH: The Traditional Hebrew Text and the New JPS Translation*, 2nd edition (Philadelphia: The Jewish Publication Society, 1999), 11.

24 Ludwig Ott, *Fundamentals of Catholic Dogma*, ed. James Canon Bastible and trans. Patrick Lynch (Cork: The Mercier Press, 1955), 217.

25 John S. Feinberg, *No One Like Him: The Doctrine of God* (Wheaton: Crossway Books, 2001), 354. Emphases original.

26 Feinberg, *No One Like Him*, 354.

27 Herman Bavinck, *Reformed Dogmatics: God and Creation*, vol. 2, ed. John Bolt and trans. John Vriend (Grand Rapids: Baker Academic, 2004), 214.

28 I assume at this point that it is coherent for a divine gracious act to extend also to God's *act to create*. While this is no insignificant assumption (since one might argue that divine *gracious* acts need to be post-creating), I follow a number of philosophers and theologians who claim that God's act of creating can be a gracious act. For instance, see Brian Hebblethwaite, *Philosophical Theology and Christian Doctrine* (Oxford: Blackwell Publishing, 2005), 41; Diogenes Allen and Eric Springstead, *Philosophy for Understanding Theology* (Louisville: Westminster John Knox Press, 2007), xxii; similarly, see William Lane Craig and J. P. Moreland, *Philosophical Foundations for a Christian Worldview*, 2nd edition (Downers Grove: InterVarsity Press, 2017), 562; William Hasker, "God Takes Risks," in *Contemporary Debates in Philosophy of Religion*, eds. Michael Peterson and Raymond J. Vanarragon (Oxford: Blackwell Publishing, 2004), 220; and Adams, "Must God Create the Best?," 324.

29 Adams, "Must God Create the Best?," 324.

30 Adams, "Must God Create the Best?," 324.

31 David H. Kelsey, *Eccentric Existence: A Theological Anthropology*, vol. 1 (Louisville: Westminster John Knox Press, 2009), 121–122.

32 Garcia, "Divine Freedom and Creation," 192. Emphasis added.

33 Rowe, "Divine Power, Goodness, and Knowledge," 26.

34 Rowe, "Divine Power, Goodness, and Knowledge," 27.

35 Rowe, "Divine Power, Goodness, and Knowledge," 27.

36 Jesse Couenhoven, "The Necessities of Perfect Freedom," *International Journal of Systematic Theology* (2012): 412.

37 Senor, "Defending Divine Freedom," 186.

38 Swinburne, *The Coherence of Theism*, 295.

39 Swinburne, *The Coherence of Theism*, 295.

40 *The Greek-English New Testament, Nestle-Aland 28th Edition and English Standard Version* (Wheaton: Crossway, 2012), 1181. Emphasis added.

41 *The Greek-English New Testament, Nestle-Aland 28th Edition and English Standard Version* (Wheaton: Crossway, 2012), 1037. Emphases added.

Chapter 5

1 See Richard A. Muller, *Dictionary of Latin and Greek Theological Terms: Drawn Principally from Protestant and Scholastic Theology* (Grand Rapids: Baker Academic, 2006), 47.

2 William Lane Craig, *God and Abstract Objects: The Coherence of Theism: Aseity* (Cham: Springer International Publishing, 2017), 3.

3 Gottfried Wilhelm Leibniz, "On God and Man," in *Leibniz on God and Religion: A Reader*, trans. and ed. by Lloyd Strickland (London: Bloomsbury Academic, 2016), 288. For further affirmation from Leibniz that God is *ens a se*, see *Leibniz on God and Religion*, 54–5, 58–9, 67–9, 72, and 86.

4 Gottfried Wilhelm Leibniz, *Theodicy: Essays on the Goodness of God, the Freedom of Man, and the Origin of Evil*, ed. by Austin Farrer and trans. by E. M. Huggard (London: Routledge and Kegan Paul, 1952), paragraph 7, 127.

5 Leibniz, *Theodicy*, paragraph 7, 127. Emphases original.

6 Hugh J. McCann, *Creation and the Sovereignty of God* (Bloomington: Indiana University Press, 2012), 7–8. Emphases original.

7 John M. Frame, *The Doctrine of God* (Phillipsburg: Presbyterian and Reformed, 2002), 232.

8 James Beilby, "Divine Aseity, Divine Freedom: A Conceptual Problem for Edwardsian-Calvinism," *Journal of the Evangelical Theological Society*, 47 (2004): 656. Emphases original. While Beilby's polemic is clearly exercised against Jonathan Edwards and those who follow him (i.e., Edwardsian-Calvinism), I nevertheless avoid explicit engagement and exposition concerning Edwards in order to simplify the discussion. In other words, I am simply drawing out the principles and arguments that Beilby—among others—utilizes while abstracting from the polemics of the original. For a response to Beilby which does, indeed, engage with an analysis and exposition of Edwards's theology, see Walter Schultz,

"Jonathan Edwards's *The End of Creation*: An Exposition and Defense," *Journal of the Evangelical Theological Society*, 49 (2006): 247–71.

9 K. Scott Oliphant, *God With Us: Divine Condescension and the Attributes of God* (Wheaton: Crossway Publishing, 2012), 230. Emphasis original.

10 For similar sentiments that divine alternativity is required for divine aseity, see R. T. Mullins, *The End of the Timeless God* (Oxford: Oxford University Press, 2016), 139–42.

11 For further discussion on the distinction between God creating in general versus God creating in particular, see Norman Kreztmann, "A General Problem of Creation: Why Would God Create Anything at All?," in *Being and Goodness: The Concept of the Good in Metaphysics and Philosophical Theology*, ed. by Scott MacDonald (Ithaca: Cornell University Press, 1991), 208–28; and Kreztmann, "A Particular Problem of Creation: Why Would God Create this World?," in *Being and Goodness: The Concept of the Good in Metaphysics and Philosophical Theology*, ed. by Scott MacDonald (Ithaca: Cornell University Press, 1991), 209–49.

12 I make this point simply because philosophers often make the distinction between (1) God creating versus not creating, and (2) God creating a particular world versus some other contrary world. In addition, given this distinction, one might say that while God must create (as opposed to not create), He is nevertheless free in the alternativity sense to create a particular world, whether that world be the best world or not. Or, conversely, (given the distinction), while God must create a particular world, namely, the best world, He is nevertheless free in the alternativity sense to create (as opposed to not create). However, while these two options endeavor to preserve an element of divine alternativity, they cannot hold true given Leibniz's commitment to the notion that God must do the best. In other words, if God must do the best, creating (versus not creating) is just as inevitable as creating a particular world, namely, the best world. For further discussion, see William E. Mann, "Divine Sovereignty and Aseity," in *The Oxford Handbook of Philosophy of Religion*, ed. William J. Wainwright (New York: Oxford University Press, 2005), 54.

13 Contrary to proponents of proposition (A), my argument in this chapter resonates quite well with the statement made by Katherin Rogers: "God, unlike created agents, does not need open options to ground his aseity." Katherin Rogers, *Anselm on Freedom* (Oxford: Oxford University Press, 2008), 190.

14 For a cumulative case that *creatio ex nihilo* is a thoroughly biblical doctrine, see Paul Copan and William Lane Craig, *Creation out of Nothing: A Biblical, Philosophical, and Scientific Exploration* (Grand Rapids: Baker Academic, 2004),

29–91. For caution that *creatio ex nihilo* is demanded by the Judeo-Christian scriptures, see Gerhard May, *Creatio Ex Nihilo: The Doctrine of "Creation out of Nothing" in Early Christian Thought*, trans. A. S. Worrall (Edinburgh: T&T Clark, 1994), 1–38; for caution that *creatio ex nihilo* is demanded by Genesis 1 (at least), see John W. Walton, *The Lost World of Genesis: Ancient Cosmology and the Origins Debate* (Downers Grove: InterVarsity Press, 2009), 41–6.

15 Theophilus, *Theophilus to Autolycus*, 2.4, in *Ante-Nicene Fathers: Fathers of the Second Century: Hermas, Tatian, Athenagoras, Theophilus, and Clement of Alexandria (Entire)*, eds. Alexander Roberts and James Donaldson (Peabody: Hendrickson Publishing, 2004), 95.

16 Saint Augustine, *Confessions* XII, 7, trans. by Henry Chadwick (Oxford: Oxford University Press, 1991), 249.

17 Saint Anselm, *Monologion*, Chapter 7, in *Basic Writings*, ed. and trans. by Thomas Williams (Indianapolis: Hackett Publishing Company, 2007), 15.

18 Augustine, *Confessions* XII, 7, 249. Emphasis added.

19 Gottfried Wilhelm Leibniz, *Leibniz's "New System" and Associated Contemporary Texts*, ed. and trans. by Roger S. Woolhouse and Richard Francks (Oxford: Oxford University Press, 1997), 164.

20 For further discussion that Leibniz is not committed to Spinoza's metaphysical monism, see Robert Adams, *Leibniz: Determinist, Theist, Idealist* (Oxford: Oxford University Press, 1994), 113–34.

21 Gottfried Wilhelm Leibniz, *Confessio philosophi: Papers Concerning the Problem of Evil, 1671–1678*, ed. and trans. by Robert C. Sleigh, Jr. (New Haven and London: Yale University Press, 2005), 117. Emphasis original.

22 Daniel J. Cook, "Leibniz on Creation: A Contribution to His Philosophical Theology," in *Leibniz: What Kind of Rationalist?*, ed. Marcelo Dascal (Springer, 2008), 451.

23 It is important at this point to emphasize the conditional "if they exist at all" because Craig, at least, in his most recent work seems to endorse the insights from fictionalism, figuralism, and pretense theory with respect to abstract objects, and thus denies the existence of abstract objects. Such an outlook on abstract objects is antirealist. As Craig summarizes, "Often we will find it convenient to speak of things like properties, propositions, numbers, and possible worlds. Such talk may be viewed as proceeding with an adopted linguistic framework in which we speak without making metaphysically heavyweight commitments. We can view the expressions of such a language as figurative or involving pretense. As I have argued, set theory seems to me a very plausible example of make-believe, whose affirmations carry no metaphysical

weight. Ordinary English seems to be just such a metaphysically lightweight language. . . . Such a combinatorial approach makes good sense of the many insights of the diversity of antirealisms. Almost all of them offer valuable insights, and we may glean from the best of the lot. I conclude that the challenge posed by Platonism to the doctrine of divine aseity can be met successfully." William Lane Craig, *God over All: Divine Aseity and the Challenge of Platonism* (New York: Oxford University Press, 2016), 207–8. Therefore, while Craig currently endorses an antirealist position on abstract objects, he nevertheless affirms that if abstract objects exist at all, then abstract objects must be created by God.

24 Paul Copan and William Lane Craig, *Creation Out of Nothing: A Biblical, Philosophical, and Scientific Exploration* (Grand Rapids: Baker Academic, 2004), 173. It is noteworthy that Copan and Craig here are motivated, like myself, to sustain divine aseity by way of *creatio ex nihilo*.

25 William Lane Craig, "Anti-Platonism," in *Beyond the Control of God: Six Views on the Problem of God and Abstract Objects*, ed. Paul M. Gould (New York: Bloomsbury Academic, 2014), 116. Emphasis added.

26 Craig, "Anti-Platonism," 115. A slightly different version of this passage can be found in Craig, *God and Abstract Objects*, 69.

27 That abstract objects are created eternally and necessarily, see Thomas V. Morris and Christopher Menzel, "Absolute Creationism," in *Anselmian Explorations*, ed. Thomas V. Morris (Notre Dame: University of Notre Dame Press, 1987), 167–78.

28 Copan and Craig, *Creation Out of Nothing*, 175, 176. Emphases original. For a developed argument of Craig's second objection to theistic activism, see Michael Bergmann and Jeffrey Brower, "A Theistic Argument Against Platonism (and in Support of Truthmakers and Divine Simplicity)," in *Oxford Studies in Metaphysics*, vol. 2, ed. D. W. Zimmerman (Oxford: Oxford University Press, 2006), 357–86. For a reply to Bergmann and Brower's objection to theistic activism, see Christopher Menzel, "Problems with the Bootstrapping Objection to Theistic Activism," *American Philosophical Quarterly*, 53 (2016): 55–68.

29 For a reply to Bergmann and Brower's bootstrapping objection to theistic activism mentioned in my note 24 (and by implication Craig's objection to theistic activism), see Christopher Menzel, "Problems with the Bootstrapping Objection to Theistic Activism," *American Philosophical Quarterly*, 53 (2016): 55–68. For others who modify theistic activism in order to avoid the bootstrapping objection, see Paul M. Gould and Richard Brian Davies, "Modified Theistic Activism," in *Beyond the Control of God?*, 51–64.

30 Greg Welty, "Theistic Conceptual Realism," in *Beyond the Control of God: Six Views on the Problem of God and Abstract Objects*, ed. Paul M. Gould (New York: Bloomsbury Academic, 2014), 81.

31 Welty, "Theistic Conceptual Realism," 81. Emphases original.

32 Walter Schultz, "The Actual World from Platonism to Plans: An Emendation of Alvin Plantinga's Modal Realism," *Philosophia Christi*, 16 (2014): 93.

33 Schultz, "The Actual World from Platonism to Plans," 95. Emphases original.

34 Schultz, "The Actual World from Platonism to Plans," 94–5. Emphasis original.

35 For a similar outlook to Welty and Schultz, see James C. McGlothlin, *The Logiphro Dilemma* (Eugene: Wipf and Stock Publications, 2017).

36 Craig, "Anti-Platonism," 100. Emphasis original. For Welty's response to Craig, see "Response to Critics," 108–9. Craig retains his worries, however, regarding conceptualism in *God over All*, 84–94.

37 Aristotle, *Metaphysics*, Book V, Part 11. Although Aristotle does not use the word "existence" here but, rather, "nature" and "substance," I follow Kit Fine in interpreting Aristotle to have an existential outlook in mind. See Kit Fine, "Ontological Dependence," *Proceedings of the Aristotelian Society*, 95 (1995): 270.

38 For further explanation and discussion on existential dependence, see Tuomas E. Tahko and E. Jonathan Lowe, "Ontological Dependence," *The Stanford Encyclopedia of Philosophy* (Spring 2015 Edition), Edward N. Zalta (ed.), URL = http://plato.stanford.edu/archives/spr2015/entries/dependence-ontological/.

39 One might highlight a possible rebuttal to PEP I, namely, if God exists, then God creates the created order. Now suppose the created order does not exist. In that case, God does not create the created order. However, in that case, God does not exist. Therefore, this argument allows us to conclude that if the created order does not exist, then God does not exist, and the argument thereby constitutes a rebuttal of PEP I. In response, what the argument highlights in concluding that "if the created order does not exist, then God does not exist" is that God is counterfactually dependent on the existence of the created order. Such a dependence, however, is completely innocuous, and thus God's aseity yet goes unscathed. Consider an analogy where "if it is raining outside, then the street is wet." Here, the fact that "it is raining outside" is counterfactually dependent on "the street being wet" since if it is not the case that the street is wet, then it is not the case that it is raining outside. However, in this case, it is plausible that the wet street cannot have any kind of causal or explanatory or whatever effect on the weather. Therefore, just as the wet street cannot have any kind of causal or explanatory or whatever effect on the weather, so too the created order cannot have any kind of causal or explanatory effect on God's essential

nature. It is simply unfortunate that the term "dependence" is part of the phrase "counterfactual dependence."

40 Tertullian, *The Treatise Against Hermogenes* (Mahwah: Paulist Press, 1956), 48.

41 For a similar distinction between existence and essence as it applies to aseity, see Mann, "Divine Sovereignty and Aseity," 36.

42 Frame, *Doctrine of God*, 232. Emphasis added.

43 Beilby, "Divine Aseity, Divine Freedom," 656. Emphasis added.

44 Beilby, "Divine Aseity, Divine Freedom," 653–4. Emphasis original.

45 Beilby makes a similar distinction between what he calls "ontological aseity" and "psychological aseity," where the former highlights that "He is uncaused, without beginning, not dependent on an external person, principle, or metaphysical reality *for his existence*," while the latter captures that "There is no lack or need in God. He is fully self-satisfied, not needing anything outside of himself *to be happy or fulfilled*." Beilby, "Divine Aseity, Divine Freedom," 648. Emphasis added. In order to avoid semantic confusion at this point, I take Beilby's ontological aseity to refer to the same thing as my existential aseity, while his psychological aseity is a subcategory of my essence aseity (assuming God's essence is to be happy and fulfilled).

46 William E. Mann, "The Metaphysics of Divine Love," in *Metaphysics and God: Essays in Honor of Eleonore Stump*, ed. Kevin Timpe (New York: Routledge Publishing, 2009), 81.

47 It is plausible to claim that Leibniz would endorse this response since he claims that God's essence includes His existence. See Gottfried Leibniz, "The Monadology," in *Philosophical Essays*, ed. and trans. by Roger Ariew and Daniel Garber (Indianapolis: Hackett Publishing, 1989), 218.

48 See E. J. Lowe, *A Survey of Metaphysics* (New York: Oxford University Press, 2002), 96. I acknowledge that there are more "fine-grained" variations of essentialism (e.g., modal essentialism and real essentialism). See also Teresa Robertson and Philip Atkins, "Essential vs. Accidental Properties," in Stanford Encyclopedia of Philosophy, ed. Edward N. Zalta, URL = https:// plato.stanford. edu/archives/sum2016/entries/essential-accidental.

49 Brian Leftow, "On God and Necessity," *Faith and Philosophy*, 31 (2014): 435. For similar remarks to that which I allude to, see Brian Leftow, "Summary: God and Necessity," *Analysis*, 75 (2015): 257–9; Brian Leftow, "Précis of 'God and Necessity,'" *European Journal for Philosophy of Religion*, 6 (2014): 1–3; and Brian Leftow, *God and Necessity* (New York: Oxford University Press, 2012), 209–47.

50 Leftow, "On God and Necessity," 436–7. Emphasis original.

51 Leftow, "On God and Necessity," 439. Emphasis original.

52 Leftow, *God and Necessity*, 209.

53 While highlighting Leftow's critique of deity theories, it is not to say that Leftow is without critics. See, for example, Chris Tweedt, "Splitting the Horns of Euthyphro's Modal Relative," *Faith and Philosophy*, 30 (2013): 205–12; see also William Lane Craig, review of *God and Necessity*, *Faith and Philosophy*, 30 (2013): 171–6. For criticism that Leftow's argument against deity theories cannot apply to all deity theories, see Walter Schultz, "A Counterexample Deity Theory," *Philosophia Christi*, 19 (2017): 7–21.

54 Thomas H. McCall, "We Believe in God's Sovereign Goodness: A Rejoinder to John Piper," *Trinity Journal*, 29 (2008): 237.

55 McCall, "We Believe in God's Sovereign Goodness," 237. Emphasis added. It is noteworthy here that McCall in this quotation, like Frame, Beilby, and Oliphant, also asserts that the idea that God must create is inconsistent with divine aseity. McCall, in other words, also seems to endorse proposition (A).

56 John M. Frame, *A History of Western Philosophy and Theology* (Phillipsburg: Presbyterian and Reformed, 2015), 721.

57 Frame, *A History of Western Philosophy and Theology*, 721. Emphasis added.

58 See John W. Cooper, *Panentheism, The Other God of the Philosophers: From Plato to the Present* (Grand Rapids: Baker Academic, 2006).

59 Cooper, *Panentheism*, 77. Emphases original.

60 Cooper, *Panentheism*, 77.

61 For a similar illustration, see Katherin A. Rogers, *Perfect Being Theology* (Edinburgh: Edinburgh University Press, 2000), 111–13.

Chapter 6

1 Laura Garcia, "Divine Freedom and Creation," *The Philosophical Quarterly*, 42 (1992): 204.

2 Edward Wierenga, "Perfect Goodness and Divine Freedom," *Philosophical Books*, 48 (2007): 208.

3 Mark Heller, "The Worst of All Worlds," *Philosophia*, 28 (2001): 263–4.

4 Gottfried Leibniz, "On Freedom and Possibility," in *Philosophical Essays*, ed. and trans. by Roger Ariew and Daniel Garber (Indianapolis: Hackett Publishing, 1989), 20–1.

5 Gottfried Wilhelm Leibniz, *Theodicy: Essays on the Goodness of God, the Freedom of Man, and the Origin of Evil*, ed. by Austin Farrer and trans. by E. M. Huggard (London: Routledge and Kegan Paul, 1952), paragraph 234–5, 272.

The quotation from M. Bayle which Leibniz refers to in order to bolster his (i.e., Leibniz's) argument can be found in *Theodicy*, paragraph 173, 235. Pierre Bayle was a seventeenth-century French philosopher who wrote a number of articles and treatises on the problem of evil. Leibniz's *Theodicy* interacts with and responds to a number of those sentiments from Bayle.

6 Roger Woolhouse, *Starting with Leibniz* (London: Continuum International Publishing, 2010), 131. Emphasis original.

7 Leibniz, "On Freedom and Possibility," 19. Emphases original.

8 Leibniz, "On Freedom and Possibility," 19.

9 Leibniz, "On Freedom and Possibility," 19.

10 Leibniz's commitment to the notion that possibility is that which does not imply a contradiction is closely related to two other ideas, namely, his idea of infinite/finite analysis and his idea of demonstrability/nondemonstrability. For, while that which is necessary (i.e., that which does imply a contradiction) has an analysis which is finite and thus demonstrable, that which is contingent has an analysis which is infinite and thus nondemonstrable. Accordingly, if a finite analysis is part and parcel of a necessary proposition, then the negation of that proposition will demonstrably entail a contradiction. In addition, if an infinite analysis is part and parcel of a contingent proposition, then the negation of that proposition will not demonstrably entail a contradiction.

11 Gottfried Leibniz, "Discourse on Metaphysics," in *Philosophical Essays*, ed. and trans. by Roger Ariew and Daniel Garber (Indianapolis: Hackett Publishing, 1989), section 6, 39.

12 Gottfried Leibniz, "Principles of Nature and Grace, Based on Reason," in *Philosophical Essays*, ed. and trans. by Roger Ariew and Daniel Garber (Indianapolis: Hackett Publishing, 1989), section 10, 210.

13 See Leibniz, "Discourse on Metaphysics," section 5, 38.

14 Leibniz, "Discourse on Metaphysics," section 5, p. 38–9. See also *Theodicy*, paragraph 234, 272.

15 There are, however, other sentiments from Leibniz which seem to suggest that the simplicity in laws and richness in phenomena are not the only elements to consider with respect to what makes a world the best. For instance, Leibniz argues that the happiness of minds is a fundamental goal of God in creating, and therefore the happiness of minds needs to be considered as part of the criteria of what makes a world valuable. If this is indeed the case (which seems plausibly true), I assume that all of what Pickup proposes here can be applied to these particular criteria as well. In other words, one might argue that contingency ought to be also found in the criterion of the happiness of minds.

16 Martin Pickup, "Leibniz and the Necessity of the Best Possible World," *Australasian Journal of Philosophy*, 92 (2014): 513.

17 Pickup, "Leibniz and the Necessity of the Best Possible World," 507.

18 Nicholas Jolley, *Leibniz*, 2nd ed. (New York: Routledge, 2020), 154.

19 Jolley, *Leibniz*, 154.

20 Another way (similar to that of the attributive and referential distinction) to exploit the ambiguity in the phrase "the best of all possible worlds" is to consult the distinction between a *de dicto* (i.e., of the word) reading of a proposition and a *de re* (i.e., of the thing itself) reading of a proposition.

21 Pickup does, indeed, highlight that the PSR is a substantial worry for his proposal, and thus Leibniz and others who follow him would likely deny the contingency of the criterion of perfection solution. As Pickup says, "The proposal, while internally consistent, is not consistent with core elements of Leibniz's metaphysics. Unfortunately, therefore, we have not discovered a viable distinction between necessity and contingency in a Leibnizian system." Pickup, "Leibniz and the Necessity of the Best Possible World," 522.

22 Wierenga, "Perfect Goodness and Divine Freedom," 208. Emphasis added.

23 Wierenga, "Perfect Goodness and Divine Freedom," 211–12.

24 Wierenga, "Perfect Goodness and Divine Freedom," 212.

25 Wierenga, "Perfect Goodness and Divine Freedom," 211.

26 Wierenga's proposal has recently been echoed and endorsed by Justin Mooney when he says "we need to follow Wierenga's lead and think in terms of God actualizing the best feasible world, rather than simply the best possible world." Justin Mooney, "Best Feasible Worlds: Divine Freedom and Leibniz's Lapse," *International Journal for Philosophy of Religion*, 77 (2015): 226. Accordingly, Mooney goes on to claim that "Wierenga rightly observes, the feasibility of worlds is a contingent matter: what is in fact the best feasible world might not have been the best feasible world . . . . [W]hich world is the best feasible world varies depending on which set of worlds happen to be feasible. Each set of feasible worlds that God might have found himself facing may be called . . . a *creaturely world-type*. Which world-type God faces is a function of which CCFs [i.e., counterfactuals of creaturely freedom] are true—a matter which is both wholly contingent and not within God's control. So God must actualize the best world that it is logically possible for him to actualize, but which world that is can vary depending on how we creatures would choose." Mooney, "Best Feasible Worlds: Divine Freedom and Leibniz's Lapse," 226. Emphasis original.

27 Katherin Rogers, *Anselm on Freedom* (Oxford: Oxford University Press, 2008), 195. For Rogers' critical remarks with respect to Molinism, see her *Freedom and*

Self-Creation: Anselmian Libertarianism (Oxford: Oxford University Press, 2015), 101–26.

28 While Mooney follows Wierenga's insights regarding feasible worlds, he suggests (like Rogers) that a non-Molinist proposal can also evade the problem of modal collapse. So Mooney says: "Supposing that God would necessarily want to actualize α, he will begin by strongly actualizing an initial segment [i.e., segment S] of α up to and including the arrival of the first set of free creatures in a certain initial set of circumstances . . . . In this scenario, precisely which S-world is ultimately actualized (whether α or some other) will depend in large part on the choices that creatures in S make. For S will have a branching future where each possible free creaturely choice constitutes a branch (and thus represents a distinct possible world or set of worlds), and as we saw above, it is not up to God how free creatures will choose to act in any given indeterministic situation. As creatures make choices within the boundaries of R [i.e., a given range of freedom], God will execute various contingency plans by performing best . . . acts in response to creaturely decisions as history progresses, always aiming for the best world he can. It is clear that modal collapse is not just evaded on this scenario, but is evaded fairly widely. The more creaturely choices that are permitted, the wider the realm of possibility will be. And it seems reasonable that α and other very good S-worlds might contain a large number of free choices." Mooney, "Best Feasible Worlds: Divine Freedom and Leibniz's Lapse," 227–8.

29 That Leibniz holds to some variant of determinism, see Robert Merrihew Adams, *Leibniz: Determinist, Theist, Idealist* (Oxford: Oxford University Press, 1994). See also Julia Jorati, "Gottfried Leibniz," in *The Routledge Companion to Free Will*, eds. Kevin Timpe, Meghan Griffith, and Neil Levy (New York: Routledge Publishing, 2017), 293–301.

30 See Alvin C. Plantinga, *God, Freedom, and Evil* (Grand Rapids: William B. Eerdmans Publishing, 1977). In addition, Plantinga states, "A state of affairs S is . . . maximal if for every state of affairs S', S includes S' or S precludes S'. And a possible world is simply a possible state of affairs that is maximal." Alvin Plantinga, *The Nature of Necessity* (Oxford: Oxford University Press, 1974), 45.

31 Lloyd Strickland, "On the Necessity of the Best (Possible) World," *Ars Disputanti*, 5 (2005): 25. Emphases original.

32 Strickland, "On the Necessity of the Best (Possible) World," 26.

33 Strickland, "On the Necessity of the Best (Possible) World," 25.

34 Strickland, "On the Necessity of the Best (Possible) World," 26.

35 Strickland, "On the Necessity of the Best (Possible) World," 26. Emphasis original.

36 Leibniz, *Theodicy*, paragraph 234, 272.

37 Franklin Perkins, *Leibniz: A Guide for the Perplexed* (London: Continuum International Publishing, 2007), 33.

38 David J. Chalmers, "Does Conceivability Entail Possibility?," in *Conceivability and Possibility*, eds. Tamar Szabo Gendler and John Hawthorne (Oxford: Oxford University Press, 2002), 145.

Chapter 7

1 Gottfried Leibniz, "Discourse on Metaphysics," in *Philosophical Essays*, ed. and trans. by Roger Ariew and Daniel Garber (Indianapolis: Hackett Publishing, 1989), 37.

2 Thomas V. Morris, *Anselmian Explorations: Essays in Philosophical Theology* (Notre Dame: University of Notre Dame Press, 1989), 170.

3 William Hasker, "God Takes Risks," in *Contemporary Debates in Philosophy of Religion*, eds. Michael Peterson and Raymond J. Vanarragon (Oxford: Blackwell Publishing, 2004), 220. Emphasis original.

4 Hasker, "God Takes Risks," 220.

5 Paul Copan and William Lane Craig, *Creation Out of Nothing: A Biblical, Philosophical, and Scientific Exploration* (Grand Rapids: Baker Academic, 2004), 175–6.

6 Sandra L. Menssen and Thomas D. Sullivan, "Must God Create?" *Faith and Philosophy*, 12 (1995): 321; see also 324.

7 While Rowe, for example, does not assert that divine alternativity is the traditional view of God's freedom, he nevertheless states that denying it would "constitute significant revisions of a major stream of thought in traditional theism." See William Rowe, "Divine Perfection and Freedom," in *Evidence and Religious Belief*, eds. Kelly James Clark and Raymond J. Vanarragon (Oxford: Oxford University Press, 2011), 183.

8 Menssen and Sullivan, "Must God Create?," 321.

9 One might be surprised, when discussing Holy Scripture, that Gen. 1:21 is overlooked when it says, "God created the great sea monsters, and all the living creatures of every kind that creep, which the waters brought forth in swarms, and all the winged birds of every kind. And God saw that this was good." *JPS Hebrew-English TANAKH: The Traditional Hebrew Text and the New JPS Translation*, 2nd edition (Philadelphia: The Jewish Publication Society, 1999), 2. Given this text, which states that what God created "was good" (but not "the best"), an objector might conclude that there is room for improvement

with respect to what God creates which is contrary to what Leibniz says. By way of response, one could argue that what is rendered "good" is simply a subcategory or even indexed under what is best. For instance, suppose I choose five professional basketball players to represent my team and that all the players are, indeed, "good" basketball players. In addition, it seems plausible, given these five professional basketball players, that one is the best player and there remains a hierarchy of talent between all five of these good players. Here we have an instance where there is a best player, but all the players are rendered "good" players. Consequently, while the best player is a good player, it is not the case that all good players are the best players. To elucidate further, supposing that Michael Jordan is the GOAT (i.e., greatest of all time, which seems like a plausible supposition), nobody would baulk at the statement, "Michael Jordan is a good basketball player." Similarly, then, with respect to God's creation—what God created is "good," but that does not negate that what He created is the best world.

10   For western formulas of the Apostles' Creed, see Heinrich Denzinger, *Enchiridion Symbolorum: A Compendium of Creeds, Definitions, and Declarations of the Catholic Church*, ed. Peter Hunermann, 43rd edition (San Francisco: Ignatious Press, 2012), 19–27.

11   *Decrees of the Ecumenical Council*, vol. 1, ed. Norman P. Tanner, S. J. (London: Sheed and Ward; and Washington, DC: Georgetown University Press, 1990), 5; see also *Documents of the Christian Church*, eds. Henry Bettenson and Chris Maunder, 4th edition (Oxford: Oxford University Press, 2011), 27.

12   Sarah Coakley, "What Does Chalcedon Solve and What Does it Not? Some Reflections on the Status and Meaning of the Chalcedonian 'Definition,'" in *The Incarnation*, eds. Stephen T. Davis, Daniel Kendall and Gerald O'Collins, S. J. (Oxford: Oxford University Press, 2004). Coakley closely follows Richard A. Norris. See Richard A. Norris, "Chalcedon Revisited: A Historical and Theological Reflection," in *New Perspectives on Historical Theology*, ed. Bradley Nassif (Grand Rapids: William B. Eerdmans Publishing, 1996), 140–58.

13   Coakley, "What Does Chalcedon Solve and What Does it Not? Some Reflections on the Status and Meaning of the Chalcedonian 'Definition,'" 161.

14   Augustine of Hippo, *On Free Choice of the Will*, trans. by Robert P. Russell, O. S. A (Washington, DC: The Catholic University of America Press, 1968), III. 5, 176.

15   Augustine of Hippo, *On Free Choice of the Will*, III. 5, 177.

16   Augustine of Hippo, *On Free Choice of the Will*, III. 9, 189.

17   Augustine of Hippo, *On Free Choice of the Will*, III. 5, 178.

18   Roland J. Teske, "The Motive for Creation According to Augustine," in *To Know God and the Soul: Essays on the Thought of Saint Augustine* (Washington, DC:

Catholic University of America Press, 2008), 161. This piece was previously published in Roland J. Teske, "The Motive for Creation According to Saint Augustine," *Modern Schoolman*, 65 (1988): 245–53.

19 Teske, "The Motive for Creation According to Augustine," 161–2.

20 Teske, "The Motive for Creation According to Augustine," 163.

21 Teske, "The Motive for Creation According to Augustine," 156.

22 Katherin A. Rogers, *The Anselmian Approach to God and Creation* (New York: Edwin Mellen Press, 1997), 61. For further discussion, see Katherin A. Rogers, "Augustine's Compatibilism," *Religious Studies*, 40 (2004): 415–35.

23 Augustine of Hippo, *The Literal Meaning of Genesis*, IV, 16, 27 in *On Genesis*, vol. I, trans. by Edmund Hill O. P. (New York: New City Press, 2002), 257.

24 Rogers, *The Anselmian Approach to God and Creation*, 62.

25 David Bradshaw, "Divine Freedom in the Greek Patristic Tradition," *Quaestiones Disputatae*, 2 (2001): 58. Emphasis original; for similar sentiments concerning Augustine's outlook, see David Bradshaw, "Divine Freedom: The Greek Fathers and the Modern Debate," in *Philosophical Theology and the Christian Tradition: Russian and Western Perspectives*, ed. David Bradshaw (Washington, DC: Council for Research in Values & Philosophy, 2012), 77–92; and Jesse Couenhoven, "The Necessities of Perfect Freedom," *International Journal of Systematic Theology*, 14 (2012): 398–419.

26 Rogers, *The Anselmian Approach to God and Creation*, 60.

27 William E. Mann, "Augustine on Evil and Original Sin," in *The Cambridge Companion to Augustine*, eds. Eleonore Stump and Norman Kretzmann (Cambridge: Cambridge University Press, 2001), 42–3.

28 Augustine of Hippo, *On Genesis: A Refutation of the Manichees*, I, 4 in *On Genesis*, vol. I, trans. by Edmund Hill O. P. (New York: New City Press, 2002), 41–2.

29 Augustine of Hippo, "Question 28 'Why did God Want to Make the World?'" in *Eighty-Three Different Questions*, trans. by David L. Mosher (Washington, DC: The Catholic University of America Press, 1982), 42.

30 See Gilbert Ryle, *The Concept of Mind* (Chicago: University of Chicago Press, 2000).

31 Augustine of Hippo, *The City of God*, 25.

32 Rogers, *The Anselmian Approach to God and Creation*, 61.

33 Teske, "The Motive for Creation According to Augustine," 159.

34 Teske, "The Motive for Creation According to Augustine," 158.

35 That "coercion" and "being forced" are synonymous with necessity according to Augustine resonates well with the Augustinian Lexicon 4 entry on "Necessitas." *Augustinus-Lexikon*, vol. 4, eds. Robert Dodaro, Cornelius Mayer, and Christof

Muller (Basel: Schwabe AG Publishing, 2012), 196. Therefore, Teske and Rogers are in agreement with the Augustinian Lexicon.

36 Anselm of Canterbury, "Why God Became Man," in *Anselm of Canterbury: The Major Works.*

37 Sandra Visser and Thomas Williams, "Anselm's Account of Freedom," in *The Cambridge Companion to Anselm*, eds. Brian Davies and Brian Leftow (Cambridge: Cambridge University Press, 2004), 193–4.

38 Visser and Williams, "Anselm's Account of Freedom," 193.

39 Katherin Rogers, *Anselm on Freedom* (Oxford: Oxford University Press, 2008), 190.

40 Rogers, *Anselm on Freedom*, 189.

41 Anselm of Canterbury, *Monologion*, Chapter 33, in *Basic Writings*, ed. and trans. by Thomas Williams (Indianapolis: Hackett Publishing Company, 2007), 44.

42 Rogers, *Anselm on Freedom*, 194.

43 Rogers, *Anselm on Freedom*, 194.

44 Rogers, *Anselm on Freedom*, 194. Emphasis added.

45 Rogers, *Anselm on Freedom*, 193.

46 Rogers, *Anselm on Freedom*, 194.

47 Rogers, *Anselm on Freedom*, 194.

48 Rogers, *Anselm on Freedom*, 194.

49 Rogers, *Anselm on Freedom*, 194. Emphasis added.

50 Rogers, *Anselm on Freedom*, 195.

51 Rogers, *Anselm on Freedom*, 195.

52 Jonathan Edwards, *Freedom of the Will*, ed. Paul Ramsey (New Haven: Yale University, 1957).

53 For a recent discussion of Edwards's understanding of the freedom of the will in general, see Richard A. Muller, "Jonathan Edwards and the Absence of Free Choice: A Parting of the Ways in the Reformed Tradition," *Jonathan Edwards Studies*, 1 (2001): 3–22; Paul Helm, "Jonathan Edwards and the Parting of the Ways?" *Jonathan Edwards Studies*, 4 (2014): 266–85; Richard A. Muller, "Jonathan Edwards and Francis Turretin on Necessity, Contingency, and Freedom of the Will. In Response to Paul Helm," *Jonathan Edwards Studies*, 4 (2014): 266–85; and Paul Helm, "Turretin and Edwards Once More," *Jonathan Edwards Studies*, 4 (2014): 286–96.

54 Edwards, *Freedom of the Will*, 357. Emphasis original.

55 Edwards, *Freedom of the Will*, 377. Emphasis original.

56 Quoted in Edwards, *Freedom of the Will*, 375.

57 Edwards, *Freedom of the Will*, 377.

58 Edwards, *Freedom of the Will*, 377. Emphasis added.

59 On the idea of moral necessity prior to Leibniz, see Michael Murray, "Pre-Leibnizian Moral Necessity," *The Leibniz Review* (2004): 1–28.

60 Samuel Clarke, *A Demonstration of the Being and Attributes of God*, ed. Ezio Vailati (Cambridge: Cambridge University Press, 1998), 84.

61 Clarke, *A Demonstration of the Being and Attributes of God*, 87. Emphasis added.

62 This point was already highlighted in Chapter 2 while explicating Leibniz's use of moral necessity.

63 Edwards, *Freedom of the Will*, 380. Emphasis original.

64 Wainwright, William, "Jonathan Edwards," *The Stanford Encyclopedia of Philosophy*, ed. Edward N. Zalta, winter 2012 edition, URL = http://plato.stanford .edu/archives/win2012/entries/edwards/. For a similar interpretation of Edwards, see Oliver D. Crisp, *Jonathan Edwards on God and Creation* (Oxford: Oxford University Press, 2012), 57–76.

65 Edwards, *Freedom of the Will*, 37.

66 Denzinger, *Enchiridion Symbolorum*, 607.

67 Here I develop in further detail some of what Timothy O'Connor says in *Theism and Ultimate Explanation: The Necessary Shape of Contingency* (Oxford: Blackwell Publishing, 2012), endnote 15, 158–9.

68 Denzinger, *Enchiridion Symbolorum*, 804–5.

69 Denzinger, *Enchiridion Symbolorum*, 607.

70 See Alan Vincelette, *Recent Catholic Philosophy: The Nineteenth Century* (Milwaukee: Marquette University Press, 2009), 50, 56.

71 Rogers, *Anselm on Freedom*, 185.

Chapter 8

1 On the alternative possibilities condition, see Robert Kane, "Introduction: The Contours of Contemporary Free-Will Debates (part 2)," in *The Oxford Handbook of Free Will*, 2nd ed., ed. Robert Kane (Oxford: Oxford University Press, 2011), 4–11; and Kevin Timpe, *Free Will: Sourcehood and Its Alternatives* (New York: Continuum, 2008), 9–17.

2 John M. Frame, *Doctrine of God* (Phillipsburg: Presbyterian and Reformed, 2002), 232. Emphasis added.

3 To clarify, the type of freedom I have in mind when saying equally as free not to create as He is/was free to create is, indeed, *divine alternativity* freedom. For

others who emphasize divine alternativity, see Thomas P. Flint, "The Problem of Divine Freedom," *American Philosophical Quarterly*, 20 (1983): 255; Thomas V. Morris, *Anselmian Explorations: Essays in Philosophical Theology* (Notre Dame: University of Notre Dame Press, 1987), 27–8; William Hasker, *Providence, Evil, and the Openness of God* (New York: Routledge Press, 2004), 166; and William Rowe, *Can God be Free?* (Oxford: Oxford University Press, 2004), 6. Historically considered, this type of freedom has been expressed as the freedom of indifference. See Muller, *Post-Reformation Reformed Dogmatics*, vol. 3, 448. For caution that the freedom of indifference entails the alternative possibilities condition, see Paul Helm, "Reformed Thought on Freedom: Some Further Thoughts," *Journal of Reformed Theology*, 4 (2010): 185–207; and Paul Helm, "Structural Indifference and Compatibilism in Reformed Orthodoxy," *Journal of Reformed Theology*, 5 (2011): 184–205.

4 Frame, *Doctrine of God*, 235.

5 "Of God's Eternal Decree," *Westminster Confession of Faith* (Free Presbyterian, 1994).

6 Jonathan Edwards, *Freedom of the Will*, ed. Paul Ramsey (New Haven: Yale University, 1957), 141.

7 Edwards, *Freedom of the Will*, 142.

8 Edwards, *Freedom of the Will*, 142.

9 There are, of course, other levels of compatibilism depending on what one supposes is the necessitating factor.

10 Frame, *Doctrine of God*, 156–7. It is noteworthy that Frame borrows this Shakespearian analogy from Wayne Grudem, *Systematic Theology: An Introduction to Biblical Doctrine* (Grand Rapids: Zondervan, 2000), 322.

11 Bruce A. Ware, *God's Greater Glory: The Exalted God of Scripture and the Christian Faith* (Wheaton: Crossway Publications, 2004), 103. Emphasis original; see also Bruce A. Ware, "Robots, Royalty, and Relationships? Toward a Clarified Understanding of Real Human Relations with the God who Knows and Decrees All That Is," *Criswell Theological Review*, 1 (2004): 191–203.

12 This view would apparently be at odds with the recent work by Hugh J. McCann, where he argues that human choices are not necessitated by secondary causes (e.g., highest desires) but that, nevertheless, God is the primary cause of all human choices. Accordingly, it is not necessarily the case that the proposition "God determines all things" entails human compatibilistic freedom, that is, Motive Compatibilism. See Hugh J. McCann, "Divine Sovereignty and the Freedom of the Will," *Faith and Philosophy*, 12 (1995): 582–98; see also Hugh J. McCann, *Creation and the Sovereignty of God* (Bloomington: Indiana University Press, 2012), 92–112.

13 For more on the intelligibility problem, see Robert Kane, "Introduction: The Contours of Contemporary Free-Will Debates (part 2)," 19–24. The intelligibility problem has also gone under the guise of the "luck objection." For further discussion, see Alfred R. Mele, *Free Will and Luck* (Oxford: Oxford University Press, 2008).

14 Ware, *God's Greater Glory*, 85–6. Emphases original. For similar appeals to the intelligibility problem while also asserting the proposition "God determines all things," see John Feinberg, "God Ordains All Things," in *Predestination and Free Will: Four Views on Divine Sovereignty and Human Freedom*, eds. David Basinger and Randall Basinger (Downers Grove: InterVarsity Press, 1986), 36; Frame, *Doctrine of God*, 138–145; and Paul K. Helseth, "God Causes All Things," in *Four Views on Divine Providence*, ed. Dennis W. Jowers (Grand Rapids: Zondervan, 2011), 42–3.

15 It is puzzling, however, that Edwards is seldom mentioned with regard to *divine* freedom, as his account of divine freedom, like human freedom, seems also to deny alternativity as a required condition for freedom. See Edwards, *Freedom of the Will*, 375–96.

16 Frame, *Doctrine of God*, 136.

17 Ware, *God's Greater Glory*, 79–80.

18 Interestingly, Frame and Ware also find interest in the doctrine of middle knowledge when accounting for compatibility between human freedom and determinism, but in a very unconventional way. They argue for what Ware calls, "Compatibilist Middle Knowledge," where God has knowledge of what compatibilistically free creatures *would* do. See Frame, *Doctrine of God*, 150–2; and 500–5; see also Ware, *God's Greater Glory*, 110–30.

19 Richard Swinburne, *The Existence of God*, 2nd edition (Oxford: Oxford University Press, 2004), 137. Emphasis original; and Richard Swinburne, *The Coherence of Theism*, rev. edition (Oxford: Oxford University Press, 1993), 137; see also David-Hillel Ruben, *Explaining Explanation*, 2nd edition (Boulder: Paradigm Publishers, 2012), 17–19.

20 Ware, *God's Greater Glory*, 87. Emphasis added.

21 Ware, *God's Greater Glory*, 87.

22 What the Theistic Compatibilists seem to endorse at this point is the following "entailment principle": if q explains p, then q entails p. For more on the entailment principle and possible objections to it, see Alexander R. Pruss, *The Principle of Sufficient Reason* (Cambridge: Cambridge University Press, 2006), 103–122.

23 Swinburne, *The Existence of God*, 76. Emphasis added.

24 It is noteworthy that Swinburne may feel the dilemma that I put forth as he elaborates on God's freedom in terms of explanation: "An action, I suggest, is a free action if and only if the agent's choosing to do that action, that is, having the intention to produce the result of that action, *has no full explanation*—of any kind." Swinburne, *The Coherence of Theism*, 146. Emphasis added.

25 My argument is something very similar to that of James F. Ross, where he states, "If it is logically possible that God should create freely [in the sense of alternativity], then it is logically possible that some event, being, or fact . . . should lack a sufficient explanation since the free creation of God and the absolute universality of the Principle of Sufficient Reason are incompatible." See James F. Ross, *Philosophical Theology* (Indianapolis: Hackett Publishing Company, 1980), 295.

26 This is not to say, however, that the Howard-Snyders are Theistic Compatibilists.

27 Daniel and Frances Howard-Snyder, "How an Unsurpassable Being Can create a Surpassable World," *Faith and Philosophy*, 11 (1994): 260; see also Daniel and Frances Howard-Snyder, "The *Real* Problem of No Best World," *Faith and Philosophy*, 13 (1996): 422–5; and Laura Garcia, "Moral Perfection," in *The Oxford Handbook of Philosophical Theology*, eds. Thomas P. Flint and Michael C. Rea (Oxford: Oxford University Press, 2009), 220.

28 For those who appeal to satisficing, see Bruce Langtry, "God and Infinite Hierarchy of Creatable Worlds," *Faith and Philosophy*, 23 (2008): 460–76; and Bruce Langtry, *God, the Best, and Evil* (Oxford: Oxford University Press, 2008), 74–83; see also William Mann, "The Metaphysics of Divine Love," in *Metaphysics and God: Essays in Honor of Eleonore Stump*, ed. Kevin Timpe (New York: Routledge, 2009), 68–71. God choosing arbitrarily and randomly has been applied not only to the act of creation but also, recently, to the certain types of evils and the number of evils which God allows in the world. See Peter van Inwagen, *The Problem of Evil* (Oxford: Oxford University Press, 2006), 89; and 103–5.

29 Frame, *Doctrine of God*, 236.

30 For further discussion on religious language and divine freedom, see David Burrell, "Creator/Creatures Relations," *Faith and Philosophy*, 25 (2008): 177–89; David Burrell, "Response to Cross and Hasker," *Faith and Philosophy*, 25 (2008): 205–12; William Hasker, "On Behalf of the Pagans and Idolaters," *Faith and Philosophy*, 25 (2008): 197–204; Richard Cross, "Idolatry and Religious Language," *Faith and Philosophy*, 25 (2008): 190–6; see also Kevin Timpe, "An Analogical Approach to Divine Freedom," *Proceedings of the Irish Philosophical Society* (2011): 88–99.

31 Frame, *The Doctrine of God*, 208. Emphases original.

32 Frame, *The Doctrine of God*, 208. Emphasis original.

33 Frame, *Doctrine of God*, 236.

34 Frame, *Doctrine of God*, 236.

35 For an affirmative answer to this question, see Peter van Inwagen, "Free Will Remains a Mystery," *Philosophical Perspectives*, 14 (2000): 1–19.

36 Robert Kane, "Libertarianism," in *Four Views on Free Will*, eds. John Martin Fischer, Robert Kane, Derk Pereboom, and Manuel Vargas (Oxford: Blackwell Publishing, 2007), 29. Emphasis original.

37 Alexander R. Pruss, "The Leibnizian Cosmological Argument," in *The Blackwell Companion to Natural Theology*, eds. William Lane Craig and J. P. Moreland (Oxford: Wiley-Blackwell Press, 2012), 55.

38 Pruss, "The Leibnizian Cosmological Argument," 55.

39 Pruss, "The Leibnizian Cosmological Argument," 55.

40 Frame, *Doctrine of God*, 47–79; and Ware, *God's Greater Glory*, 67–78.

41 Recall, however, that the supposition here is at odds with McCann's work mentioned in note 12.

42 See Steven B. Cowan, "Compatibilism and the Sinlessness of the Redeemed in Heaven," *Faith and Philosophy*, 28 (2011): 416–31; for a response to Cowan, see Timothy Pawl and Kevin Timpe, "Heavenly Freedom: A Response to Cowan," *Faith and Philosophy*, 30 (2013): 188–97.

43 See Feinberg, "God Ordains All Things," 34–5.

44 Paul Helm, *Eternal God: A Study of God Without Time*, 2nd edition (Oxford: Oxford University Press, 2011), 180.

45 Helm, *Eternal God: A Study of God Without Time*, 180.

46 Katherin Rogers, *Anselm on Freedom* (Oxford: Oxford University Press, 2008), 198–9.

47 Other than Wierenga, Rogers, and Talbott (which were discussed in Chapter 3), for other contemporary accounts of God's freedom where alternativity is denied, see Keith Ward, *Religion and Creation* (Oxford: Oxford University Press, 1996), 318–21; James E. Dolezal, *God without Parts: Divine Simplicity and the Metaphysics of God's Absoluteness* (Eugene: Wipf and Stock Publishers, 2011), 188–212; Timothy O'Connor, *Theism and Ultimate Explanation: The Necessary Shape of Contingency* (Oxford: Wiley-Blackwell Press, 2012), 111–29; and Hugh J. McCann, *Creation and the Sovereignty of God*, 155–75.

48 See Frame, *Doctrine of God*, 252; and Ware, *God's Greater Glory*, 55–6.

Chapter 9

1 One will quickly notice that the type of necessity in question here is *de re* necessity (i.e., necessity of the thing) as opposed to *de dicto* necessity (i.e., necessity of what

is said). Accordingly, wisdom and goodness are part of the nature or very essence of God, which is just to say that God would cease to be God provided He did not possess these properties.

2 Katherin A. Rogers, *Perfect Being Theology* (Edinburgh: Edinburgh University Press, 2000), 121.

3 Laura L. Garcia, "The Essential Moral Perfection of God," *Religious Studies*, 23 (1987): 142.

4 Garcia, "The Essential Moral Perfection of God," 143.

5 Scott A. Davison, *Petitionary Prayer: A Philosophical Investigation* (Oxford: Oxford University Press, 2017), 61.

6 Davison, *Petitionary Prayer*, 61.

7 Paul Helm, *The Providence of God: Contours of Christian Theology* (Downers Grover: InterVarsity Press, 1993), 155. Emphases original.

8 Gottfried Wilhelm Leibniz, *Theodicy: Essays on the Goodness of God, the Freedom of Man, and the Origin of Evil*, ed. by Austin Farrer and trans. by E. M. Huggard (London: Routledge and Kegan Paul, 1952), paragraph 9, 128–9. Emphases original.

Bibliography

Adams, Robert M. *Leibniz: Determinist, Theist, Idealist*. Oxford: Oxford University Press, 1994.

Adams, Robert M. "Must God Create the Best?" *Philosophical Review*, 81 (1972): 317–32.

Adams, Robert M. "Moral Necessity," in *Leibniz: Nature and Freedom*, ed. by Donald Rutherford and J. A. Cover, 181–93. Oxford: Oxford University Press, 2005.

Allen, Diogenes and Eric Springstead. *Philosophy for Understanding Theology*. Louisville: Westminster John Knox Press, 2007.

Anselm, *Monologion*, in *Basic Writings*, ed. and trans. by Thomas Williams, 1–74. Indianapolis: Hackett Publishing Company, 2007.

Anselm. "Why God Became Man," in *Anselm of Canterbury: The Major Works*, ed. by Brian Davies and G. R. Evans, 260–356. Oxford: Oxford University Press, 2008.

Aristotle. *Metaphysics*, Book V, Part 11.

Augustine. *On Free Choice of the Will*, trans. by Robert P. Russell, O.S.A. Washington, DC: The Catholic University of America Press, 1968.

Augustine. "Question 28 'Why did God Want to Make the World?'" in *Eighty-Three Different Questions*, trans. by David L. Mosher, 54. Washington, DC: The Catholic University of America Press, 1982.

Augustine. *Confessions* XII, 7, trans. by Henry Chadwick. Oxford: Oxford University Press, 1991.

Augustine. *The Literal Meaning of Genesis*, IV, 16, 27 in *On Genesis*, vol. I, trans. by Edmund Hill O.P. New York: New City Press, 2002.

Augustine. *On Genesis: A Refutation of the Manichees*, I, 4 in *On Genesis*, vol. I, trans. by Edmund Hill O.P. New York: New City Press, 2002.

Augustinus-Lexikon, "Necessitas," vol. 4, ed. by Robert Dodaro, Cornelius Mayer, and Christof Muller, 196. Basel: Schwabe AG Publishing, 2012.

Bavinck, Herman. *Reformed Dogmatics: God and Creation*, vol. 2, ed. by John Bolt and trans. by John Vriend. Grand Rapids: Baker Academic, 2004.

Beilby, James. "Divine Aseity, Divine Freedom: A Conceptual Problem for Edwardsian-Calvinism," *Journal of the Evangelical Theological Society*, 47 (2004): 647–58.

Bergmann, Michael and Jeffrey Brower. "A Theistic Argument Against Platonism (and in Support of Truthmakers and Divine Simplicity)," in *Oxford Studies in*

Metaphysics, vol. 2, ed. D. W. Zimmerman, 357–86. Oxford: Oxford University Press, 2006.

Bradshaw, David. "Divine Freedom in the Greek Patristic Tradition," *Quaestiones Disputatae*, 2 (2001): 56–69.

Bradshaw, David. "Divine Freedom: The Greek Fathers and the Modern Debate," in *Philosophical Theology and the Christian Tradition: Russian and Western Perspectives*, ed. by David Bradshaw, 77–92. Washington, DC: Council for Research in Values & Philosophy, 2012.

Burrell, David. "Creator/Creatures Relations," *Faith and Philosophy*, 25 (2008): 177–89.

Burrell, David. "Response to Cross and Hasker," *Faith and Philosophy*, 25 (2008): 205–12.

Catechism of the Catholic Church, "V. Prayer of Praise."

Chalmers, David J. "Does Conceivability Entail Possibility?," in *Conceivability and Possibility*, ed. by Tamar Szabo Gendler and John Hawthorne, 145–200. Oxford: Oxford University Press, 2002.

Clarke, Samuel. *A Demonstration of the Being and Attributes of God*, ed. by Ezio Vailati. Cambridge: Cambridge University Press, 1998.

Coakley, Sarah. "What Does Chalcedon Solve and What Does it Not? Some Reflections on the Status and Meaning of the Chalcedonian 'Definition'," in *The Incarnation*, ed. by Stephen T. Davis, Daniel Kendall, and Gerald O'Collins, SJ, 143–63. Oxford: Oxford University Press, 2004.

Cook, Daniel J. "Leibniz on Creation: A Contribution to His Philosophical Theology," in *Leibniz: What Kind of Rationalist?*, ed. by Marcelo Dascal, 449–62. Springer, 2008.

Cooper, John W. *Panentheism, The Other God of the Philosophers: From Plato to the Present*. Grand Rapids: Baker Academic, 2006.

Copan, Paul and William Lane Craig. *Creation out of Nothing: A Biblical, Philosophical, and Scientific Exploration*. Grand Rapids: Baker Academic, 2004.

Couenhoven, Jesse. "The Necessities of Perfect Freedom," *International Journal of Systematic Theology*, 14 (2012): 396–414.

Cowan, Steven B. "Compatibilism and the Sinlessness of the Redeemed in Heaven," *Faith and Philosophy*, 28 (2011): 416–43.

Craig, William Lane. review of *God and Necessity*, *Faith and Philosophy*, 30 (2013): 171–6.

Craig, William Lane. "Anti-Platonism," in *Beyond the Control of God: Six Views on the Problem of God and Abstract Objects*, ed. by Paul M. Gould, 113–26. New York: Bloomsbury Academic, 2014.

Craig, William Lane. *God over All: Divine Aseity and the Challenge of Platonism*. New York: Oxford University Press, 2016.

Craig, William Lane. *God and Abstract Objects: The Coherence of Theism: Aseity*. Cham: Springer International Publishing, 2017.

Craig, William Lane and J. P. Moreland. *Philosophical Foundations for a Christian Worldview*, 2nd ed. Downers Grove: InterVarsity Press, 2017.

Cross, Richard. "Idolatry and Religious Language," *Faith and Philosophy*, 25 (2008): 190–6.

Davison, Scott A. *Petitionary Prayer: A Philosophical Investigation*. Oxford: Oxford University Press, 2017.

Decrees of the Ecumenical Council, vol. 1, ed. by Norman P. Tanner, S.J. London: Sheed and Ward; and Washington, DC: Georgetown University Press, 1990.

Denzinger, Heinrich. *Enchiridion Symbolorum: A Compendium of Creeds, Definitions, and Declarations of the Catholic Church*, ed. by Peter Hunermann, 43rd ed. San Francisco: Ignatious Press, 2012.

Documents of the Christian Church, ed. by Henry Bettenson and Chris Maunder, 4th ed. Oxford: Oxford University Press, 2011.

Dolezal, James E. *God without Parts: Divine Simplicity and the Metaphysics of God's Absoluteness*. Eugene: Wipf and Stock Publishers, 2011.

Edwards, Jonathan. *Freedom of the Will*, ed. by Paul Ramsey. New Haven: Yale University, 1957.

Feinberg, John. "God Ordains All Things," in *Predestination and Free Will: Four Views on Divine Sovereignty and Human Freedom*, ed. by David Basinger and Randall Basinger, 17–44. Downers Grove: InterVarity Press, 1986.

Feinberg, John S. *No One Like Him: The Doctrine of God*. Wheaton: Crossway Books, 2001.

Fine, Kit. "Ontological Dependence," *Proceedings of the Aristotelian Society*, 95 (1995): 269–90.

Flint, Thomas P. "The Problem of Divine Freedom," *American Philosophical Quarterly*, 20 (1983): 255–65.

Frame, John M. *The Doctrine of God*. Phillipsburg: Presbyterian and Reformed, 2002.

Frame, John M. *A History of Western Philosophy and Theology*. Phillipsburg: Presbyterian and Reformed, 2015.

Franks, W. Paul. "Divine Freedom and Free Will Defenses," *Heythrop Journal*, 56 (2015): 108–19.

Garcia, Laura L. "The Essential Moral Perfection of God," *Religious Studies*, 23 (1987): 137–44.

Garcia, Laura L. "Divine Freedom and Creation," *The Philosophical Quarterly*, 42 (1992): 191–213.

Garcia, Laura L. "Moral Perfection," in *The Oxford Handbook of Philosophical Theology*, ed. by Thomas P. Flint and Michael C. Rea, 217–40. Oxford: Oxford University Press, 2009.

Gould, Paul M., ed. *Beyond the Control of God?: Six Views on the Problem of God and Abstract Objects*. London: Bloomsbury Academic, 2014.

Gould, Paul M. and Richard Brian Davies. "Modified Theistic Activism," in *Beyond the Control of God?: Six Views on the Problem of God and Abstract Objects*, 51–64. London: Bloomsbury Academic, 2014.

Grudem, Wayne. *Systematic Theology: An Introduction to Biblical Doctrine*. Grand Rapids: Zondervan, 2000.

Hasker, William. "God Takes Risks," in *Contemporary Debates in Philosophy of Religion*, ed. by Michael Peterson and Raymond J. Vanarragon, 317–25. Oxford: Blackwell Publishing, 2004.

Hasker, William. *Providence, Evil, and the Openness of God*. New York: Routledge Press, 2004.

Hasker, William. "On Behalf of the Pagans and Idolaters," *Faith and Philosophy*, 25 (2008): 197–204.

Hebblethwaite, Brian. *Philosophical Theology and Christian Doctrine*. Oxford: Blackwell Publishing, 2005.

Heller, Mark. "The Worst of All Worlds," *Philosophia*, 28 (2001): 255–68.

Helm, Paul. *The Providence of God: Contours of Christian Theology*. Downers Grover: Intervarsity Press, 1993.

Helm, Paul. "Reformed Thought on Freedom: Some Further Thoughts," *Journal of Reformed Theology*, 4 (2010): 185–207.

Helm, Paul. *Eternal God: A Study of God without Time*, 2nd ed. Oxford: Oxford University Press, 2011.

Helm, Paul. "Structural Indifference and Compatibilism in Reformed Orthodoxy," *Journal of Reformed Theology*, 5 (2011): 184–205.

Helm, Paul. "Jonathan Edwards and the Parting of the Ways?" *Jonathan Edwards Studies*, 4 (2014): 266–85.

Helm, Paul. "Turretin and Edwards Once More," *Jonathan Edwards Studies*, 4 (2014): 286–96.

Helseth, Paul K. "God Causes All Things," in *Four Views on Divine Providence*, ed. by Dennis W. Jowers, 25–52. Grand Rapids: Zondervan, 2011.

Howard-Snyder, Daniel. "The Puzzle of Prayers of Thanksgiving and Praise," in *New Waves in Philosophy of Religion*, ed. by Yujin Nagasawa and Erik J. Wielenberg, 125–49. Palgrave Macmillan, 2008.

Howard-Snyder, Daniel and Frances Howard-Snyder. "How an Unsurpassable Being Can Create a Surpassable World," *Faith and Philosophy*, 11 (1994): 260–8.

Howard-Snyder, Daniel and Frances Howard-Snyder. "The *Real* Problem of No Best World," *Faith and Philosophy*, 13 (1996): 422–5.

Jolley, Nicholas. *Leibniz*, 2nd ed. New York: Routledge, 2020.

Jorati, Julia. "Gottfried Leibniz," in *The Routledge Companion to Free Will*, ed. by Kevin Timpe, Meghan Griffith, and Neil Levy, 293–301. New York: Routledge Publishing, 2017.

Jorati, Julia. "Gottfried Leibniz: Philosophy of Mind," *The Internet Encyclopedia of Philosophy*, ISSN 2161-0002, https://www.iep.utm.edu/, February 19, 2020.

JPS Hebrew-English TANAKH: The Traditional Hebrew Text and the New JPS Translation, 2nd ed. Philadelphia: The Jewish Publication Society, 1999.

Kane, Robert. "Libertarianism," in *Four Views on Free Will*, ed. by John Martin Fischer, Robert Kane, Derk Pereboom, and Manuel Vargas, 5–43. Oxford: Blackwell Publishing, 2007.

Kane, Robert. "Introduction: The Contours of Contemporary Free-Will Debates (part 2)," in *The Oxford Handbook of Free Will*, 2nd ed., ed. by Robert Kane, 3–35. Oxford: Oxford University Press, 2011.

Kelsey, David H. *Eccentric Existence: A Theological Anthropology*, vol. 1. Louisville: Westminster John Knox Press, 2009.

Kreztmann, Norman. "A General Problem of Creation: Why Would God Create Anything at All?," in *Being and Goodness: The Concept of the Good in Metaphysics and Philosophical Theology*, ed. by Scott MacDonald, 208–28. Ithaca: Cornell University Press, 1991.

Kreztmann, Norman. "A Particular Problem of Creation: Why Would God Create this World?," in *Being and Goodness: The Concept of the Good in Metaphysics and Philosophical Theology*, ed. by Scott MacDonald, 229–49. Ithaca: Cornell University Press, 1991.

Langtry, Bruce. *God, the Best, and Evil*. Oxford: Oxford University Press, 2008.

Langtry, Bruce. "God and Infinite Hierarchy of Creatable Worlds," *Faith and Philosophy*, 23 (2008): 460–76.

Leftow, Brian. *God and Necessity*. New York: Oxford University Press, 2012.

Leftow, Brian. "On God and Necessity," *Faith and Philosophy*, 31 (2014): 435–59.

Leftow, Brian. "Précis of 'God and Necessity'," *European Journal for Philosophy of Religion*, 6 (2014): 1–3.

Leftow, Brian. "Summary: God and Necessity," *Analysis*, 75 (2015): 257–9.

Leibniz, Gottfried. "2a. The Principle of Sufficient Reason," in *Leibniz: Selections*, ed. by Philip P. Wiener, 93–96. New York: Charles Scribner's Son, 1951.

Leibniz, Gottfried. *Theodicy: Essays on the Goodness of God and the Freedom Man and the Origin of Evil*, ed. by Austin Farrer and trans. by E. M. Huggard. London: Routledge and Kegan Paul, 1952.

Leibniz, Gottfried. "Discourse on Metaphysics," in *Philosophical Essays*, ed. and trans. by Roger Ariew and Daniel Garber, 35–68. Indianapolis: Hackett Publishing, 1989.

Leibniz, Gottfried. "Monadology," in *Philosophical Essays*, ed. and trans. by Roger
    Ariew and Daniel Garber, 213–224. Indianapolis: Hackett Publishing, 1989.

Leibniz, Gottfried. "On Freedom and Possibility," in *Philosophical Essays*, ed. and trans.
    by Roger Ariew and Daniel Garber, 19–22. Indianapolis: Hackett Publishing, 1989.

Leibniz, Gottfried. "Principles of Nature and Grace, Based on Reason," in
    Philosophical Essays, ed. and trans. by Roger Ariew and Daniel Garber.
    Indianapolis: Hackett Publishing, 1989.

Leibniz, Gottfried. "A Vindication of God's Justice Reconciled with His Other
    Perfections and All His Actions," in *Monadology and Other Philosophical Essays*,
    trans. by Paul Schrecker and Anne Martin Schrecker. Indianapolis: The Bobbs-
    Merrill Company, Inc, 1965.

Leibniz, Gottfried. *Leibniz's 'New System' and Associated Contemporary Texts*, ed. and
    trans. by Roger S. Woolhouse and Richard Francks. Oxford: Oxford University
    Press, 1997.

Leibniz, Gottfried. *Confessio Philosophi: Papers Concerning the Problem of Evil,
    1671–1678*, ed. and trans. by Robert C. Sleigh, Jr. New Haven and London: Yale
    University Press, 2005.

Leibniz, Gottfried. "On God and Man," in *Leibniz on God and Religion: A Reader*,
    trans. and ed. by Lloyd Strickland, 286–299. London: Bloomsbury Academic, 2016.

Leibniz, Gottfried. "On Scripture, the Church and the Trinity," in *Leibniz on God
    and Religion: A Reader*, ed. by Lloyd Strickland, 227–232. London: Bloomsbury
    Academic, 2016.

Leibniz, Gottfried and Samuel Clarke. *Correspondence*, ed. by Roger Ariew.
    Indianapolis: Hackett Publishing, 2000.

Look, Brandon C. "Gottfried Wilhelm Leibniz," *The Stanford Encyclopedia of
    Philosophy* (Summer 2017 Edition), ed. by Edward N. Zalta, URL = https://plato.s
    tanford.edu/archives/sum2017/entries/leibniz/

Lowe, E. J. *A Survey of Metaphysics*. New York: Oxford University Press, 2002.

Mann, William E. "Augustine on Evil and Original Sin," in *The Cambridge
    Companion to Augustine*, ed. by Eleonore Stump and Norman Kretzmann,
    98–107. Cambridge: Cambridge University Press, 2001.

Mann, William E. "Divine Sovereignty and Aseity," in *The Oxford Handbook of
    Philosophy of Religion*, ed. by William J. Wainwright, 35–58. New York: Oxford
    University Press, 2005.

Mann, William E. "The Metaphysics of Divine Love," in *Metaphysics and God: Essays
    in Honor of Eleonore Stump*, ed. by Kevin Timpe, 60–75. New York: Routledge
    Publishing, 2009.

May, Gerhard. *Creatio Ex Nihilo: The Doctrine of 'Creation out of Nothing' in Early
    Christian Thought*, trans. by A. S. Worrall. Edinburgh: T&T Clark, 1994.

McCall, Thomas H. "We Believe in God's Sovereign Goodness: A Rejoinder to John
    Piper," *Trinity Journal*, 29 (2008): 235–46.

McCann, Hugh J. "Divine Sovereignty and the Freedom of the Will," *Faith and Philosophy*, 12 (1995): 582–98.

McCann, Hugh J. *Creation and the Sovereignty of God*. Bloomington: Indiana University Press, 2012.

McGlothlin, James C. *The Logiphro Dilemma*. Eugene: Wipf and Stock Publications, 2017.

Mele, Alfred R. *Free Will and Luck*. Oxford: Oxford University Press, 2008.

Menssen, Sandra L. and Thomas D. Sullivan. "Must God Create?" *Faith and Philosophy*, 12 (1995): 321–41.

Menzel, Christopher. "Problems with the Bootstrapping Objection to Theistic Activism," *American Philosophical Quarterly*, 53 (2016): 55–68.

Mooney, Justin. "Best Feasible Worlds: Divine Freedom and Leibniz's Lapse," *International Journal for Philosophy of Religion*, 77 (2015): 219–29.

Morris, Thomas V. *Anselmian Explorations: Essays in Philosophical Theology*. Notre Dame: University of Notre Dame Press, 1989.

Morris, Thomas V. and Christopher Menzel. "Absolute Creationism," in Thomas V. Morris, *Anselmian Explorations*, 167–78. Notre Dame: University of Notre Dame Press, 1987.

Muller, Richard A. "Jonathan Edwards and the Absence of Free Choice: A Parting of the Ways in the Reformed Tradition," *Jonathan Edwards Studies*, 1 (2001): 3–22.

Muller, Richard A. *Dictionary of Latin and Greek Theological Terms: Drawn Principally from Protestant and Scholastic Theology*. Grand Rapids: Baker Academic, 2006.

Muller, Richard A. "Jonathan Edwards and Francis Turretin on Necessity, Contingency, and Freedom of the Will. In Response to Paul Helm," *Jonathan Edwards Studies*, 4 (2014): 266–85.

Mullins, R. T. *The End of the Timeless God*. Oxford: Oxford University Press, 2016.

Murray, Michael J. "Pre-Leibnizian Moral Necessity," *The Leibniz Review*, 14 (2004): 1–28.

Murray, Michael J. "Spontaneity and Freedom in Leibniz," in *Leibniz: Nature and Freedom*, ed. by Rutherford, Donald and J. A. Cover, 194–216. Oxford: Oxford University Press, 2005.

Norris, Richard A. "Chalcedon Revisited: A Historical and Theological Reflection," in *New Perspectives on Historical Theology*, ed. by Bradly Nassif, 140–58. Grand Rapids: William B. Eerdmans Publishing, 1996.

O'Connor, Timothy. *Theism and Ultimate Explanation: The Necessary Shape of Contingency*. Oxford: Wiley-Blackwell Press, 2012.

Oliphant, K. Scott. *God With Us: Divine Condescension and the Attributes of God*. Wheaton: Crossway Publishing, 2012.

Ott, Ludwig. *Fundamentals of Catholic Dogma*, ed. by James Canon Bastible and trans. by Patrick Lynch. Cork: The Mercier Press, 1955.

Pawl, Timothy and Kevin Timpe. "Heavenly Freedom: A Response to Cowan," *Faith and Philosophy*, 30 (2013): 188–97.

Perkins, Franklin. *Leibniz: A Guide for the Perplexed*. London: Continuum International Publishing, 2007.

Pickup, Martin. "Leibniz and the Necessity of the Best Possible World," *Australasian Journal of Philosophy*, 92 (2014): 507–23.

Plantinga, Alvin. *The Nature of Necessity*. Oxford: Oxford University Press, 1974.

Plantinga, Alvin C. *God, Freedom, and Evil*. Grand Rapids: William b. Eerdmans Publishing, 1977.

Pruss, Alexander R. *The Principle of Sufficient Reason: A Reassessment*. Cambridge: Cambridge University Press, 2006.

Pruss, Alexander R. "The Leibnizian Cosmological Argument," in *The Blackwell Companion to Natural Theology*, ed. by William Lane Craig and J. P. Moreland, 24–100. Oxford: Wiley-Blackwell Press, 2012.

Robertson, Teresa and Philip Atkins, "Essential vs. Accidental Properties," in *Stanford Encyclopedia of Philosophy*, ed. by Edward N. Zalta. https://plato.stanford.edu/arc hives/sum2016/entries/essential-accidental

Rodriguez-Pereyra, Gonzalo. "The Principles of Contradiction, Sufficient Reason, and the Identity of Indiscernibles," in *The Oxford Handbook of Leibniz*, ed. by Maria Rosa Antognazza, 45–64. Oxford: Oxford University Press, 2018.

Rogers, Katherin A. *The Anselmian Approach to God and Creation*. New York: Edwin Mellen Press, 1997.

Rogers, Katherin A. *Perfect Being Theology*. Edinburgh: Edinburgh University Press, 2000.

Rogers, Katherin A. "Augustine's Compatibilism," *Religious Studies*, 40 (2004): 415–35.

Rogers, Katherin A. *Anselm on Freedom*. Oxford: Oxford University Press, 2008.

Rogers, Katherin. *Freedom and Self-Creation: Anselmian Libertarianism*. Oxford: Oxford University Press, 2015.

Ross, James F. *Philosophical Theology*. Indianapolis: Hackett Publishing Company, 1980.

Rowe, William L. *Can God be Free?*. Oxford: Oxford University Press, 2004.

Rowe, William L. "Divine Power, Goodness, and Knowledge," in *The Oxford Handbook of Philosophy of Religion*, ed. by William Wainwright, 15–34. Oxford: Oxford University Press, 2007.

Rowe, William L. "Response to: Divine Responsibility without Divine Freedom," *International Journal for Philosophy of Religion*, 67 (2010): 37–48.

Rowe, William L. "Divine Perfection and Freedom," in *Evidence and Religious Belief*, ed. by Kelly James Clark and Raymond J. Vanarragon, 175–85. Oxford: Oxford University Press, 2011.

Ruben, David-Hillel. *Explaining Explanation*, 2nd ed. Boulder: Paradigm Publishers, 2012.

Ryle, Gilbert. *The Concept of Mind*. Chicago: University of Chicago Press, 2000.

Schultz, Walter. "The Actual World from Platonism to Plans: An Emendation of Alvin Plantinga's Modal Realism," *Philosophia Christi*, 16 (2014): 81–100.

Schultz, Walter. "A Counterexample Deity Theory," *Philosophia Christi*, 19 (2017): 7–21.

Senor, Thomas D. "Defending Divine Freedom," in *Oxford Studies in Philosophy of Religion*, vol. 1, ed. Jonathan Kvanvig, 168–95. Oxford: Oxford University Press, 2008.

Strickland, Lloyd. "On the Necessity of the Best (Possible) World," *Ars Disputandi*, 5 (2005).

Strickland, Lloyd, "Staying Optimistic: The Trials and Tribulations of Leibnizian Optimism," *Journal of Modern Philosophy*, 1 (2019): 1–21.

Swinburne, Richard. *The Coherence of Theism*, Revised ed. Oxford: Oxford University Press, 1993.

Swinburne, Richard. *The Existence of God*, 2nd ed. Oxford: Oxford University Press, 2004.

Tahko, Tuomas E. and E. Jonathan Lowe. "Ontological Dependence," *The Stanford Encyclopedia of Philosophy* (Spring 2015 Edition), ed. by Edward N. Zalta, URL = http://plato.stanford.edu/archives/spr2015/entries/dependence-ontological/

Talbott, Thomas. "God, Freedom, and Human Agency," *Faith and Philosophy*, 26 (2009): 378–97.

Tertullian. *The Treatise Against Hermogenes*. Mahwah: Paulist Press, 1956.

Teske, Roland J. "The Motive for Creation According to Saint Augustine," *Modern Schoolman*, 65 (1988): 245–53.

Teske, Roland J. "The Motive for Creation According to Augustine," in *To Know God and the Soul: Essays on the Thought of Saint Augustine*, ed. by Roland J. Teske. Washington, DC: Catholic University of America Press, 2008.

The Greek-English New Testament, Nestle-Aland 28th Edition and English Standard Version. Wheaton: Crossway, 2012.

Theophilus. *Theophilus to Autolycus*, 2.4, in *Ante-Nicene Fathers: Fathers of the Second Century: Hermas, Tatian, Athenagoras, Theophilus, and Clement of Alexandria (Entire)*, ed. by Alexander Roberts and James Donaldson. Peabody: Hendrickson Publishing, 2004.

Timpe, Kevin. *Free Will: Sourcehood and Its Alternatives*. New York: Continuum, 2008.

Timpe, Kevin. "An Analogical Approach to Divine Freedom," *Proceedings of the Irish Philosophical Society*, (2011): 88–99.

Timpe, Kevin. *Free Will in Philosophical Theology*. New York: Bloomsbury Academic, 2014.

Tweedt, Chris. "Splitting the Horns of Euthyphro's Modal Relative," *Faith and Philosophy*, 30 (2013): 205–12.

van Inwagen, Peter. "Free Will Remains a Mystery," *Philosophical Perspectives*, 14 (2000): 1–19.

van Inwagen, Peter. *The Problem of Evil*. Oxford: Oxford University Press, 2006.

Vincelette, Alan. *Recent Catholic Philosophy: The Nineteenth Century*. Milwaukee: Marquette University Press, 2009.

Visser, Sandra and Thomas Williams. "Anselm's Account of Freedom," in *The Cambridge Companion to Anselm*, ed. by Brian Davies and Brian Leftow, 179–203. Cambridge: Cambridge University Press, 2004.

Voltaire. *Candide, or, Optimism: A New translation, Backgrounds, Criticism*, ed. by Robert Martin Adams. New York: Norton, 1966.

Wainwright, William. "Jonathan Edwards," *The Stanford Encyclopedia of Philosophy* (Winter 2012 Edition), ed. by Edward N. Zalta, URL = http://plato.stanford.edu/archives/win2012/entries/edwards/.

Walton, John W. *The Lost World of Genesis: Ancient Cosmology and the Origins Debate*. Downers Grove: InterVarsity Press, 2009.

Ward, Keith. *Religion and Creation*. Oxford: Oxford University Press, 1996.

Ware, Bruce A. *God's Greater Glory: The Exalted God of Scripture and the Christian Faith*. Wheaton: Crossway Publications, 2004.

Ware, Bruce A. "Robots, Royalty, and Relationships? Toward a Clarified Understanding of Real Human Relations with the God who Knows and Decrees All that Is," *Criswell Theological Review*, 1 (2004): 191–203.

Welty, Greg. "Theistic Conceptual Realism," in *Beyond the Control of God: Six Views on the Problem of God and Abstract Objects*, ed. by Paul M. Gould, 81–96. New York: Bloomsbury Academic, 2014.

Westminster Confession of Faith, "Of God's Eternal Decree," Free Presbyterian, 1994.

Wierenga, Edward. "The Freedom of God," *Faith and Philosophy*, 19 (2002): 425–36.

Wierenga, Edward. "Perfect Goodness and Divine Freedom," *Philosophical Books*, 48 (2007): 207–16.

Woolhouse, Roger. *Starting with Leibniz*. London: Continuum International Publishing, 2010.

Index

Index to Scripture